INTEGRATED SECURITY SYSTEMS DESIGN

INTEGRATED SECURITY SYSTEMS DESIGN

Concepts, Specifications, and Implementation

Thomas Norman, CPP, PSP, CSC

AMSTERDAM • BOSTON • HEIDELBERG • LONDON
NEW YORK • OXFORD • PARIS • SAN DIEGO
SAN FRANCISCO • SINGAPORE • SYDNEY • TOKYO
Butterworth-Heinemann is an imprint of Elsevier

Acquisitions Editor: Pamela Chester
Acquisitions Editor: Jennifer Soucy
Assistant Editor: Kelly Weaver
Project Manager: Melinda Ritchie
Cover Designer: Eric DeCicco

Butterworth-Heinemann is an imprint of Elsevier
30 Corporate Drive, Suite 400, Burlington, MA 01803, USA
Linacre House, Jordan Hill, Oxford OX2 8DP, UK

Library of Congress Cataloging-in-Publication Data
Norman, Thomas.
  Integrated security systems design : concepts, specifications, and implementation / By
Thomas Norman.
    p. cm.
Includes index.
ISBN-13: 978-0-7506-7909-1 (alk. paper)
ISBN-10: 0-7506-7909-3 (alk. paper)
1. Computer networks-Security measures. 2. Information storage and retrieval
systems-Security measures. 3. Computers-Access control. 1. Title.
TK5105.59. N45 2005
005.8–dc22

                         2006038020

British Library Cataloguing-in-Publication Data
A catalogue record for this book is available from the British Library.

ISBN 13: 978-0-7506-7909-1
ISBN 10: 0-7506-7909-3

For information on all Butterworth-Heinemann publications
visit our Web site at www.books.elsevier.com

Printed in the United States of America
07 08 09 10 11 10 9 8 7 6 5 4 3 2 1

Working together to grow
libraries in developing countries

www.elsevier.com | www.bookaid.org | www.sabre.org

ELSEVIER   BOOK AID   Sabre Foundation
             International

Dedication

This book is dedicated to the memory of Former Lebanese Prime Minister Rafik al-Hariri. Mr. Hariri was tragically assassinated by the enemies of freedom on February 14, 2005 in Beirut, Lebanon. Rafik Hariri was a visionary leader with a program to unite Lebanese of all religions together under a common Lebanese flag, independent of outside influences.

Rafik al-Hariri was a hero to all who knew and loved him. He saw the future, and the future was peace and prosperity, not conflict and failure. He was a champion of democracy and did much to further the cause of the Lebanese people whom he loved so much.

We miss him every day.

Table of Contents

viii   *Contents*

Preface

The leap from traditional proprietary alarm/access control system infrastructures and analog intercom and video infrastructures to newer Ethernet based system infrastructures is a difficult one for many security practitioners. Clients, consultants, integrators, technicians and even those in security sales have found the change to be mysterious, daunting and intimidating.

I was an early advocate of Information Technology (IT) based infrastructure because it offered something that older security system infrastructures could not: true enterprise capability. Ethernet infrastructures permit the distribution of a security system across the organization's facilities all over the world. That just isn't possible with older infrastructures.

While I was delighted to see the security manufacturing industry adopt Ethernet infrastructures, I was distressed to see that the industry was not seriously addressing the need to provide for the security of the security system itself on the new Ethernet infrastructure. When I asked manufacturers why they were not addressing network security, I received answers like: "Oh, that is the IT Department's responsibility," or "Security integrators have their hands full just learning how to deal with Ethernet based systems; we'll get to network security later."

So here now was an industry that was responsible for securing the entire organization's assets, and the security system itself was often not secure. The idea that such a startling vulnera-bility should itself be so vulnerable was unacceptable to me. So it was clear that it was important for security professionals to understand IT theory in order to efficiently design networks and practical network security.

Soon the security industry will move to systems in which there are no analog or proprietary wired devices at all; where all devices connect directly to the Ethernet infrastructure. The knowledge of how to design efficient network systems and how to secure those systems is paramount to successful security systems. This is the future of security technology.

In this book, I also bring the reader insight into some of the most sophisticated design concepts anywhere in the security industry. We'll be discussing design concepts that are able to make ordinary systems perform extraordinary functions. This is the one and only book you will need for all security design concepts.

Acknowledgments

a. Most of all, I thank my longsuffering and pure-hearted wife, Cynthia Kamalo-Norman, who has traveled around the world to be my partner. I can never enough repay her kindness, her support, her warmth and affection.
b. I am thankful for the help and support of my confidant and business associate, Michael Crocker, CPP, CSC, President of Michael Crocker, CPP & Associates, Inc. and Vice-President of ASIS International Region 6, as he patiently encouraged me in the writing of this book, and whose comments and suggestions have been invaluable.
c. I am grateful for the diligent review of the manuscript by:

- John R. Dew, CPP, Northeast Regional Director of Protection Partners International (PPI)
- Harvey M. Stevens, PhD, CPP, President of Stevens Associates, Inc.
- Mr. John Brady, ConocoPhillips
- Mr. Kevin Henson, Asier Technology
- Mr. Paul Williams, Gray Hat Research
- Mr. Nabil el Khazen, Engineered Systems International, Beirut, Lebanon
- and my protégés Mr. David Skusek and Mr. Adel Mardelli

d. I am lucky to have had the help of two of the top minds in Information Technology today to assist in Chapters 10 and 11.

- Paul Williams is one of the leading minds in Information Technology Security today. Paul is President of Gray Hat Research, which is a member of Protection Partners International.
- Dr. Jack Nisson holds some remarkable patents in WiFi Antenna Applications. Dr. Nisson has designed antennas that are significantly more immune to out-of-phase signals, resulting in far better performance. Dr. Nisson contributed to the section on Wireless Data. Dr. Nisson is President and Founder of WiFi-Plus, Inc.

e. I am enormously grateful to my publisher and friends, Ms. Jennifer Soucy, Ms. Pamela Chester, Ms. Kelly Weaver, and Ms. Melinda Ritchie, for their encouragement and continuous support, and to Butterworth-Heinemann/Elsevier for their continued support of the Security Community.
f. I am also especially grateful to ASIS International for their important and foundational support of the Security Industry and of this small book.
g. And I am also thankful for the support of all of the readers of my articles and previous book, who constantly encourage me to keep writing, despite having actually read what I have written.
h. For each above, I am humbled by their knowledge and kindness. Their contributions have been invaluable.

Introduction to Integrated Security Systems

1

Introduction and Organization of the Book

Most integrated security systems installed today are designed to protect unknown vulnerabilities against unknown threats. They often use techniques and products that work well to the advantage of the vendor but not always so well to the advantage of the client, and they are often more expensive than is necessary. We can change that.

This book is about designing convergence-based integrated security systems and enterprise integrated security systems (which are also convergence based). These are security systems that have three major defining attributes:

- Integrated security systems comprise numerous subsystems together into one complete, highly coordinated, high-functioning system. Typical subsystems include alarm, access

3

control, closed-circuit video, two-way voice communication, parking control, and other related systems. System integration is the basic concept for all that follows.

- System integration involves both the integration of components and the integration of functions. High-level functions can be obtained by integrating components into a comprehensive working system, instead of individual disconnected subsystems.

- Convergence-based integrated security systems are integrated security systems that utilize TCP/IP Ethernet infrastructure as the basic communications media. This is the result of a convergence of industries (the security technology industry and the information technology industry). Most new integrated security systems are convergence-based systems.

- We will also discuss enterprise integrated security systems concepts in depth. Enterprise integrated security systems are those security systems that have been integrated with other systems, including elevators, private automatic branch exchanges, human relations programs, and security video and intercommunications systems, at the corporatewide (the enterprise) level to perform a wide variety of automated security-related tasks in a manner consistent with corporate or agency policies and procedures and that do so uniformly across the entire enterprise. For example, when an employee is terminated, the act of pressing OK on the human resources software screen can cause the employee to also be terminated from the access control system and information technology system and even shut down access to his or her telephone and voice mail. Such integration can prevent a hostile terminated employee from gaining outside access to valuable data or leaving a forwarding or even antagonistic message on his or her voice mail. Virtually all but the very earliest enterprise integrated security systems are convergence based, and almost all of the earliest systems utilize some convergence concepts.

Although you may not need to design enterprise-class integrated security systems, understanding their design concepts will make you a better designer of any convergence-based integrated security system, so it is worthwhile to be attentive to the enterprise-class concepts when they are discussed herein.

WHO SHOULD READ THIS BOOK

This book is designed for new and experienced system design consultants, designers, and project managers who build these complex systems and for the building owners, security directors, and facilities directors who operate them. Each will benefit from the expansive array of issues covered. Many of these subjects have only rarely or perhaps have never been discussed before in any book to my knowledge. These include such aspects as how to make your security system virtually disappear on the information technology system infrastructure, as though it were not there at all to anyone but the system administrator (Chapter 17); a complete discussion on how to use security technology to delay, confound, and take down aggressors in very high security environments (Chapter 4); and secrets on system implementation that help ensure a stable, reliable, and high-functioning system (Chapters 9 and 18). There is some discussion about pitfalls out of which the potential for lawsuits have arisen for well-meaning but unsuspecting project participants. My goal is to help you gain command of every aspect of the process necessary to ensure your success, the success of the project team, and especially the success of your client.

Designing enterprise integrated security systems seems daunting to most who have only designed systems for single buildings or for small campus environments. The challenge has become ever more important with the advent of terrorism and the move toward using electronic security systems to augment homeland security. The challenge of helping to protect our nation's transportation, economic, and cultural infrastructure raises the importance of designing what used to be esoteric systems. Today, these systems are becoming more commonplace. However, many of them are being designed using old skill sets and outdated techniques, resulting in outmoded and therefore unsuitable products.

A BRIEF BACKGROUND

In 2003, the security technology industry crested a hill. Behind us, in the rearview mirror, is yesterday's technology. Ahead of us toward the horizon is the technology of tomorrow. It is different from the past. It is information technology (IT) based. Many in the security industry are afraid of it. They will resist the change. They will lose.

In the 1990s, large corporate and government clients began to understand that they are better served by enterprise-class security systems. Enterprise systems differ from older approaches in that they permit the uniform application of security policies and procedures across the entire organization. They permit centralized monitoring of security, business processes, and adherence to policy. They reduce liability and operating costs. They permit a user from one facility to freely access any other if his or her access level permits.

Nearly every manufacturer has embraced the enterprise security concept, but they are still trying to make it work in the context of older system architectures. These will all be replaced by pure IT infrastructures in the near future. By reading this book, you will be ahead of the game and be able to make design decisions that will save you and your client tens of thousands of dollars and many headaches.

These large-scale enterprise-level integration projects raise the bar, and we must all train well enough to jump over it. This book presents everything you will need to know to achieve success on these complex projects.

A FRAMEWORK FOR UNDERSTANDING THE DESIGN PROCESS

I frequently receive calls from designers who are challenged with projects beyond their experience, asking how to approach the task. I tell them the first question is not how, but why? Now, do not misunderstand me: I do not mean why should I bother? I mean that the process should begin with a clear and complete understanding of the following:

• What assets are we trying to protect?

- From whom are we protecting them?
- And against what kinds of attack or misuse?
- How can I use integration to improve the operations of my client and disrupt the operations of criminals and terrorists?

Only after these questions are understood and answered can we begin to consider what to design and how to approach it. This book will help you learn how to design large integrated security systems, beginning with how to approach the project with the question, why?

GOALS OF THE BOOK

After finishing this book, you will have a new command of the following:

- Strategic issues

   The importance of integrating electronics and physical security with a solid foundation of good security management.
   How to work with the client's best interests in mind.
   How to know when to integrate systems and when it does not benefit the client.
   The difference between strategic integration and haphazard integration.
   The difference between component integration and integration of functions.
   How to dramatically improve security at a facility using good integration strategies.
   How to lower system and staffing costs and improve employee productivity using good system integration practices.
   How to create a solid basis for design, including

      What is security and what is not.
      How to determine the appropriate level of security.

   We will examine why you need to know more about IT systems and cover issues most designers did not know were important (to their ultimate peril and that of their clients).

We will discuss the esoteric side of integration, including how to design deployable delaying barriers and when and how to use reactive electronic automated protection systems that can actively intervene in a security event, stopping it immediately, from the security command center.

• Technical issues

How to budget systems and plan phased implementation.

We will fully explore the system design elements, including drawings of each type, and how to write quality specifications that stand up to challenges and clearly state the client's needs. We will examine what can be achieved by integrating with other building systems and explore the many ways to interface with them.

We will also examine the foundation of how to design, including

Drawing hierarchies.
Specification hierarchies.
How to completely integrate drawings and specification into a single, thorough, and perfectly understandable set of construction documents.

We will explore in great detail how to design each type of drawing required, including

Title sheets
Site plans
Floor plans
Elevations
Detail plans
Physical mounting details
Riser diagrams
Single line diagrams
System interface diagrams
System schedules

We will cover every typical aspect of security system specifications, including how to make them actually communicate the client's best interests in a way that the contractor understands what to do, how to do it, and how to know he or she has succeeded.

We will explore how to select the best technologies to use for each project with considerations to the client's best long-term interests, short-term budget concerns, installation cost factors, visual aesthetics, long-term maintenance and reliability considerations, the ability to expand the system flexibility, and the ability to scale the system size.

We will discuss how to secure the security system from various kinds of attacks, including insider attacks.

- Tactical issues

We will discuss how to manage client relations so that our design work is always in his or her best interest and he or she understands that and has constant confidence in us.

We will examine the differences between what needs to be in bid documents, construction documents, and as-built documents.

We will examine each type of technology and explore its benefits and limitations, including alarm and access control systems, analog and digital security video elements and systems, security communications systems, system infrastructure options, system integration options, and security command center options.

We will also discuss how to provide bidding support to clients that gives them a truly empirical standard of evaluation for which bidder to select.

We will explore the important and delicate matter of how to review system installation to help ensure the success of the consultant, the contractor, and the client.

We will also examine legal considerations and how good system design coupled with quality construction management and good relationship management can work together to the success of all project participants, avoiding problems, confrontations, and lawsuits.

Designing enterprise integrated security systems is exciting, challenging, and highly rewarding. A well-designed system can

save a client millions of dollars over its life in improved operations efficiency, improved safety, and avoided security losses.
The best enterprise integrated security system designers are
highly prized for this reason.

ARRANGEMENT OF THE BOOK

This book is arranged to go from the strategic to the technical to the tactical. Strategic subjects are covered primarily
in Chapters 1–3, technical subjects are covered primarily in
Chapters 4–10, and tactical subjects are covered primarily in
Chapters 11–19. The strategic section covers the "why" of design,
including some important history that provides insight into how
to stay in the path of industry development and not be side-
tracked as it goes by, the technical section explains how it is
done, and the tactical section provides the cultural knowledge
that leads to project success. If at any time (especially in the
technical section) it gets to be a little too much at once, it is ok
to jump around a bit. If you are not interested in the history of
electronic systems, or any other specific section, feel free to skip
that section; however, each section provides important insight
to the total process. For example, the section on history provides important insight into how to spot industry trends before
they occur. I have provided advice and consulted with manufacturers on important industry developments many years before
they were thought to be important by the manufacturers. Those
who listened and modified their designs accordingly moved out
in front of the industry. Those who did not were left behind.
How did I know where the industry was going? The seeds of
the future are in the past. Understanding how the founders of
the industry dealt with the technical problems they faced provides us with insight into why things work the way they do
today. Understanding what we want to achieve and how other
industries have dealt with similar problems provides us with
insight into how to manipulate technology to achieve it. The
great body of knowledge is always out there. We only have to
see and not just look. Understanding the industry from strategic, technical, and tactical viewpoints gives us the ability to solve
problems in a way that endures as technology develops and as

the organization grows. It is helpful to understand strategic and tactical aspects first to help understand why the technical details are so important. Although the challenge is considerable, the information is easily digestible if you take it in small bites.

The book is also arranged in a way that is useful as a learning tool and then can be used for years as a reference guide. You will find that some information is repeated. That is intentional. All the information herein is organized in a way that guides the user from the simple to the complex. So you will find a concept presented first, then a discussion of its strategic value, then tactical applications, and, finally, a discussion on the technical implementations of the technology.

Welcome to convergence-based integrated security systems design and thank you for reading.

2

Integrated Security System Design Benefits and Philosophy

WHY INTEGRATE SYSTEMS?

Why a Strategic Approach to Security Design Is Necessary

Everything operates within a hierarchy, and security is no exception. When an organization is founded, it establishes a mission. For Detroit automakers, that mission is to make money by building cars; for a chain of home hardware centers, it is to earn profits by selling hardware; for a hospital, it is to provide health care; for some nonprofit organizations, it is to assist developing countries; and for the United Nations, it is the pursuit of world peace. Each of these missions requires the establishment of business programs and organizational structures to support the mission. For a corporation, those programs could include manufacturing, distribution, and sales; for a health care organization, programs could include hospitals, clinics, and outreach programs; and for a nonprofit organization, the programs could include fund-raising and assistance programs. Almost all organizations also have accounting, information technology, filing, and administrative support programs. Once the programs are established, the organization must acquire assets to support the programs. Assets could include factories, warehouses, depots, shelved products, networks, furniture, and office buildings. In fact, each business program has a mission, subprograms, and assets. All assets need protection from misuse and harm. Enter the security program. The security program also has a mission, subprograms, and assets, like any other business program. One of those programs is the electronic component (high-tech systems, of which there may be several, including electronic security systems and information technology security systems).

Uniform Application of Security Policies

In order to get consistent results, it is imperative to use consistent processes and procedures. Imagine how chaotic it would be for a multinational corporation to allow every department at each site in each business unit to perform their accounting using their own choice of different software programs and different accounting techniques. It would be very difficult for the organization's management to consolidate all these different reports into a single cohesive picture of the organization's finances, and that could easily result in corporate losses and intense scrutiny by regulatory bodies and shareholders. It is also unwise for any organization to allow its business units and individual sites to establish their own individual security policies and procedures, guard-force standards, etc., which results in the potential for legal liability where different standards are applied at different business units. Enterprise-class security systems provide the platform for the uniform application of enterprise security policies across the entire organization. Enterprise-class security systems can also provide visibility regarding how other company policies are being applied and followed. What follows, then, can be better management when that information is made available to management in a cohesive way.

Force Multipliers

Integrated security systems are force multipliers. That is, they can expand the reach of a security staff by extending the eyes, ears, and voice of the console officer into the depths of the facility where he could not otherwise reach. The use of video guard tours enhances the role of patrol officers because many more guard tours can be made with video than with patrol staff alone. Detection and surveillance systems alert security staff of inappropriate or suspicious behaviors, and voice communications systems allow console officers to talk with subjects at a building in another state or nation while their behavior is observed on-screen.

Multiple Systems

The integration of alarm, access control, security video, and security voice communications into a single hardware/software platform permits much more efficient use of security manpower. Enterprise-class security systems are force multipliers. The better the system integration, the better the organization will be able to use its security force.

Multiple Buildings

When security systems span multiple buildings across a campus, the use of a single security system to monitor multiple buildings further expands the force multiplication factor of the system. The more buildings monitored, the higher is the value of the system.

Multiple Sites

Like multiple buildings on a single site, the monitoring of multiple sites further expands the system's ability to yield value. It is at this point that a true enterprise-class security system is required because monitoring multiple sites requires the use of network or Internet resources. Monitoring multiple sites can be tricky due to network bandwidth. We discuss how to get the most out of network bandwidth later in the book.

Multiple Business Units

Some large organizations also have multiple business units. For example, a petrochemical company may have drilling, transportation, refining, terminaling, and retailing units. Each of these can benefit by inclusion in an enterprise-wide security program.

Improved System Performance

Enterprise-class systems also provide significantly improved system performance. The integration of multiple systems at multiple sites into a cohesive user interface allows for simple, straightforward command and control. Gigantic systems become manageable.

Improved Monitoring

System monitoring is usually dramatically improved over nonenterprise systems. The integration of alarms, access control, video, and voice communications across the platform provides the console officer with coherent and timely information about ongoing events and trends. This is especially true of systems that utilize situational awareness software that put the alarms and alerts into a dynamically updating context of the site and floor plans so that the console officer can clearly see evolving suspicious activity in relation not only to the surroundings, but also to security response assets. In elegantly designed systems, when a visitor at a remote site presses an intercom call button and identifies himself or herself as an authorized user who has forgotten his or her access card, the console officer can pull up the record for that user quickly and confirm both the identity of the person at the intercom and that person's validity for that door. In this design, the system knows the user, the door, and the date and time. As the console officer drops the person's icon onto the door icon, the system either grants or denies access to the door based on the person's authorization for that door for that time. (This application requires custom software.)

Reduced Training

Enterprise-class security systems also require less training. The most basic console operator functions for a truly well-designed enterprise-class system can be learned in just a few minutes (answering alarms, viewing associated video, and answering the intercom). Because the interface is standardized across the enterprise, cross-training between buildings and facilities is practical. Also, operators from one site can provide support for a console officer or guard at another.

Better Communications

The system also provides for better communications. Imagine a single software platform that integrates security intercoms, telephone, cell phones with integral walkie-talkie functions, two-way radios, and paging into one easy-to-manage platform. Imagine a console officer who can wear a wireless headset, wear a wired headset, or use the computer's microphone and speakers and trigger the push-to-talk button with a footswitch or a mouse press. Efficiency of the system is further improved when the system queues the appropriate intercom automatically each time a camera is selected. The more the system presents the console operator with the tools to act as though he or she were there at the scene, the better the system serves the security purpose. (This function is best performed by situational awareness software in addition to conventional integrated security system software.)

COST BENEFITS

Improved Labor Efficiency

For many of the reasons stated previously, enterprise-class security systems enhance labor efficiencies. There are fewer consoles, fewer guards, no redundant monitoring, no nighttime live monitoring where it was not cost-effective before, and mutual aid between sites and buildings. All these factors free up guards to be on patrol and in live communication with the central console.

Reduced Maintenance Costs

Enterprise-class security systems are generally built on the use of a common technology across the entire platform. Counterintuitively, they are also generally built on simpler technology than less sophisticated systems. The key to success is often the elegant combination of simple technologies into a highly refined system. This inherent architectural simplicity often also results in lower maintenance costs. Although the results are elegant and sophisticated, the underlying technology is actually simpler than in times past. The key is to combine simple Boolean algebra logical functions (and, or, not, counting, timing, etc.) in elegant ways.

Improved System Longevity

Security systems are notoriously short lived. Contemporary security systems are composed of numerous delicate components that either fail mechanically or are unable to upgrade as the system scales. Thus, when upgrades are necessary, it is often necessary to throw out components that are only a few years old because they are not compatible with newer technologies. This inbuilt obsolescence has a long tradition in security systems, much to the consternation of building owners and consultants. Most building systems are expected to last 15 to 20 years. Some building systems, including the basic electrical infrastructure, are expected to last the life of the building. However, most electronic security systems made by major manufacturers and installed by major integrators last less than 7 years. A well-designed enterprise-class security system should last 10 to 15 years between major architectural upgrades. This is achievable using the principles taught in this book.

HOW INTEGRATION IS ACHIEVED

System integration involves both the integration of components and the integration of functions. High-level functions can be obtained by integrating components into a comprehensive working system instead of individual disconnected subsystems.

Systems integration is not a challenge of electronics; it is of course a technical challenge, but more importantly, it is a challenge of imagination. Sometimes, investigation, exploration, and invention are required. Consider it a puzzle to be solved. Look at the pieces and the objective. Do not accept at face value what you are told by the manufacturers about the capabilities and limitations of their systems. As a systems designer, you should know more than the manufacturers about how to integrate systems.

This book will help guide the designer along the path of understanding the technology and perhaps how to stimulate the imagination toward the goal.

SUMMARY

Each organization has a mission. It develops programs in support of that mission and acquires assets to support the programs. Those assets need protection to avoid their misuse, theft, or destruction.

Security system integration provides the following benefits:

- Uniform application of security policies
- Integrates multiple systems into one for operational simplicity
- Can integrate systems from multiple buildings and multiple sites for operational simplicity
- Can integrate the services for multiple business units for consistency

System integration can also provide the following:

- Improved monitoring
- Reduced training

- Better communications
- Cost benefits from improved labor efficiency, reduced maintenance costs, and improved system longevity

Integration is achieved through understanding the capabilities of the systems, combining basic elements together to perform higher functions, and using imagination.

3

History of Electronic Security

You may not be inclined to read a chapter on history, but you would be missing some important strategic principles. Otherwise, read on.

THE HISTORY OF INTEGRATED SECURITY SYSTEMS

Most industry folks believe that security systems are pretty well evolved today. Well, if that is true, many of them are deformed mutants. Early in the evolution of the systems, a particular thing happened that has served well the manufacturing community and not so well the integrators, designers, and clients. The good news is that the convergence of information technology infrastructure with security systems is changing that.

First, let's discuss the five generations of the technology and how it evolved.

THE FIRST GENERATION

As we travel through the history of electronic security systems, pay special attention to the evolution of alarm and access control systems, for in the failure of that industry to adapt to emerging technology were the seeds of today's and tomorrow's systems.

In the beginning, there were alarm systems. In 1851 in Boston, the first McCulloh loop telegraph-type alarm system was installed (Fig. 3-1). These systems involved sending a

Figure 3-1 McCulloh loop tape printer. Photo courtesy of the Los Angeles Police Department.

20-milli-amp current down a loop of wire and monitoring the current on the wire. If there were any change in current, it would cause a relay to change state or move a pen on a paper tape, sending a coded message. These were also heavily used in police and fire pull stations. Early intercom systems date back to the 1940s. The first magnetic stripe access control cards appeared in the 1960s. In 1961, the London police began using closed-circuit television (CCTV) to monitor activities in train stations. All of these were discrete, individual systems. For example, there were no camera switchers, but each camera reported to an individual monitor. Taping video was not done because it was too expensive. Alarm recording was done by hand notes. The idea was to be alerted to crime problems, to deter criminals, and to help those in need. These were the first generation of electronic security systems. By today's standards, these were very basic systems.

The first generation of access control systems is still in use today in the form of single-door hotel card systems (Fig. 3-2).[1] In the first generation of security technology, CCTV and intercom systems were a rarity. CCTV systems were primarily limited to one camera displayed on a single monitor. For those few systems that had more than one camera, typically a monitor was used for each camera. Where intercoms were used at all, they were typically either custom installations or an extension of a business intercom.

THE SECOND GENERATION

The second generation of access control systems networked eight card readers together to a dedicated computer that was approximately the size of a huge early electronic desk calculator (Fig. 3-3).[2] There were typically a pair of keypads, a nixie tube display, and a 3-in. paper tape. When a person presented a card to the front door of a facility, one would hear the paper tape chatter and the nixie tubes would display something like 1CO3-AG. One would then refer to a book that would indicate that card CO3 was granted access to door 1.

The second generation of alarm systems replaced the difficult to read meters and paper tapes with colored lamps and an audible alarm (Fig. 3-4).[3] Each alarm had three colored

Figure 3-2 First-generation card reader.

lamps—green for secure, red for alarm, and yellow when bypassed. There was a switch to bypass the alarms. The second generation began in approximately 1945 and continues today. CCTV systems were still little used, but intercom systems were becoming slightly less than obscure.

THE THIRD GENERATION

The third generation began in 1968 and continued until approximately 1978. Third-generation systems combined alarm and

Figure 3-3 Second-generation card access system.

Figure 3-4 Second-generation alarm panel. Image used with permission of Flair Electronics, Inc.

access control into one system. Up to 64 card readers and up to 256 alarm points were wired individually back to a PDP-8 or IBM Series 1 minicomputer with core memory, a beehive® terminal, and a line printer. A basic 16 card reader system could cost more than $100,000. During this time, CCTV began to be used by corporations and there were a few instances of intercom systems (Fig. 3-5).

Figure 3-5 Third-generation alarm/access control system. Image courtesy of Computer History Museum.

THE FOURTH GENERATION

In 1971, Intel introduced the first 4-bit microprocessor, the 4044, designed by Intel designer Ted Hoff for a Japanese calculator company. The processor boasted more than 2300 transistors—more switches than ENIAC had, which filled an entire room and required a dedicated air-conditioning system just for the computer (Fig. 3-6). The 6502 and 8088 8-bit microprocessors soon followed. These became the basis for a new breed of alarm and access control system technology called distributed controller systems.

Until 1974, each alarm and access control field device was wired individually back to the minicomputer, where a jumble of wires fed into custom-made circuit boards. All that wire was costly and often cost-prohibitive for most organizations. In 1974, one of the first distributed controller microcomputer-based alarm and access control systems was christened (by Cardkey®). It brought for the first time the ability to multiplex alarms and card readers into controller panels and network panels together into a distributed system. This was a radical change.

Figure 3-6 ENIAC computer. Image courtesy of the United States Army.

Finally, the cost of wiring, which was a major cost of early systems, was dramatically reduced. The earliest fourth-generation systems still terminated all these controllers into a central minicomputer, computer terminal, and line printer (early Cardkey 2000 system). The computers often had what I like to call a "user-surly" interface. When a person presented a card at the front door, the terminal still dutifully displayed something like "1CO3-AG" as the line printer chattered the same message. The console officer then looked that code up in a book.

Corporations began using intercoms and CCTV more extensively, although prices were still prohibitive for most users, with basic cameras costing as much as $1,200 each.[4] Major advances in CCTV occurred during this period as well. For the first time, it was possible to use just a couple of video monitors to view many cameras because the cameras were finally being terminated into sequential switchers that switched the monitor view from camera to camera in a sequence.[5]

As the industry progressed, costs decreased dramatically and the systems became much more user-friendly.

CCTV systems saw major advances. First, the advent of consumer videocassette recorders helped reduce the price of video storage to practical levels. In the early 1990s, video was being multiplexed by splitting the 30 frames per second that the recorder used between various cameras so that each camera was recorded two or more times per second onto a single tape. This economized video storage even further. In the alarm and access control system industry during this time, minicomputers gave way to PCs and server-based networked systems.

The laggard was intercom technology, for which there was no single industry standard and little compatibility between manufacturers, and it was difficult to network together buildings or sites. Intercom usage was minimal in most systems, usually reserved to assist access at remote gates and doors.

By the mid-1990s, however, the manufacturers realized that organizations wanted to integrate their various systems, and they had begun to integrate alarm, access control, and CCTV and intercoms into truly integrated systems. These systems could detect an intrusion, automatically call up an appropriate video camera to view the alarm scene, and if an intercom was nearby, they could sometimes queue the intercom for response. They would also display not only the video but also a map showing the area of the alarm to help the console operator better understand what he or she was seeing on the video monitor. This was the earliest attempt at what would later become known as situational awareness software.

These systems were able to detect and respond in real time to emerging security events. However, the system interfaces were highly proprietary and clumsy. Achievement of an interface between any two brands and models of systems would usually not apply to any other brands or models. Each time integration was desired, it was always new turf.

Stalled Progress

Many leading consultants believed that true systems integration would be performed by alarm and access control systems.[6] However, they were wrong. Significant progress stalled for more than a decade from the mid-1980s until after 2000. There was a fundamental reason for this that dates back to the foundation of the industry. In the early days of fourth-generation microprocessor-based systems, 64 kilobytes of random access memory (RAM) cost more than $1,000.[7] Because memory was so expensive, the founders of the industry solved the problem by putting the "personality" of the systems into erasable programmable read-only memory (EPROM). This meant that the systems functions were totally defined by the contents of their EPROMs. For the most part, their functions were not very field programmable. By the end of the 1990s, some of the leading systems had a seemingly infinite parts list, with a part for every function. This was because the industry had failed to change with the times. By 2000, it was possible to buy 64 megabytes of memory for approximately $10. That means that one could buy 1000 times the amount of memory for nearly 1/100 of the price of the 64 kilobytes of RAM in 1980. That is like getting a 747 airplane for the price of a pizza! As the computer industry surged forward with regard to capabilities and prices decreased dramatically, some consultants and integrators considered that the access control system industry was desperately trying to maintain its margins and was not generally implementing advances in system architecture. Accordingly, at the same time that microcomputer costs were decreasing, there were no significant reductions in access control system costs. The access control system industry was also hanging onto a long-term strategy of keeping its architecture as proprietary as possible while clients were increasingly asking consultants to design nonproprietary open-architecture systems. This strategy was doomed to fail.

Fourth-generation alarm and access control system architecture functions were defined by their physical attributes. They did what they did because of the programming attributes of the EPROM. Their functions were controlled by their physical environment.

A key strategic principle is that it is important to understand that good security is achieved by the ability to control the environment. Any device that cannot control its environment outside of what the product development designer imagined that environment to be is inherently limited in its ability to serve the needs of the client in controlling appropriate behavior. If you cannot control the environment, the environment controls you.

The fourth generation of alarm and access control systems was doomed by its failure to adapt to emerging trends of network technology and trying to hold tenaciously to controller-based systems. Enter the fifth generation.

FIFTH-GENERATION TECHNOLOGY

The problem with alarm and access control systems was that their manufacturers thought they were making alarm and access control systems (you read that correctly). What they were actually making was programmable logic controllers (PLCs), which were equipped with an alarm and access control system database. This is an important distinction because in their failure to understand this, they clung to EPROM architecture. Although EPROMs solved the industry's early problems of high memory costs, as memory costs plummeted, the industry confined its systems to the functions that its designers imagined for each box and implemented into the EPROM in the controller box. However, corporate and government clients all had special needs that could only be met with changes in the logic structure of the controller. For example, if a client needed a local alarm to sound at a door if it was held open too long during the daytime but wanted that door to alarm at the console immediately after hours, the client was sold an adapter box to perform this function for each door. Most manufacturers responded to such needs by building a long list of adapter boards and boxes to make their system perform each unique need. For those manufacturers who did not make a large assortment of these products, there were third-party manufacturers who did.

This strategy served the manufacturing community well but did not serve the clients so well because of the additional hardware and custom equipment required to perform perfectly logical functions needed by the average client. For example, if a client wanted to have confirmation of perimeter alarms by two detection systems (requiring both to trigger in order to cause an alarm but using each individually to cause an alert), most fourth-generation systems required each detection system to have its own inputs (providing the alert—the "or" function). Then the system would reflect the status of those inputs on output relays, which would then be hardwired together to create "and" functions, and those hard-wired outputs would be wired to additional inputs as "and" function alarms. This may not sound like a challenge, but for perimeter systems comprising 50 or more detection zones in each detection system, the cost of hardwire and wiring was often thousands of dollars more than the cost of a PLC-based system.

However, a few industry experts understood that there is no function desired by any client that cannot be performed by a simpler, not a more complicated, system architecture. Every imaginable function can be performed by a simple combination of inputs, outputs, memory, logic cells, counters, and timers. Like dancing, in which endless variety can be achieved with only a few basic steps, an endless variety of functions can be achieved with only these few basic logic objects. That structure defines PLC architecture. A few manufacturers introduced PLC-based alarm and access control systems, notably those who made building automation systems (BAS) that were already based on PLC architecture. However, these products never made a significant impact in the marketplace because the manufacturers continued to focus their marketing efforts on their BAS product lines instead of their access control system products.

The key to fifth-generation alarm and access control systems is that they are all based on entirely software-based functions, whereas earlier systems were based on functions that were defined in hardware. In the late 1980s and 1990s, however, the industry was driven to integrate multiple buildings and sites. The industry struggled with a variety of unsuccessful system architectures until it gradually adopted a network infrastructure already in place in most businesses—the local area network (LAN), municipal area network (MAN), and wide area network (WAN) Ethernet architecture. As the manufacturers began adapting their systems to Ethernet architectures, a convergence of security systems began to occur, bringing together alarm, access control, CCTV, and voice communication systems into a single integrated system.

That convergence continues today. In its next phase, distributed alarm and access control system controllers will possibly totally disappear as CCTV manufacturers realize that they can totally integrate alarm and access and intercom functions into their CCTV Ethernet architecture. This will result in a system that is composed entirely of "edge devices" (cameras, intercoms, door access hardware, etc.) and a server/workstation for the user interface. These are interfaced together on the LAN.

Today's digital video cameras already have digital signal processing (DSP) chips and up to 64 megabytes of RAM. Soon, each individual door's access devices will be served by a single tiny controller in a junction box above the door. That tiny circuit board will comprise inputs, outputs, a card reader port, door lock output, and an exit device port, all served by a DSP chip and several megabytes of memory. A database of all users for that door will be contained in the DSP's memory board. A single centrally located controller may manage all of the microcontrollers in the entire building.

As these edge devices begin to connect directly to the LAN without an intervening controller, costs will decrease dramatically. Although the industry seems to be concerned about this development, in fact it will result in a substantially higher use of the systems. The industry need not fear. In the same way that CCTV manufactures feared the price drop below $1,000 per camera, only to find that camera sales soared, so too will alarm and access control and intercom sales soar as the introduction of microcontrollers causes prices to decrease. When these devices are combined with PLC programmability, which will allow an infinite variety of applications without an endless stock of hardware, the industry will finally have arrived. Within the next few years, the industry will very likely be served by only edge devices and software, connected together on a security LAN.

AVOIDING OBSOLESCENCE

Obsolescence is a funny thing. When we specify obsolete equipment, it does not seem so at the time. How can we tell what is going to be obsolete? How long is a good enough life cycle? How about a migration path to the future? There are signs.

Planned Obsolescence

At one time, a major access control manufacturer had in its current line five different access control systems in which each was designed to serve a different market growth segment, from a small system that could support only approximately 32 readers to a large system that could serve multiple sites and could handle thousands of alarms, card readers, etc. None of those systems could migrate to the next. If a consultant were to specify a smaller system from this manufacturer, and the client outgrew that system in only 2 years, for example, the client would have to abandon much of the capital investment and purchase a new system. That is built-in obsolescence. That company does not exist anymore. It was bought by a big corporate integrator. It is their problem now (and their clients' problem too).

Unplanned Obsolescence

The industry is undergoing a sea change as this book is written. Much of today's access control and video technology will not exist in any form within the next few years. How do I know? Market forces, that's how. Some have argued that the industry has long been based on serving the manufacturers, not the clients. If that is true, information technology-based systems will largely end that. It is possible that someday the industry will manufacture edge devices and software, nothing else—no digital video recorders, no access control panels, nothing but small microcontrollers and digital cameras that connect field devices directly to and that are powered by the Ethernet and software. It is a good bet that all those bent metal boxes that manufacturers sell will be obsolete soon. This is about to become a very thin market with very few manufacturers (but with many software vendors in the early years). As this book was being written, the very first of these systems was introduced.

SUMMARY

There are five generations of security system technology:

- The first generation included stand-alone card readers and McCulloh loop alarms.

- The second generation included centralized card readers on rudimentary processors and lamp-type alarm panels. Early CCTV cameras began to see some limited use.
- The third generation of systems included integrated alarm/access control systems on early minicomputers, slightly more CCTV usage, and the first use of business intercom systems for security.
- The fourth generation of systems introduced distributed processing panels for alarm/access control systems, major advancements in CCTV, and dedicated-use security intercoms. Systems integration began in the fourth generation.
- The fifth generation will likely be based on DSP-type microprocessors for alarm/access control system, with integral TCP/IP switchers that may integrate digital cameras and intercoms, all local to the door.

CHAPTER NOTES

1. An example of first-generation card access systems is the Ving Card® system.
2. Examples of second-generation access control systems include the Rusco® 500, the early Cardkey 1200, and numerous Secom® systems.
3. An example of a second-generation alarm system is the Flair® alarm panel.
4. RCA Vidicon® camera typical pricing as of 1980.
5. One of the first sequential switchers was made by Vicon.
6. Surprisingly, one of the earliest full-integration platforms came from a small company in Branson, Missouri, called Orion Technologies. Other major video manufacturers quickly followed suit, leaving alarm/access control system manufacturers as systems to be integrated instead of being the primary integration platform.
7. Typical price for static RAM circa 1980.

Security System Design

4

Security System Design Elements

When it comes to integrated security systems designs, I do not recommend napkins. This is especially true for enterprise security systems. These systems are highly integrated into their environments and often highly integrated into other systems. Knowledge is required. Skill is needed. Integrators who work from the "seat-of-the-pants" often leave the project with their pants on fire. Enterprise security systems design involves a set of tools and a process. The following is a brief description of the tools and the process, which will be elaborated on in Chapters 5–9.

THE TOOLS

The tools of design include drawings, specifications, interdiscipline coordination, product selection, project management, and client management.

Drawings

Drawings are the heart of the design. Drawings are discussed in detail in Chapter 10, but it is important to understand their strategic role in the process, which is described here. Drawings should show the following:

- The relationship of devices to their physical environment (plans, elevations, and physical details)
- The relationship of devices to the conduit system and to power (plans and risers)
- The relationship of devices to each other (single line diagrams)
- The relationship of devices to the user (programming schedules)

  Drawings must serve five distinct types of users:

- The bid estimator: The bid estimator must determine what materials are needed. Helpful drawing tools include device schedules (spreadsheets listing devices and their attributes) and plans showing device locations and conduit lengths, sizes, and wire fills. Other drawings useful to the bid estimator include single line diagrams, riser diagrams, and system interfacing diagrams.
- The installer: The installer needs drawings that show both the big picture and the smallest details. Therefore, it is helpful if the drawings are formatted in a hierarchical fashion. Single lines show the big picture. Plans show device locations and their relationship to the building and conduit system. Physical details and interface details show the smaller details.
- The project manager: The project manager needs to manage the progress of the installation, including coordinating the

ordering and arrival of parts and supplies and coordinating manpower to the project at the correct time, in the correct place, and in coordination with other trades to get all devices mounted and all connections made. He or she will primarily rely on schedules for provisioning logistics, plans to measure installation progress, and single line diagrams to gauge how close the system is to start-up.

- The maintenance technician: After the system is installed, it is the maintenance tech's turf. He or she will need single line diagrams to determine how the system interconnects, plans to determine where devices are located and how they connect in the physical space, and risers and power schedules to know where to go from floor to floor and the source of power for each device. The integrator should be required to provide maintenance manuals that have all these drawings. I also recommend that the integrator be required to place a pocket on the inside door of each electronics assembly with an envelope containing the system single line diagram, riser, and plans appropriate to service the equipment in that rack. Also, he or she should be required to install a field intercom station at each service location to communicate with the console to facilitate communications with another technician or console operator.

- The next engineer expanding the system: Many systems undergo expansion on an irregular basis. You may not be the next engineer, but someone will be. He or she will need all of your drawings in order to understand how to expand the system. The client should receive all your drawings in AutoCAD® form and specifications in Adobe PDF form.

Specifications

Specifications are discussed in detail in Chapter 10, but it is important to understand their strategic role in the process, which is described here.

If drawings are the heart of the design, specifications are the head. Specifications generally take precedent in legal disputes. Drawings are just there to illustrate the standards and practices written into the specifications. If you are very long in your career, you will see some pretty bad specs. We used to joke in our office about someday seeing a set of specifications that simply say "Make it work real good." Some come pretty close to that. We have seen security system specifications that are only 5 pages long. There is a lot of room there for serious mistakes by a well-meaning contractor. Many security system contracting problems are the result of incomplete or wrong specifications.

With possibly very few exceptions, most integrators I have met sincerely want to do well for their clients. It is the designer's job to provide the integrator with enough information to do well. To the extent that drawings and specifications are incomplete, inaccurate, or misleading, the contractor can make unintended errors that will be costly and aggravating to the installer, the integrator for whom he or she works, and most certainly the system's owner.

Specifications should include a description of what the project entails; descriptions of the whole integrated system and each subsystem; a description of the services the contractor will provide; and a list of acceptable products and acceptable installation, testing, acceptance, training, and warranty practices. Different specification formats prevail in different areas of the world, and occasionally these may change as building code authorities evolve in their preferences. This will all be covered in detail in Chapter 10.

Product Selection

Specifying the correct products for the job can result in a wonderful system that can easily exceed the owner's expectations. The wrong products can leave the owner upset with the installer, the manufacturer, and the designer. Here is where the designer has to have free reign to do what is in the best interest of the client. To the extent that the designer is placed under pressure to specify one brand or another due to market forces, I assure you that the owner will suffer. If the owner suffers, everyone suffers. The operator suffers, the maintenance tech suffers, the integrator who has to listen to an unhappy client suffers, the manufacturer suffers, and the industry suffers. Countless manufacturers and integrators have lost repeat work (and lost client referrals) due to expediencies in product selection. Respect the client's interests in product selections. Have a pure heart on this. You will enjoy a strong reputation among your clients, peers, and competitors. Your professional reputation is one of your most valuable assets, and at all times it is in your own hands. The future is yours to build or to ruin.

Interdiscipline Coordination

This is where enterprise and integrated security systems make it or break it. Some designers are especially adroit at coordinating the interfaces of related systems. Their interfaces work beyond all expectations and their clients are extremely satisfied. Learn this skill and you will master a career. Chapter 14 focuses on this art. Read it thoroughly and you will be well respected by your peers.

These higher skills mark the difference between journeyman and master designers. I was once presented with a challenge to design an alarm/CCTV/voice communications system to protect an unmanned offshore oil platform where there was only a 60-kb satellite up/downlink throughput and only 24 watts of power available to power the security system equipment. A normal system design would have required the client to spend an additional $6,000 per month on satellite throughput and a new capital investment of $100,000 in additional solar panels to power it. Our design incorporated the existing satellite throughput and required no additional power investment. This was done with off-the-shelf equipment simply by using an existing SCADA system and programmable logic controller to do alarm processing instead of adding a separate alarm system and by manipulating the video data packet size and system operation so that only one camera was ever on the satellite at one time to limit video throughput. We also designed custom software that sequenced one frame of video at a time across the satellite link in order to prevent contention between the cameras or trying to stuff too much data across a too small pipe. This sort of design expertise makes very happy clients and can be the difference between impossible and doable designs.

Project Management

The designer has to manage the design portion of the project. Design project management is all about delivering a design that meets the client's needs, the integrator's needs, and the client's project manager's needs. The designer must do all this while working on other projects; he or she must provide the project deliverables on time and complete, and keep all parties happy. If the designer is very busy, on a normal project this can be a nearly unachievable task, like running a marathon while balancing spinning plates on sticks. On some projects, if the client's project manager does not control the restless troops, it is more like running a marathon while balancing spinning plates with one's hair on fire.

Project management has four main phases:

- Initiating the project
- Planning the project
- Executing the project
- Controlling and closing the project

A number of things in each project need management. The Project Management Institute (PMI) certifies project managers with both the Project Management Professional (PMP) and PMI certifications. The PMP process includes the following:

- Establishing the framework for project management
- Managing the scope of the project
- Managing time
- Managing cost
- Managing quality
- Managing people
- Managing communications
- Managing risk
- Managing procurement
- Managing the project's integration aspects
- Maintaining a high level of professionalism throughout the project

There are three main aspects to each project:

- Project scope of work
- Project schedule
- Project cost

Although it is beyond the scope of this book to teach project management, I will state that it is an essential skill for any engineer. Unless the reader is already professionally trained in project management, I strongly encourage the reader to invest in several books on project management and spend several weeks getting familiar with the principles. Project management is all about providing structure and planning to what seems to many to be an intuitive process. However, without the necessary structure, project management quickly descends into crisis management and then frequently damage control. Millions of dollars are lost each year by firms that entrust large projects to unqualified project managers. Your career will flourish if you have the requisite project management skills.

One of the most important aspects of project management is design management. One of the secrets to good design management is to keep the process simple and batched. That is, do the work in batches, not strung out over weeks. Accumulate tasks, accumulate coordination information, and then design. Do not spend many hours on a project until the design task is ready. Take endless notes and organize them into design, product selection, coordination with other parties, interdiscipline coordination, and client interfaces. Then, when all is ready, close the doors, don't take calls, and concentrate on the drawings.

Designers who allow the project to pass over them like a wave spend their careers lying sideways in the public trough like there is no tomorrow. It is a fact. There are time bandits on each project. They will ask for endless nuances of revisions and endless questions; they will want information before it can possibly be ready, certainly before their work is ready. Here is the priority:

- Get project requirements.
- Get environmental information.

- Get and give coordination requirements information.
- Design the system.
- Check for accuracy.
- Revise design.
- Deliver the final design.

Tips on Schedule Management

Throughout the project, keep everyone else on your schedule. Get the client's project manager to agree on a schedule for your work. Deliver a copy of the schedule to the project manager. Stick to the schedule. Remind others of your schedule when they want it now. There will be those who push you unreasonably for a schedule because they waited too long in the project to hire you. However, you must be thorough in your design and not make rash decisions that are not adequately researched. Remember, if they want it bad, they'll likely get it bad. Everyone will suffer, especially your reputation.

All the previous discussion is purely technical. When the client arrives, the spotlight is on you. Successful project management is the intersection of schedule control, scope control, and cost control. Experience helps more than a little. Project management is a science, but it is also an art. I recommend two fine books to help with this:

- *PMP® Exam Prep—A Course in a Book* (RMC Publications, ISBN 0-9711647-3-8): This book is associated with the Project Management Institute, which certifies project managers with the PMP certification. It is a wonderful book to help prepare students for the rigorous PMP certification. I highly recommend pursuing the PMP certification. It is a tough one, but it will help you succeed in every project and certainly distinguishes its holders among their peers.
- *Project Rescue* by Sanjiv Purba and Joseph J. Zucchero (McGraw-Hill/Osborne): This book deals with how to recognize projects that may be headed for disaster and how to recover them. This is one of the best books I have read on project management.

Client Management

Tips on Relationship Management

Someday, you will find yourself sitting in a conference room full of people. They will include the owner's representative, the project manager (these two might be the same person), perhaps several architects (building shell and core, structural, interiors, and landscape), consultants (electrical, mechanical, plumbing, etc.), contractors (general contractor, electrical contractor, security contractor, etc.), and stakeholders (security director, information technology director, etc.). At some point in the meeting, they will all turn to you, the security designer, and ask for your presentation or opinion. It is important to understand that each of these people has at least three agendas:

- The first agenda is their role in the project. The interiors architect has a different agenda than the shell and core architect; the general contractor has a different agenda than the electrical contractor. The information technology director does not care about the agenda of the landscape contractor.
- The second agenda is that of their employer. The employer may have a technology bias or a business culture that is aggressive or conservative.
- The third agenda is that of the individual. He or she may be humble or pompous, technically competent or covering up a feeling of inadequacy.

One difference between good designers and great designers is how well they understand and implement the way they relate to each of these parties and each of their agendas in a project. Early in the project, one must learn the participants and their agendas. Then, it is important to talk to the person, asking the questions that speak to his professional agenda, his employers' agenda, and in a muted way to his personal agenda. This must be done while speaking in a broad way to the audience at large and, most important, it must be done in the context of advancing the security project scope on schedule and within budget.

THE PLACE OF ELECTRONICS IN THE OVERALL SECURITY PROCESS

Security design most of all is a process. Electronic security systems are only one of many tools in the process. Important though they are, they are also most often depended on to deliver results beyond their ability, and most often they are not coupled with the other countermeasures that can make them the effective tool they can be. The most important element of a world-class security system is to design it in its proper context so that it can deliver the best results. When a security system is properly designed and applied as part of a comprehensive security program, it can properly serve its client.

The Security Program

I am fascinated that so many organizations that pay so much attention to best business practices and are diligent in their accounting and manage their productive assets efficiently in the context of producing revenues or fulfilling the organization's mission nonetheless give very little regard to the same level of professionalism in their security organization. Security is not a commodity. It is a value. Much like accounting, it shares two attributes in support of the organization's mission. Security and accounting both serve to support the organization's ability to comply with codes and regulations, and they both minimize losses in the organization. However, accounting departments are historically much better equipped to account for their successes. Security managers and directors historically come from a law enforcement background where the emphasis is on crime reaction, not crime prevention, and where there is little focus on cost/benefit calculations.[1] This has not served security management well in their ability to obtain required resources, and it has not served the organizations well in that required resources are seldom forthcoming until after a serious event that could easily have been prevented. Security, like any other business program, should be built on a sound and documentable financial basis.

ESTABLISH ELECTRONIC SECURITY PROGRAM OBJECTIVES

Security Policy: The Foundation of All Countermeasures

There should be a good foundational reason for any security countermeasure, and that reason should be founded in security policy. If a contractor, consultant, or owner cannot point to a specific security policy as a reason for a specific countermeasure, then either there is not a good reason for the countermeasure or there is a flaw or gap in the policy. This is one of the most important principles of good security system design, and I cannot emphasize it enough. Countermeasures without policy give skillful litigation attorneys room to criticize the lack of uniform application of security policy, which is a major focus of security litigation.

Designs that are created without a basis in a comprehensive security policy will leave vulnerabilities in the protection of the organization and its assets. These are vulnerability holes in the security program that are created by the system designer's lack of awareness of some critical asset needing protection or some unanalyzed threat, or of some vulnerability that is unknown without a comprehensive security risk assessment, security master plan, and security policies and procedures. If you are asked to design a security system without these prerequisites, you should first recommend these steps; if still you are asked to proceed, be sure to indicate in your contract that the system may not provide adequate protection against any unknown vulnerabilities.

The following is the order of battle for protecting any asset:

- Perform a security risk assessment.[2]

    Understand what assets there are to protect.
    Understand what threats exist that could be interested in destroying, damaging, or misusing the assets. What are their motivation, history, and capabilities? What entry

methods do they use? What tools do they use? What attack scenarios do they use? How do they plan attacks? Is the threat one of terrorism or simply O.D.C. (ordinary decent crime).[3]

Understand what vulnerabilities exist that these threats could exploit and what existing countermeasures are in place to protect the assets.

What is the overall likelihood of attack, and how attractive are these assets to potential attackers?

- Create a security plan.

  Evaluate what additional countermeasures are required in order to fully protect the assets. Budget and prioritize the countermeasures based on cost, ease of implementation, and effectiveness.

- Create a schedule of implementation.

  Immediate action items (this will include the establishment of security policies and procedures).
  Phased implementation:

  > High-risk conditions
  > Low-risk conditions
  > As budget becomes available

  Understand that any unimplemented countermeasure is a remaining vulnerability. Be prepared to accept or transfer that risk.

- Establish security policies and procedures.

  Define what risks are to be protected.
  Define how they will be protected and by what type of countermeasures.

  > High-tech: electronic security systems, information technology security, telephone system security, etc.

Low-tech: locks, barriers, landscaping, lighting, signage, etc.

No tech: policies and procedures, security programs, security awareness training, guard programs, bomb and drug dogs, etc.

Define how employees, visitors, and contractors are to be handled and their responsibilities relative to the organization's security.

Define how the organization will detect, assess, and manage threats and which behaviors will be tolerated and which will not.

Design a security program to address the security management objectives, including employee awareness training and rules for management, employees, guards, and visitors and contractors.

Design an environment that facilitates appropriate behavior, including area segregation for employees and visitors and trespass identification signage.

Design an electronic security system to help management detect, assess, and manage inappropriate behavior.

Understand and implement the project in accordance with pertinent regulations and codes, which could be from any of the following sources or regulatory agencies:

Department of Defense

Coast Guard

International and Uniform Building Codes and Municipal Building Codes and Authorities Having Jurisdiction (local agencies)

National Fire Protection Association and municipal fire safety codes

Occupational Safety and Health Act

Office of Statewide Health Planning and Development, the California Earthquake Code

International Ship and Port Security and Maritime Security requirements

Codes of Federal Regulations

Specific industry standards

Special compliances—Secret Service, etc.

TYPES OF DESIGN EFFORTS

New Construction

New construction projects are typically driven by the architect, and all consulting disciplines follow the architect's lead with regard to design standards, project management, and schedule. New construction projects typically are predictable. There is clear direction on what disciplines need coordination and each person in those trades understands that coordination is part of the effort. All are working under one leader toward a common goal—a successful project on a specific completion date. The architect will closely guard access to the owner, so all direction comes from the architect alone unless he or she arranges a meeting with the owner for input and review.

Renovation or Retrofit

Renovation projects vary in size and scope. Generally, the security system upgrade is part of a larger upgrade effort, and in many ways these projects are similar to new construction projects, except that there are usually fewer trades and the construction cycle is not as long. Again, the architect will take the lead on the project, unless the owner has designated a specific project manager to represent his or her interests.

Government-Driven Projects

Government projects are often regulation driven. They may also be driven by new construction or renovation requirements, but the common thread is that there will be an agency or multiple agencies involved whose specific security needs are defined in an international, federal, state, or local regulation to which they must comply.

The government entity will usually have a set of standards for the system specification, for how the system is designed, approved, and built, and for how it operates. The designer must follow these guidelines or regulations exactly; his or her success will be judged by someone whose job it is to find fault with every system. If there is any fault, it will be found, so it pays to get it right the first time. There should be no shortcuts, no adaptations to personal preference, and no designing the system to suit one's own point of view. No point of view matters except that of the reviewer who will be judging the outcome against the code or regulation. Know your codes.

Even when the project is privately owned, codes and regulations may rule. For example, the security for any seaport, airport, or river terminal is guided by a set of specific codes, regulations, and rules. In many cases, the project may have to respond to multiple standards from multiple agencies. The very acceptance of the project by public agencies may hinge on how well the security designer understands these rules. It is not uncommon, for example, for liquified natural gas (LNG) projects to rest entirely on the fulfillment of security regulations. The owner may risk hundreds of millions or even a billion dollars on the quality of the security consulting effort.

It is very dangerous indeed for security designers who are unfamiliar with the regulations to attempt to design facility security for such a project. This can be a path to bankruptcy for both the designer and the owner who hired him or her. In one case, the owner of a functioning and prestigious high-rise commercial building in San Francisco faced a forced closure of his building by the fire department because the building manager had hired a security contractor to equip all stair tower doors with electric locks. The security contractor won the contract because his price was by far the lowest. However, the building manager did not know that what made the price so low, the use of electric strikes instead of approved stair tower door locks, also put the building out of compliance with building fire codes. The installation of strikes corrupted the fire-rated door frames, voiding their fire rating, and ultimately the owner was required to replace all the affected stair tower doors and new frames with approved assemblies at a cost that was significantly higher than the highest of the original bids. The owner was out a lot of money and the security contractor went bankrupt. This was an expensive way for both the owner and the security contractor to learn the fire code. Know your codes.

Commercial Projects

Commercial projects are often a delight to work on. Unlike government projects, where regulations and process rules, a commercial enterprise is always interested in getting to the finish as fast as possible and with as little cost and process as necessary. The commercial entity is usually not interested in the best system but, rather, a system that is good enough. Uniform building codes and fire/life safety codes will always apply. In many commercial projects, the designer is working directly for the project owner, so lines of communication are short and it is easier for the designer to understand the owner's needs and accommodate them efficiently. That personal relationship can also make the project more personally rewarding since the owner often expresses his or her satisfaction directly to the designer after the project is complete.

Facilities-Driven Projects

Major and minor renovations alike are often placed under the jurisdiction of the facilities department of an organization. Facilities managers have a set of project processes that they follow and that the designer must understand. In these projects, the facilities manager will be the main point of contact, and the architect, consultants, and contractors will all work directly for the facilities manager. The facilities manager is often a contractor rather than an employee of the company he or she serves, so there is often not a direct path to the owner for decisions and decisions are often driven more by cost than functions.

User-Driven Projects

In rare cases, the designer may have the opportunity to work directly for the user. These projects are generally smaller, and the user usually wants the project to cost as little as possible and be done to a high standard. It is easy to understand the requirements because there is direct access to the user. Often, however, there can be severe time and budget constraints on the work. Another type of user-driven project is that in which the designer is called in to solve problems that were created by another design. These projects are unique opportunities to be creative and achieve high success.

PROJECT DRIVERS

There is always some reason why the owner wants a security system designed. It is important to know the reasons, both expressed and unexpressed, because whether the owner tells the designer or not, he or she expects those concerns to be addressed. So it is incumbent upon the designer to find out why the project is important to the owner and what problems the owner wants addressed.

Construction Effort

The drivers for a construction effort on the surface seem obvious; there is construction and the owner needs a new security system to protect the new building or office suite. However, there will still be hidden drivers that the designer must know. These could include the specific security needs of each department in the building and how the area crime statistics affect the risk of the owner.

Regulation Compliance

Sometimes, the project flows out of a need to meet a new code or regulation. It cannot be stressed enough the need to know and understand the code and regulation requirements for each project.

Event Driven

Often, one or more security events may occur that create a groundswell of concern among employees or the owner's assets may be found to be at risk due to an event. Nothing creates awareness like a loss or the threat of a loss. Even where an asset is not compromised, the mere evidence of an attempt is enough to cause the owner to seek the help of a qualified consultant.

Insurance Driven

In some cases, the owner's insurer may dictate that certain measures be taken in order to qualify for insurance at an attractive rate.

Hidden Agendas

In almost every project, there are hidden agendas that are real, if not obvious, drivers for the project. It may be difficult to get the owner to divulge these, but if the designer senses that the owner is not telling him or her everything, it is better to ask than to work in ignorance. The owner will judge the success of the project by its ability to meet this hidden agenda, spoken or not.

SUMMARY

The tools of security system design include drawings, specifications, interdiscipline coordination, product selection, project management, and client management.

Drawings should show the relationship of the devices to their physical environment, the relationship of devices to the conduit system and power, the relationship of devices to each other, and the relationship of devices to the user. Drawings should be designed to serve the bid estimator, the installer, the project manager, the maintenance technician, and the engineer who will later expand the system.

Specifications describe what the system is, what products are acceptable, and how it should be installed. The specifications detail the requirements for interdiscipline coordination and project management.

The design process should begin with the establishment of a security program based on a comprehensive risk assessment. No part of a system should be designed without knowing what role it serves in the security policy.

Project types include

- New construction
- Renovation or retrofit

- Government-driven projects
- Commercial projects
- Facilities-driven projects
- User-driven projects

Project drivers include

- Construction effort
- Regulation compliance
- Event driven
- Insurance driven
- Hidden agendas

CHAPTER NOTES

1. "In new era, corporate security looks beyond guns and badges." *New York Times*, May 27, 2002.
2. A variety of security assessment models exist, from the simple to the highly detailed. One of the best is by the American Petroleum Institute/National Petrochemical and Refiners Association. Although originally intended for chemical and petrochemical sites, this is so complete that it can be used effectively at any type of facility.
3. From *To Catch a Thief* by John Mortimer: "What the British police used to call O.D.C. (ordinary decent crime) has suffered a sad decline in this era of predominantly indecent and extraordinary offenses." The *New York Times* on the Web – August 24, 1997. Available at http://www.nytimes.com/books/97/08/24/reviews/970824.24mortimt.html?_r=1.

5

Electronics Elements (High-Level Discussion)

No matter what, all elements of security can only achieve one or more of the following five basic functions:

- Deterrence
- Detection
- Assessment
- Reaction (delay and response)
- Evidence gathering

Electronic systems can act as a deterrent, perform detection, assist in the assessment of the event with regard to its severity, assist in reaction, and gather evidence. Each element of electronic security systems can perform one or more of these tasks.

ACCESS CONTROL ELEMENTS

One of the basic concepts of security is to limit access only to people who share a common interest with the organization— people who intend to interact with the best interests of the organization in mind. In other words, do not allow entry to criminals who will harm the organization's people, take or misuse its physical property or intellectual property, or harm its good name. Organizations use access control systems to help achieve this goal. Access control systems use something that the person is (biometric comparison), has (a token or a smart card), or knows (a password) to make judgments as to whether the person should be allowed into a secure area.[1]

The systems commonly use a credential to identify the subject as a person who is authorized to be in a certain area at a certain time. Most credentials are in the form of an identification badge that the subject can wear. This may display the person's image and name, and it may use a color or pattern scheme that identifies to others "in the know" that the subject is permitted in the organization's premises and sometimes indicates which areas. This card also often has an electronic coding that is used with card readers to allow the enterprise security system to make judgments on behalf of the organization regarding whether the bearer is permitted through a door, gate, or portal at a specific time or day. Sometimes, keypads are used instead of cards.

More secure systems use a biometric credential—a fingerprint, hand geometry, retinal scan, iris scan, voice comparator, facial recognition, finger blood vessel scan or other measure—to determine that the person is authorized. Often, biometric readers simply confirm that the person is who he or she claims to be (by having presented a card or key code). In the most sophisticated variant, the biometric systems actually identify the user by matching the biometric sample against a vast database of other previously taken samples.

DETECTION ELEMENTS

If deterrence is the ultimate goal of security countermeasures, then detection is where deterrence begins.[2] The ability to detect is at the heart of eliminating the probability of success of the criminal or terrorist mission. Detection is a process that includes sensing, processing, and transmitting the detection, and reporting it to someone who can act.[3]

Alarm Sensors

There are many types of alarm sensors, including the following:

- Point detection (e.g., door, window, duress [panic switch] and floor-pad switches).
- Beam detection (photoelectric or laser beams).
- Volumetric: The sensing of unwanted motion in a defined area.
- Relay detection: Sensing the condition of another process or system.
- Capacitance detection: These commonly include numerous perimeter detection systems that detect the presence of a person in an area where he or she should not be.
- Intelligent detection: Utilization of microprocessors and software to cause detection of a specific behavior or condition in specific circumstances.

Alarm Processors

In most cases involving sophisticated electronic security systems (including all enterprise security systems), the detection is processed locally before it is transmitted. Processing may involve simple decisions such as whether or not the detection is occurring during an appropriate time period (no volumetric alarms in a office building lobby during normal working hours). The processing may be more extensive, such as checking to determine if a group of conditions are right to trigger the alarm. The processing typically occurs in an alarm and access control system controller. Usually, the processor will also perform a check to ensure that the detection was received ok.

Alarm Transmission

Once the alarm is processed, it must be transmitted to someone who can take action on the detection. In the past, this occurred over RS-485 or similar data lines. Today, almost all integrated system alarm transmissions are over TCP/IP Ethernet connections. These are sometimes converted to fiber-optic or wireless (802.11 or other) mediums.

Alarm Reporting

The detection is received by a monitoring device and is acknowledged by a person who can act on it. In enterprise security systems, the detection is almost always displayed on a computer with specialized software that is also capable of integrating access control, CCTV, voice communications, and ancillary systems integration, which may include two-way radio, private automatic branch exchange (PABX), elevators, building automation, information technology, and other systems.

Follow-On Action

Following detection and assessment, the security system should assist in preventing an adversary from successful completion of a malevolent action against a facility.[4] Follow-on action is that integration element which allows the enterprise security system to do some amazing things. For example, based on detection of an intrusion into a highly restricted area, the system can implement delaying barriers that might include dispatching personnel, activating vehicle or pedestrian barriers (e.g., rising bollards or roll-down doors), dousing all lights, and disorienting audio signals (sounding alarms within the structure, which raises the anxiety level of the aggressor) to disrupt the progress of the attackers.[5] Follow-on actions can also facilitate access for a legitimate user, such as turning on lights from a parking garage through lobbies, corridors, and to the exact office suite of a card holder.

ASSESSMENT AND VERIFICATION ELEMENTS

Some alarm notifications are a display of nuisance conditions and not a real alarm, so it is important to vet all alarms so as not to respond to a tree branch falling against a perimeter fence. There are several ways that assessment can be achieved:

- Guard response assessment: One can dispatch a guard to check out the alarm condition. This takes time and is costly. The delay before assessment is not desirable, and it is possible that by the time the guard arrives at the alarm site, the person who caused it may be gone so no verification is possible, even though the alarm was real. Guard response assessment is not ideal.
- Second alarm sensor assessment: An alarm can also be verified by the activation of a second alarm. Although it is possible for a single nuisance alarm to occur, it is less likely that two nuisance alarms could occur in rapid succession. In a well-designed integrated security system, alarms are often coupled to confirm each other.
- Audio assessment: In parking structures and other remote areas, audio alarms are often used that respond to specific sounds such as a person screaming in alarm or fear. The same microphone that caused the alarm can then be used to confirm it. By listening to the area where the alarm occurred, a console guard can confirm that the noise that activated the alarm was a real event.
- Video assessment: One of the most common forms of assessment is with video cameras. A guard can observe the conditions at the scene of the alarm. This is a quick and precise way of verifying alarms.

REACTION ELEMENTS

After an alarm is verified, the organization may choose to act on it. Options include deterring the aggressor, delaying him or her, or disrupting the attack. This requires reactive electronic automated protection systems (REAPS). There are three common types of REAPS:

- Communications elements: The most basic and least expensive method is to communicate with the aggressor. Only the most determined aggressor will continue after he or she is interrupted in the act. Security intercoms are an effective and economical tool that can be used to stop attacks in their tracks.

- Deployable barriers: More sophisticated systems utilize deployable barriers, including rising bollards and wedges to stop vehicles and electrified locks, roll-down doors, and deployable operable walls to delay pedestrians. Environment disruption devices can be used to delay an attack until a more formidable response force can arrive and take control of the offender.
- Attack disruption: Ultimately, in high-security environments it may be necessary to actually disrupt the attack. This can include deployable smoke, fast setting and sticky foam dispensing systems, drop chains, explosive air bags, automated weaponry, deluge water systems, acoustic weapons, and other effective, if rarely used, systems. All of these have the common element of making it much more difficult for an attack to continue and can result in the capture of the attacker. There are two types of attack disruption systems—nonlethal and lethal. Even some nonlethal systems can cause injury. In either case, it is important to implement safety measures in the activation mechanism to ensure that accidental activation does not occur and possibly injure innocents.
- Evidence gathering, storage, and retrieval: One of the key elements of enterprise security systems is their ability to log alarms and events and to record video and audio that can serve as the evidence required to build a case against a criminal offender.
- Policy enforcement: This is where it all comes together to serve the organization. One of the key capabilities of enterprise security systems is their ability to support safety, business ethics, and security policy enforcement. The ability to detect improper behavior, assess it as a real event, and use the evidence to support additional training or enforcement is of tremendous value to any organization. The systems can also help identify chronic or determined policy abusers and provide the evidence necessary to weed out employees or contractors who are working against the best interests of the organization. On the most basic level, access control systems

do a wonderful job of controlling who goes where, helping to ensure that sensitive areas are limited to those with clearance and that visitors do not walk the halls unescorted.

SUMMARY

A complete security program includes deterrence, detection, assessment, response, and evidence collection and disposition.

Security begins with denying criminals access to the organization's assets. Access control systems employ credentials, codes, or biometrics to limit access to authorized users. Access control elements include card readers, electrified locks, door position switches, and request to exit devices. Access credential readers can be based on what a person has (a card), what a person knows (a code), or what a person is (biometrics).

Detection systems limit the probability of success of a criminal act. Detection sensors include alarm sensors (point sensors, volumetric sensors, beam detectors, relay detection, capacitance detection, and intelligent detection systems). Each alarm must be processed, transmitted, and reported for follow-on action. Assessment and verification elements may include guard assessment, second alarm sensor assessment, audio assessment, and video assessment. After assessment, action may be necessary. Reaction elements may include communications elements, deployable barriers, and attack disruption.

Security systems also provide evidence collection and a means to enforce policy.

CHAPTER NOTES

1. U.S. Department of Defense and Defense Information Systems Agency (2006, January 11). *Access Control Security Technical Implementation Guide*, Version 1, Release 0, p. 16. U.S. Department of Defense, Washington, DC.
2. U.S. Department of Energy, Office of Security Affairs Office of Safeguards and Security (1994). *Manual for Protection and Control of Safeguards and Security Interests*, DOE M 5632.1C, 7-15-1994, Chapter V,1.b. U.S. Department of Energy, Washington, DC.

3. U.S. Department of Energy, Office of Security Affairs Office of Safeguards and Security (1994). *Manual for Protection and Control of Safeguards and Security Interests*, DOE M 5632.1C, 7-15-1994, Chapter V,1.f. U.S. Department of Energy, Washington, DC.
4. Garcia, Mary Lynn (2001). *The Design and Evaluation of Physical Protection Systems*, p. 6. Butterworth/Heinemann, Newton, MA. (ISBN 0-7506-7367-2)
5. A good description of various dispensable barriers is provided in Mary Lynn Garcia's book, *The Design and Evaluation of Physical Protection Systems*, (2001), beginning on p. 216.

6

Electronics Elements (Detailed Discussion)

ALARM/ACCESS CONTROL SYSTEMS

The basic elements of most current alarm and access control systems are discussed in the sections that follow.

Identification Devices

Identification devices include card/key/barcode[1]/radio frequency identification readers, keypads, and biometric[2] readers. As introduced in Chapter 5, access control systems can determine your identity by what you know, by what you have, or by who you are.

The most basic types of identification (ID) readers are keypads. Basic keypads are simple 12-digit keypads that contain

Figure 6-1   Alarm keypad.

the numbers 0–9 and ✳ and # signs (Fig. 6-1). The most desirable attributes of keypads are that they are simple to use and they are cheap. The most undesirable attribute of keypads is that it is relatively easy for a bystander to read the code as it is being entered, and then you have been duplicated in the access control database (i.e., now two people know your code so now no one is sure if the person who used the code is really you). Also, the pizza delivery guy usually knows a code since there is usually someone in the organization who gives out his or her code for such things. This defeats the purpose of access control since now management has no idea who has the codes. Although shrouds for keypads are available, they are cumbersome and do not seem to be well accepted, and the pizza delivery guy still knows the code.

Two other variants are the so-called "ashtray" keypad, which conceals the code quite well (Fig. 6-2), and the Hirsch™ keypad, which works very well. The Hirsch keypad displays

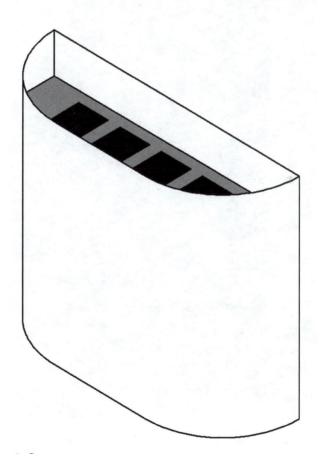

Figure 6-2 Early access control keypad.

its numbers behind a flexible, transparent cover using seven-segment LED modules. Then, to confuse the guy across the room with the binoculars, it scrambles the position of the numbers so that they almost never show up in the same location on the keypad twice. This ensures that even though the guy with binoculars can see the pattern of button pressing, it will be useless since that pattern does not repeat often (Fig. 6-3). We have also found that in many organizations, there is something about the high-tech nature of the Hirsch™ keypad systems that seems

Figure 6-3 Hirsch ScramblePad®. Image used with permission of Hirsch Electronics, Inc.

to make its users more observant of the need not to give out the code to unauthorized people.

One step up the scale of sophistication from keypads are ID cards and card readers. Access control cards come in several variants, and there are a number of different card reader types to match both the card type and the environment.

Common card types include the following:

- Magnetic stripe
- Wiegand wire
- Passive proximity
- Active proximity
- Implantable proximity
- Smart cards (both touch and touchless types)

Increasingly rare types include

- Barcode
- Barium ferrite
- Hollerith
- Rare-earth magnet

Magnetic Stripe Cards

Magnetic stripe cards (Fig. 6-4) have a magnetic band (similar to magnetic tape) laminated to the back of the card. These were invented by the banking industry to serve automatic teller machines (ATMs). Typically, there are two or three bands that are magnetized on the card. The card can contain a code (used for access control identification), the person's name, and other useful data. Usually in access control systems, only the ID code is encoded. There are two types of magnetic stripe cards: high and low coercivity (how much magnetic energy is charged into the magnetic stripe). Bank cards are low coercivity (300 Oersted) and most early access control cards were high coercivity (2750 or 4000 Oersted). However, as clients began to complain that their bank cards failed to work after being in a wallet next to their access card, many manufacturers switched to low coercivity for access cards as well. Desirable attributes of magnetic stripe cards are

Figure 6-4   Magnetic stripe card.

that they are easy to use and inexpensive. Undesirable attributes are that they are easy to duplicate and thus not suitable for use in any secure facility.

Wiegand Cards/Keys

The Wiegand effect is named after its discoverer, John R. Wiegand. The Wiegand effect occurs when a specially made wire is moved past a magnetic field causing it to emit a very fast magnetic pulse in response (10 μsec) to the magnetic field. Wiegand wires are placed into cards and keys in a pattern of north/south such that they create ones and zeros when read by a Wiegand card/key reader. In the early days of access control, a wiring protocol was established to accommodate Wiegand effect readers, called the Wiegand wiring scheme for card readers. Today, manufacturers refer to their proximity card readers to be wired with this Wiegand wire interface.

Barcode Cards

Barcode cards use any of several barcode schemes, the most common of which is a conventional series of lines of varying thicknesses. Barcodes are available in visible and infrared types. The visible type looks similar to the UBC barcode on food articles. Infrared barcodes are invisible to the naked eye but can be read by a barcode reader that is sensitive to infrared light. The problem is that either type can be easily read and thus duplicated; so barcodes are also not suitable for secure environments.

Barium Ferrite Cards

Barium ferrite cards are based on a magnetic material similar to that used in magnetic signs and refrigerator magnets. A pattern of ones and zeros is arranged inside the card, and because the material is essentially a permanent magnet, it is very robust. Barium ferrite card readers can be configured for insertion or swipe type. For swipe types, these are often in the form of an aluminum plate placed within a beveled surface. The user simply touches the card to the aluminum surface and the card is read. Swipe and insertion barium ferrite cards and keys are almost nonexistent today, relegated only to legacy systems. The aluminum touch panel is still common in some locales.

Hollerith

The code in Hollerith cards is based on a series of punched holes. The most common kind of Hollerith card is that which is used in hotel locks. Some Hollerith cards are configured such that their hole patterns are obscured by an infrared transparent material. One brand of Hollerith is configured into a brass key (Fig. 6-5). Hollerith cards are not commonly used in secure facilities.

Rare-Earth Magnets

An extremely rare type of access credential is the rare-earth key. The rare-earth magnets are set in a pattern of four wide by eight long and each can be positioned so that north is pointing left or right, making a pattern of ones and zeros. Such keys are very difficult to duplicate and are suitable for high-security facilities, although their cost is high since each key must be handmade.

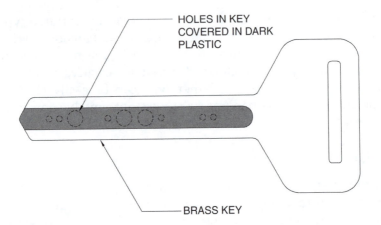

HOLES IN KEY
COVERED IN DARK
PLASTIC

BRASS KEY

Figure 6-5   Hollerith access key.

Photo Identification Elements

Access cards grant access and identification cards provide visual evidence that the bearer is authorized to be in the area. Identification badges can have many visual attributes, including a photo of the bearer, a logo of the organization (not necessarily a wise thing), the bearer's name, and a color scheme that may identify areas where the person is authorized. Sometimes, a color or code may designate if the bearer is a contractor or vendor.

To help verify the authenticity of the card, it is common to laminate a holographic overlay that provides a visual indication that the card has not been tampered with.

Some organizations use separate access cards and identification cards, but most have combined the two functions into a single credential.

Multitechnology Cards

As organizations grow, it is common for some employees to need to travel to multiple offices and facilities where different card technologies may be used. There are three solutions to this problem. One solution is to have the traveling employees carry a different card for each facility they visit. Another is to convert the entire organization's access control system to a single card standard, which can be expensive. Finally, technology can come to the rescue by creating a card that contains codes that are readable by two or more access control systems. Multitechnology cards can include magnetic stripes, Wiegand, proximity, and even smart cards all in one card. Implantable chips can provide access to very high-security facilities with an assurance that the credential has not found its way into the wrong hands.

Card Readers

Card readers have been configured in a number of different ways. Early card readers were of the insertion type (Fig. 6-6). These were prone to getting dirty and thus reading intermittently. Swipe readers came next (Fig. 6-7). These were easier to keep clean and more reliable. These mostly eliminated the problem of chewing gum and coins being inserted and were also easy to use. However, reliability was still a problem.

Proximity card readers date back to the early 1970s, and they continue to evolve (Fig. 6-8). Reliability issues have been virtually eliminated for all but intentional abuse. Proximity card readers have been designed for many unique environments, including normal interior walls (for mounting to single-gang

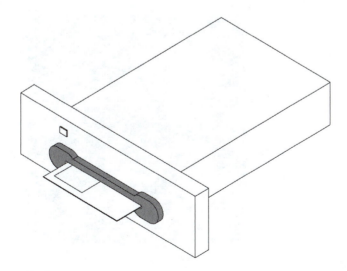

Figure 6-6 Insertion card reader.

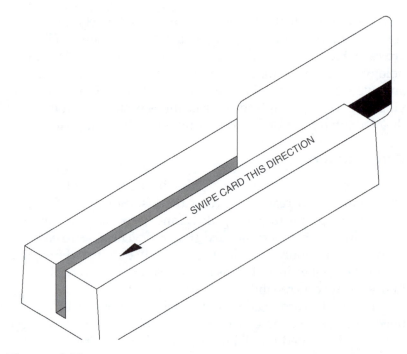

Figure 6-7 Swipe card reader.

Figure 6-8 Proximity card reader. Image used with permission of HID Global.

Figure 6-9 One-gang proximity reader. Image used with permission of HID Global.

electrical box) (Fig. 6-9) and door frames (mullion readers) (Fig. 6-10). There are also long-range readers for use in car parks and garages so that the user does not need to roll down the car window and be exposed to the weather (Fig. 6-11).

Proximity cards and readers work by passing a handshake set of radio frequency signals (traditionally in the 60- to 150-kHz range). Basically, the reader is always transmitting a low power signal through one of two antennas in the card reader. When a card comes into the radio energy field, the radio frequency energy is picked up by one of two antennas on the card and is used to charge a capacitor. When the capacitor voltage reaches a critical level, it "dumps" its energy into an integrated circuit (chip) on the card, which is programmed with a unique card number. The chip also has a radio frequency transmitter, and it transmits the unique card number through a second antenna on

Figure 6-10 Mullion proximity reader. Image used with permission of HID Global.

Figure 6-11 Long-range proximity reader. Image used with permission of HID Global.

the card. All this occurs in milliseconds. When the card reader picks up the transmission from the card, it passes the card number to the reader input board of the access control system, where a grant/deny access decision is made based on the facility code and card number, which together make up the unique card number code, and the day and time of presentation of the card.

Newer proximity cards and readers use smart-card technology that can also receive, store, and process information from the card reader back to the card, allowing more complicated transactions. For example, the card can be used like a credit card to purchase food in a vending machine or gas at a gas pump. The card can store a history of transactions, such as where the user has gone and with what readers he or she has interacted. Some transactions may be unknown to the user such that it is possible to track a user's position in a facility at any given time or for other special purposes. One exotic access control credential is the implantable chip. Only slightly larger than a grain of rice, the chip can be implanted in a user's arm and can provide access to high-security areas. These chips have been implanted

Figure 6-12 Veri-Chip implantable access control credential. Used with permission from Veri-Chip Corporation.

in agricultural animals and pets for many years to help track an animal's health and locate its owner when lost. It is the closest thing to biometrics (Fig. 6-12).

TWIC Cards

The U.S. Transportation Security Agency (TSA) has implemented the Transportation Worker Identification Credential (TWIC) program. The TWIC card can be used for all personnel who require unrestricted physical or computer access to TSA-controlled facilities. TWIC credentials are used at facilities that are under the jurisdiction of the Aviation and Transportation Security Act and the Maritime Transportation Security Act. TWIC positively ties the person to his or her credential and to the person's threat assessment. The credential can then be used to allow unrestricted access to the cardholder for appropriate areas of the facility. TWIC cards will help ensure that cardholders who travel from facility to facility can be recognized with a single card.

   Biometric readers come in many forms, but all share the function of identifying a person by his or her unique physical attributes. Common biometric readers include fingerprint readers, hand geometry readers, iris scanners, voice recognition systems, handwriting recognition systems, and finger blood vessel pattern recognition systems.

Other Field Devices

These include electrified locks, door position switches, request-to-exit devices, and gate operators. Electrified locks are discussed in detail in Chapter 7.

There are a nearly infinite number of types and applications of electrified locks. This is one of the areas that set the master designer apart from the journeyman. It pays to learn electrified locks exceptionally well since many codes stipulate how certain types of electrified locks can be applied. Also, each project has a unique set of security requirements that, combined with door types, directions of travel, fire exit paths, and codes, makes for an infinite combination of lock types. There are several basic types of locks.

Electrified Strikes

Electrified strikes replace the conventional door strike into which a typical door latch closes. Unlike a conventional door strike, which requires that the door latch be retracted in order for it to open, the electric strike unlocks the door by simply folding back to release the door latch as the user pulls the door open. It springs back instantly as the door latch clears the strike so that it is ready to receive the latch as the door closes again. There are many types of electric strikes, but they all operate the same way. A few electric strikes are strong enough to be considered security devices, but most should not be relied on for high-security environments. Unfortunately, most electric strikes are not rated for their strength, which makes it difficult to determine whether or not one should rely on it to resist a forced attack. Any strike that does not list its physical strength should be assumed to be incapable of resisting a forced attack. One of the favorable attributes of electric strikes is that they do not draw power except when they unlock. This makes them suitable for environments in which power availability is a concern.

Electrified Mortise Locks

A mortise lock is a lock that is built into a routed pocked or "mortise" in the door. These locks are very strong since the lock is sizable relative to the latch and dead bolt and the lock is effectively part of the door, so it is essentially as strong as the door. When a mortise lock is placed in either a solid-core door or a hollow metal door, these are placed into a hollow metal frame. The result is a very strong door and lock. Mortise locks are available in a variety of configurations, the most common being office and storeroom types. The office lock is equipped with only a latch bolt, and the storeroom type is equipped with both a latch bolt and a dead bolt. Electrified mortise locks are simply normal mortise locks in which the latch bolt has been attached to a solenoid within the lock body so that upon triggering the solenoid the latch bolt retracts, unlocking the door. There are a few electrified storeroom mortise locks, but most are of the office type.

Magnetic Locks

Often considered the staple of electrified locks, the magnetic lock is little more than just an electromagnet attached to a door frame, and there is an armature attached to the door. When the electromagnet is energized and the armature on the door is against the lock, the lock engages. These are typically very strong locks, usually having 800–1500 lbs of holding force. This lock is sometimes stronger than the door to which it is attached. Magnetic locks should be used with a redundant means of unlocking to ensure that a person inside the locked area can always exit. A "Push to Exit" button or crash bar that interrupts power to the magnetic lock is always advised.

Electrified Panic Hardware

Where a door is located in the path of egress, panic hardware is often used, depending on the occupancy rating. Panic hardware is required on any door where there could be a large number of people needing exit in an emergency. Panic hardware is easily identified by the push bar (formerly called a crash bar) that the users press as they push through the door. Panic hardware facilitates a single exit motion since users have only to push on the door as they are moving through it. This facilitates the rapid exit of large numbers of people since no one has to wait behind anyone else while they stop to turn a door handle. In a severe emergency such as a fire, such momentary delays can compound to cause a crush of people behind a door that is unlocked but which can become a barrier if someone has difficulty with the door handle. There are several basic types of panic hardware configurations, depending on the requirements of the door to which the panic hardware is mounted. Panic hardware is electrified by one of several methods, usually involving a solenoid that releases a latch on the door.

Specialty Locks

Most people pay little attention to doors and locks; they just use them. However, there are a remarkable number of variations of doors, frames, locks, and electrification methods. Some unusual locks have been developed for special needs (see Chapter 7).

Switches

Door and gate position switches (DPS) sense if the door or gate is opened or closed. A variant of the DPS is the monitor strike, which determines if the door is not only closed but also whether a latch bolt or dead bolt is in fact engaged. The typical DPS is composed of a magnetically sensitive switch and a magnet placed close to the switch.

Typically, the switch is placed on the door frame and the magnet is placed on the door or gate. When the door or gate is opened, the switch also opens, sending a signal to the alarm system. Variants of DPSs include surface and concealed mounting versions (Figs. 6-13 and 6-14), wide- and narrow-gap sensing areas, and conventional or balanced bias types. Wide-gap DPSs were developed to prevent accidental triggering by nuisance conditions, such as when the wind blows against a sliding glass door.

To prevent an intruder from simply placing a magnet against the DPS while opening the door, balanced-bias switches

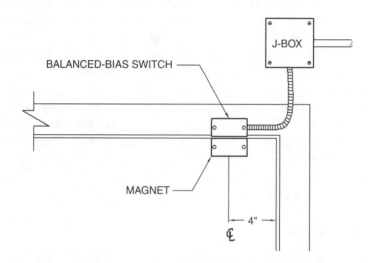

Figure 6-13 Surface-mounted door position switch.

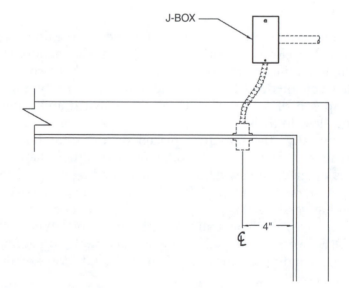

Figure 6-14 Concealed door position switch.

were developed that place the switch in a closely controlled magnetic field. If another magnet is brought near the switch when the door is closed, that act alone will trigger an alarm even before the door is opened.

Other types of DPSs include plunger type, Hall effect, and mercury switches. These are sometimes used in areas where it is not possible to place a magnet in the door or gate, or where a device must be alarmed if it is moved. The plunger switch alerts when the object that is pushed against it is moved. These are often mechanical switches and can be unreliable for high-security applications. Hall effect switches rely on the presence of a magnetic field within a confined area to alert. They also work by moving the object. Mercury switches are sometimes placed inside an object that should not be moved in any dimension and can be made to alert to the slightest movement. These are often used with radio frequency transmitters.

Duress Switches

Duress switches are usually placed under a desk or counter to alert security if the person at the counter feels threatened. The two most common types are finger activated and footswitch activated. If the person believes he or she needs assistance, he or she can either push a shrouded button (or two buttons together to prevent false alarms) or place a toe under and lift a footswitch. Another type used in cash drawer applications is the bill trap. This type activates when the last bill in a drawer is removed, indicating a robbery.

Request-to-Exit (REX) Sensors

It is good that a security system can alert when a door is opened, but what about a DPS at a door equipped with a card reader? When a person is exiting that door legally, there must be some way to sense that the exit is not an alarm and bypass the DPS for the duration of the door opening. This is what a REX sensor does.

There are two common types of REX sensors, infrared and push switch. An infrared REX sensor is placed above the door on

the secure side and constantly monitors the door handle searching for human motion. When motion is sensed in the approach
area to the door, the sensor activates and thus alerts the access
control electronics that the pending door opening is a legal exit,
not an alarm.

The push switch type is configured either as a labeled button near the door (required in most municipalities for magnetic
locks) or can be a switch that is configured into the handle of a
mortise lock or the electrified panic hardware push bar. These
are more intuitive.

Even when other types of REX sensors are used on magnetically locked doors, it is still important to configure a labeled
"Push to Unlock" button near the door. This button should be
wired both to the access control system electronics to signal a
legal exit and to the lock through a timer to ensure that if the
access control system electronics should fail, the user may still
exit the door. It is not only embarrassing but also can be legally
costly and even deadly if a user is ever trapped inside a building
with no way to exit.

Door and Gate Operators

Door and gate operators are mechanical devices that automatically open and close doors and gates in response to a command.
Door operators are common in public buildings and assist in the
movement of large numbers of people with little effort or assist
handicapped persons through the door. Gate operators are commonly used to automatically open vehicle gates in response to a
command.

Door operators are often used with magnetic locks such
that the access control system may both unlock and then open a
door. This is common at main public and commercial building
doors, and this combination is also frequently used where there
is a requirement to assist the handicapped. Wherever door operators are used with magnetic locks, it is imperative to sequence
the operation such that the door unlocks first and then opens.
If this sequencing is not built into the design, the automatic operator may fail after a short period of time. Better door operator
companies have incorporated a special circuit for this purpose,

but it must be specified. I designed one of the first such interfaces for a major door operator manufacturer. Doors that are in the path of egress must be equipped with safety devices to ensure that a person can exit in an emergency with no special knowledge. This typically means that there must be a labeled push button or some other type of code-approved method of egress. Codes will always prevail on any magnetically locked door. Do not assume that a code from one city is acceptable in another. Know your codes.

Gate operators that are electrically locked must also be interfaced in order to function correctly.

Revolving Doors and Electronic Turnstiles

Revolving doors and electronic turnstiles are sometimes used to provide positive access control. That is, each person must enter and leave using an access credential, and only one person may transit the portal at a time for accountability purposes.

Revolving doors (Fig. 6-15) can be equipped with a special operator that will allow only one person at a time through a

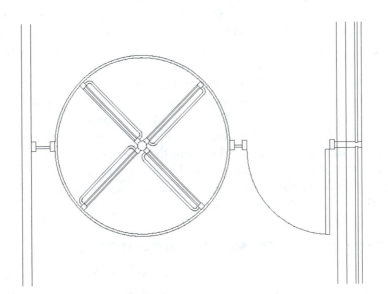

Figure 6-15 Revolving door.

rotating (X) pane. Like door operators, revolving doors can be locked between uses, but even when unlocked, they can be controlled by the operator so that only one rotation is permitted. Early revolving door operators were sometimes problematic. However, modern operators by major manufacturers are well developed, and most work well. It is wise to coordinate directly with the manufacturer of the revolving door operator to achieve the desired functions. These may include the following:

- Card reader controlled
- Remote bypass from a security console
- Auto-reverse if two or more people enter on one card use
- Auto-reverse if an unauthorized person attempts to use the door at the same time as an authorized user but from the opposite side of the revolving door
- Audio alert of improper use with instructions

Such doors are also available with status alerts on alarm, on reverse, with user count, etc.

Revolving doors for access control should be configured to the "X" rather than "+" configuration when waiting for next use.

Electronic turnstiles (Fig. 6-16) are similar to the old-fashioned turnstiles used at subways and ballparks, except that the rotating member is replaced by an infrared photo beam that detects when someone passes through. There is also a type of electronic turnstile that uses paddle arms or glass wings to act as a physical barrier. These devices are designed to control access to a commercial or government building with a high degree of speed (throughput) and elegance. Electronic turnstiles must be used with an access control system that can deliver speedy card executions in order to be accepted by the users. As for revolving doors, the designer should coordinate the specifications carefully with the turnstile manufacturer.

Electronic Processing Components

Electronic processing components include reader interface boards, alarm input boards, output relay boards, and controllers. Every alarm and access control system made today uses some

Figure 6-16 Electronic turnstiles with paddle barriers.

form of controller between the workstations/servers and the field devices (Fig. 6-17). These vary slightly from manufacturer to manufacturer, but the theme is the same. Each has three basic elements:

- A microprocessor with connectivity to the server and other controllers
- Memory
- Field device interface modules (reader interface boards, alarm input boards, and output relay boards)

The configuration may vary (some systems combine these elements together into one board, whereas in others they are components that can be distributed or wired together in one electrical box), but all systems use these same elements. However, that will change soon.

When I began writing this book, the concept of microcontrollers, which I had long proposed, was scoffed at by most in

Figure 6-17 Alarm/access control panel. Image used with permission of DSX Access Systems, Inc.

the industry. However, by the time this book is published, at least one manufacturer will be making small microcontrollers that control a single door, with some auxiliary inputs and outputs. The new generation of microcontrollers will contain their own memory and microprocessor. They will fit in a small box above the door. Also, they will eventually incorporate a mini data switch connected by Ethernet.

This design will revolutionize the industry. The alarm and access control industry has been based for years on metal bending—that is, on the sale of hardware. This is about to become a software industry. It is part of the sea change mentioned previously.

Soon, it will be possible to connect a card reader, DPS, REX, and lock, together with an intercom outstation and a video camera, into a single small electronic smart switch that will contain its own central processing unit and memory. I have been predicting this for more than a decade, and now it is occurring.

SERVER (AND BUSINESS CONTINUITY SERVER)

All enterprise-class alarm and access control systems depend on servers to store and manage the master databases on which all system operations rely. Smaller systems may incorporate the server functions directly into the system's workstation. Servers operate basically two kinds of services: system operation and archiving. On simple systems, these are both contained within a single server. On larger, more complex systems, these functions may be separated into separate boxes.

On larger systems, it is common to have a backup server that duplicates the database and functions of the primary server. This second server is usually configured to take over in the event the primary server experiences some unexpected failure or planned shutdown. Smart designers place the backup server in another building or even in another state to act as a business continuity server, not just a fail-over server. There are two basic functions on backup servers: mirrored operation and fail-over operation. Mirrored backup servers are used to maintain a constant and instantaneous backup of archived data (both alarm/access control data and video image data). Fail-over servers wait until the primary server fails, then they take control of the system instantaneously or, in simpler systems, by having the operator switch to the fail-over server. Fail-over servers should be used for system operating services and for archiving where the backup server is in the same physical area as the primary server. For true business continuity servers, the backup servers should be located off-site and all archiving should be mirrored to ensure that if a catastrophic event occurs at the primary server location, no data are lost.

WORKSTATIONS

Workstations are the human interface that manage and communicate with the controllers and servers. In simple systems, one workstation may do it all—server, card programming, system programming, report printing, identification badging, and alarm monitoring. However, on enterprise-class alarm and access control systems these functions are divided among a variety of workstations.

On a recent system designed by the author, for a corporate headquarters of a major petrochemical company, a single building had five workstations—one for card and system programming, one to capture pictures and program data for the photo identification system, one at the main lobby desk to monitor alarms and the electronic turnstiles access, and two for alarm monitoring in the security command center. The same system used five servers in two different buildings. All these workstations and servers resided on just one campus. This system is capable of monitoring hundreds of sites in multiple countries. There can be multiple workstations at each site, resulting in dozens to hundreds of workstations.

The point is that there is no practical limit to the number of workstations in a system. Workstations can be connected directly to the server, to the Ethernet backbone, to a controller, or to the Internet using a web browser so that a security manager can make decisions remotely while on vacation or during a weekend. Enterprise-class systems provide infinite choice.

Data Infrastructure Basics

When the user presents a card to a card reader and the card reader passes that information to a controller, a decision is made to unlock the door. That information, along with alarm detection information, is transmitted along a data infrastructure to the server, and then it is distributed to appropriate workstations. The data infrastructure is the backbone of the system. In older systems, there was a unique data infrastructure for the alarm and access control system, but most modern systems have converted to an Ethernet communications protocol. Older protocols included RS-485, Protocol A, Protocol B, 20-ma current loop, and other methods. The newer Ethernet protocol supports worldwide systems architectures that can be connected in many different ways to meet the special needs of each client, each site, and each security environment. Additionally, Ethernet protocols can also communicate CCTV and voice technologies all on a single data infrastructure. Ethernet can be easily converted to fiber optics, 802.11a/b/g, laser, or geostationary satellite to facilitate unique environmental requirements where normal wired infrastructures present design challenges. It would be easy to write an entire book(s) on the subject of security system data infrastructures, and it is a difficult subject to boil down to its basics. More information on this subject is presented here and in the System Commissioning section of this book.

Interfaces to Other Building Systems

Alarm and access control systems begin to perform wonders when they are interfaced to other building systems. Typical interfaces include fire alarm systems, elevators, parking control systems, lighting control systems, signage, roll-down doors, private automatic branch exchange (PABX) systems, paging systems, water features, irrigation control systems, and even escalators. The primary purposes for interfacing alarm and access control systems to other building systems is to control access to things other than doors and gates, enhance safety or convenience to building users, automate building functions that would otherwise be handled manually or by numerous other systems, or insert a delay into the path of an intruder.

ADVANCED ELEMENTS

Legacy Systems Integration

One of the key challenges facing enterprise security systems designers is how to integrate the new technology into older, legacy systems. Typically, government entities and large corporations have developed their security systems in a somewhat haphazard fashion. This resulted from the fact that electronic security was initially addressed at the local level in almost all large organizations, and only later did they come to realize that there was a value to having a single standard across the entire organization. The result was that most organizations had many different types of products across various sites that were difficult to blend into a single contiguous system. To complicate this problem, the security industry has a long tradition of proprietary systems that are not based on any single standard (with the exception of CCTV systems, which had to conform to the preexisting NTSC standard). Virtually every alarm and access control system and every major security intercom system used components that could not be interchanged.

This problem was compounded by the early introduction of digital video systems that were based on proprietary compression technologies, which again ensured that the stored data could not be shared with their competitors' products. The first piece of good news is that the entire suite of enterprise security system components connects to Ethernet data infrastructures.

The bad news is that there are three not entirely small problems:

- Older and current alarm and access control systems still use proprietary software interfaces that in most cases are not intended to link their data with other competing systems. Manufacturers still seem to hope against all logic that their clients will gleefully abandon all installations made by other manufacturers and replace them with equipment made by them.
- Different digital CCTV manufacturers have adopted varying video compression technologies, making interfacing to a single standard difficult. Some manufacturers have even modified existing compression algorithms to become proprietary to them alone.
- As security intercom manufacturers move to digital products, they are also adopting numerous different compression protocols, again making a single platform more difficult.

Now the second piece of good news: Computers are very good at operating multiple protocols together on the same platform. That means that unless the compression protocol is truly unique, it is possible to combine multiple protocols into a single operational platform.

The third piece of good news is that some of the alarm and access control system manufacturers are beginning to make uniform interfaces to create multisystem interoperability.

The fourth piece of good news is that, in almost all cases, it is not necessary to fully interface different systems together in order to get them to cooperate in truly meaningful ways. Interfacing methods are discussed in detail in Chapter 14.

Data vs. Hardware Interfaces

Alarm and access control systems are often interfaced to other building systems, such as elevators and building automation systems. There are two ways to accomplish these interfaces. They can be realized either by exchanging data information or by handshaking with dry contacts between the two systems. There are advantages and disadvantages to both approaches.

Data interfaces have wonderful advantages. First, a single data interface (one little wire) can last a lifetime, no matter how many times the systems are expanded, adapted, and upgraded. Once the original data interface is connected and the software is interfaced, the systems can be adapted repeatedly to expand the quantity and functions of the interfaces.

Second, that single wire can control an empire. Once an interface is conducted on a network, it is global. It is not necessary to interface each and every site if the systems can communicate by a data interface.

Although data interfaces are wonderful, because they rely on software, they are vulnerable to software upgrades. When software is upgraded, it is not uncommon for software programmers to forget the little details of the last issue that almost nobody used. Nobody used it; it cannot be important enough to keep updated while we are under a tight schedule to meet the upgrade release date. We can pick that up in a patch later. Thus, the poor unsuspecting client eagerly awaiting his or her new software upgrade installs it and the interface does not work anymore—instant software data interface vulnerability. There are indeed organizations that have had to reinstall obsolete software in order to maintain an old data interface.

Likewise, there are advantages and disadvantages to hardware interfaces. Hardware interfaces are accomplished by connecting the dry contact of a relay in one system to the input point of another system. This allows the first system to signal the second system that some condition has changed and the second system should do something about it. This simple principle is multiplied to accommodate as many individual connections as each system needs. Relays can be combined to perform logic (and, or, not, and if), and they are reliable. Once a relay interface is set up and tested, it does not matter how many times the software is updated on either system. It will always work.

The disadvantage of hardware interfaces is that they are generally site specific and they are entirely inflexible. If the system is expanded, and more interface points are needed, more relays and more inputs will be required—more expense every time there is a change or expansion. Thus, it is a trade-off. Each system requires an individual decision as to what is in the best interest of the organization.

CCTV SYSTEMS

Evolution of Analog Video Systems

The Bookends of Time

There was once a time when video cameras were a very rare element in security systems. Any system that had even one video camera was considered the pinnacle of high-technology security systems. Now security video cameras are just about blister-packed for 99 cents. In the old days, the ability to see outside the building was considered extraordinary. Today, cameras are used to determine if a particular person in a crowd of 50 is acting suspiciously without human intervention and then alert a security officer to that fact for further analysis. This kind of automation can be occurring across 1000 cameras over an entire subway system, vastly increasing the value of the security organization to the city it serves.[3]

How Analog Video Works

Television video was invented by Philo Farnsworth, who was an employee of Thomas Edison. This inventive genius worked out that if you could control the movement of a directed electronic beam against a phosphorous surface affixed to glass within a vacuum tube, you could "paint" the phosphor with a luminous line. Vary the intensity of the beam and you can make it glow brighter and darker. Cause the beam to return to its origin and shift it down a bit over and over again and you can paint a picture on the phosphorous screen. Carefully select the phosphor so that it glows for exactly the time it takes to write one complete frame and time that to be slightly faster than the persistence of the sensitivity of the human retina and you have moving images. Television—What a concept!

The earliest security video systems hardly qualified to fit the term, having only one or two tube-type (black-and-white Vidicon™) cameras, some coaxial cable, and one or two black-and-white video monitors. Vidicon's™ tubes and monitors required annual replacement. A huge advance in sophistication occurred when RCA invented the sequential video switcher. This handy box connected up to 16 video cameras and displayed them on two video monitors. One sequenced through all the cameras, and the second displayed one's favorite camera view.

The Branch

Then video evolution took a branch that still continues today. On one branch was the development of a device called a "quad." This device displayed four video cameras on a single screen and recorded them all on a single tape. On the other branch was an extension of the old sequencer, the video matrix switch. The video switch allowed the connection of many cameras (as few as 16 and as many as 64 in the early days) and could display them on up to four (or eight) video monitors. A keyboard gave the user the ability to program any camera to any monitor and could also sequence cameras to one or more monitors.

Videotape

It was at approximately this time that videotape recorders became useful for security projects. Prior to that, videotape recorders used reel-to-reel tape, with early recorders using 2-in. tape to record only 1 hour of video, and the recorders were the size of a small chest of drawers. Recorders did not become practical for any security application until RCA invented the enclosed $3/4$-in. U-Matic videotape cartridge. The U-Matic tape recorder was the size of a piece of luggage but would record up to 2 hours. Soon after, Phillips invented the VHS tape recorder and the U-Matic was history. The VHS tape recorder was small and could record up to 6 hours of video. Then in the early 1990s, a company called Robot introduced a VHS recorder that was able to record up to 24 hours in combination with a totally new device, the video multiplexer.

The major problem was that at that time it was not common to break video images down, which stream at a rate of 30 frames per second, to a series of individual frames at a rate of 4 frames per second.[4] Such a device would have to be able to store one image from each camera and discard the next three.

The multiplexer was specifically made to work with the new 24-hour recorder and vice versa. What was truly unique about this new pair was that it worked in a totally new way to achieve the remarkable result of 24-hour recording. A Robot researcher determined that although the VHS recorder could not record a continuous stream of video any slower than 6 hours, it could nonetheless record a huge number of individual frames of video if they were sequenced to the recorder in individual images. This approach resulted in its ability to record almost exactly two frames per second for 16 cameras. VHS recorders were designed to record a single stream of video that fed at a rate of 30 frames per second. The new multiplexer sampled a frame from each camera every half second and fed that frame as a still image to the video recorder. Thus, the new 24-hour VHS recorder stored one frame from each camera in sequence until all were recorded and then began again with the first camera. The new multiplexer passed a single frame of video from each of 16 cameras in sequence to the video recorder and then started all over again. In order to do this, the multiplexer had to do something completely new. It converted the analog scanned video into a series of digitized single frames. It was then possible to store digital frames individually on tape moving much slower than one could store an analog frame. At the time, the digitization of video was a footnote to the achievement of the multiplexer. Hardly anyone took notice. However, a few of us in the industry took note and began predicting the future.

I began talking about the coming digital revolution as early as 1993.

HOW DIGITAL VIDEO DIFFERS FROM ANALOG

Capturing and Displaying Analog Video

Analog video is created in a video camera by scanning an electron beam across a phosphor. The beam intensity is determined by the amount of light on each small area of the phosphor, which itself responds to the light being focused on it by a lens. That beam is then transmitted to a recording, switching, or display device. Analog switchers simply make a connection between devices by closing a relay dry contact. Recorders simply record the voltage changes of the electron beam onto tape, and display devices convert the voltage back into an electron beam and aim it at another phosphorous surface, which is the display monitor that is viewed.

Capturing and Displaying Digital Video

Digital video images are captured entirely differently. Light is focused by a lens onto a digital imager. This is an integrated circuit in which the "chip" is exposed rather than covered by the plastic body of the chip, as in a normal integrated circuit. It is a little known fact that virtually all integrated circuits respond to light. Early electronic programmable read-only memory chips were in fact erased of their programming by "flashing" them with light. This phenomenon was utilized to make an integrated circuit that comprised hundreds of thousands (today millions) of individual light-sensitive chips. When light was focused on this chip, it responded by creating a different voltage in each individual picture element (pixel) in direct proportion to the amount of light striking that particular element. A matrix was formed from the output voltages of each row and column of chips, and this lattice was then scanned to replicate the voltage of a conventional tube-type video imager. The result was the world's first digital imager. Video can be displayed in much the same way as it is gathered. The most common technologies today are liquid crystal displays (LCD) and plasma displays for directly viewed displays and digital light processor (DLP) devices for projected video. All of these are variations of the same basic concept. A semitransparent color pixel (blue, green, red) is arrayed in front of an illuminator. The video image is fed to the display and the pixels do their job, displaying the video images. LCD displays have become the de facto standard for smaller displays, and plasma and LCD displays are both common for large screens. DLP projectors accommodate most displays over 60 in. diagonal, except for video walls, which are composed by grouping arrays of LCD, plasma, or projected video box displays.

Archiving Analog and Digital Video

Analog video is transmitted as a fluctuating voltage with codes embedded for color, hue, and gamma. This fluctuating voltage is processed and fed to a recording head. The basic analog recording head for video works on the same principle as an analog audiotape recorder; that is, a current is fed to a specially formed electromagnet, which is formed to present a smooth surface to the tape that is being swept across the head by a pair of rotating reels. The electromagnet has a very tiny gap, across which a magnetic flux is developed in response to the fluctuating current. As the tape is rolled across the tiny gap in the recording head, the tape is magnetized in direct proportion to the current in the electromagnetic head. To play the tape back, the same tape is moved past another playback head, and the magnetic signals recorded on the tape are converted back to electrical currents, corresponding to the originally recorded signal. Videotape differs from audiotape in that the heads are slightly tilted and spun in order to record a series of diagonal stripes, each corresponding to a field of a video frame (Fig. 6-18). There are two fields for each video frame, and these are interlaced such that the first field records or displays 525 stripes of video. The beam is then shifted down to an area between the first and second stripes of the first field, and then the process is repeated for the second field of 525 stripes. When both fields are displayed together, the result is that the two fields are combined together to form

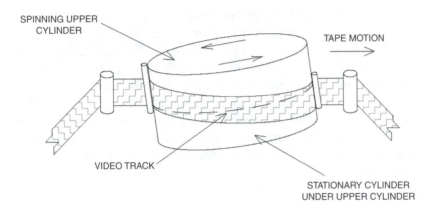

Figure 6-18 Helical scan recording head.

a single video frame. Two fields are used because by painting the entire screen twice, and by shifting the second field slightly down from the first field so that its lines lie in between the lines on the first field, the image is of higher resolution than that of just one field and they are interlaced so that the eye does not catch the time difference from the first stripe at the top of the screen to the last stripe at the bottom.

Digital video is transmitted instead by a string of data packets. Each packet is composed of ones and zeros in a designated format. The packet has a header, footer, data, and, sometimes, encryption.[5] The header has the packet address (where it comes from and where it is going, what kind of data are in the packet, how much data are in the packet, the camera identifier, date and time, and other information). The footer has information that closes the packet so that the destination device knows it has received the whole packet. Each packet of video is stored on digital disk or digital tape, and the video can be retrieved based on its time code, camera number, the alarm condition that the video is recording, or any other criteria that may have been stored in the header.

Digital Transmission Systems

Digital video packets are transmitted in either of two basic protocols: Transport Control Protocol (TCP) or User Datagram

Protocol (UDP)/RDP. TCP (Transport Control Protocol) is a one-to-one communication relationship—one sending device and one receiving device. Well, that is not entirely true. TCP packets can in fact be broadcast to many destination addresses, but it requires opening an individual one-to-one session for each destination device. Where many cameras and several monitoring stations are involved, this can consume so much of the network's resources that the entire system can freeze from data overload. For these situations, the network designer selects UDP or RDP protocols.

Digital Basics

One cannot really understand digital video without understanding digital systems. In order to understand digital systems, one must understand the TCP/Internet Protocol (IP), on which all digital video systems are based. Protocols are the basic language and culture of digital systems. In the beginning, there were numerous noncompeting digital protocols and languages. Each was developed by scientists and engineers for a specific purpose and application. There were two challenges: how to get computers to talk the same language regardless of the operating system or program language, and how to get the signals from here to there in the physical world. These were separate problems, but both had to be solved in order for networks to work at all. Basically, the early data communications solutions broke down into methods that were specific to either military or academia. In fact, the military funded most early digital communications efforts, and academia began working on the problem for the military (the beginning of a long and prosperous funding relationship for academia). Soon after the first viable computer was built, at which time there existed only several computers in several universities and military research agencies, the idea of networking these computers occurred to the users. The Applied Research Programs Agency (ARPA; a branch of the U.S. military) funded a program to develop a network that would network the various computers together. ARPA-NET was born. Now, early in the development of any new technology, there are competing ideas that are developed to solve the unique problems of the organization that it serves. Some of these turn out to be really good ideas, but most do not. They might have gotten the job done for the specific application, but networking requires a simple, robust way of getting many different computers to exchange communications through a common language. It is necessary to make sure that the communication has actually occurred and that only the intended recipients get the message. There were many challenges. Just getting signals across the nation was a major task since only telephone lines existed to get the job done. ARPA-NET did just that, along with the development of the digital modem, which converted digital pulses into audio tones and then reassembled the tones back to data at the receiving end. ARPA-NET later evolved into the World Wide Web.[6] At the same time that ARPA-NET was evolving into the World Wide Web, other scientists were struggling with how to get the signals from here to there in the physical world. Basically, three ways evolved. The first worked for point-to-point communications, connecting any two computers together, and this involved the invention of modems. The second and third ways involved connecting many computers together in a true network and two approaches developed, from which a truly rich tapestry of interconnections has evolved. The first is a ring network and the second is a line, hub, and tree family of networks. Both approaches functioned by connecting individual digital devices (nodes) onto a network. In early ring networks, a token (thus the term token ring) was passed from node to node like a baton in a relay race. Whoever has the token can talk. Everybody else gets ready to listen.[7] When the node with the token is done dumping data on the ring, the token is passed on to the next node on the ring. It examines the data to determine if it is the addressee and, if it is, it downloads the data; otherwise, it passes it on to the next node, after adding its own message to the data. Token rings are robust because there can be no collisions of data messages on the network. They work well as long as the data being sent is relatively small. When the data movement becomes large, token rings break down under the weight of all the data, and the ring moves slower and slower as each node processes what it does not want and adds its own to the message. Remember, however, there is never a collision because only one node can be on the ring at any given time.

The other method that was developed was collision based. The earliest of these were line communications systems in which each node attached to a common communications line, such as a coaxial wire. Any node could get on the line at any time and transmit, and every node was in listen mode if it was not transmitting. The great idea of this approach was that nodes did not have to wait for a token to be passed to them in order to listen; they were pretty much always listening. This greatly reduced total traffic on the network. The problem was that if two nodes tried to transmit at the same time, there was a collision and no other node could hear because the data turned into noise, like a room full of people arguing where no one can be understood. This approach required a protocol that could handle the collisions. Two methods were used to handle the collisions. The first was that the single long data streams of token rings were broken down into smaller individual packets of data that would be transmitted and then reassembled at the receiving end. The second was an embedded code that told the receiving node that it had in fact received all the packets of the message to which the packet belonged. So if a message consisted of 25 packets and only 23 were received, the receiving node would call out on the network for the 2 missing packets, and the sending node would resend only those 2 packets. When all the packets of the message were received, the receiving node would call back to the sending node with a message that all packets had been received and that communication was over. This approach took some working out for several years until the highly robust and reliable TCP/IP protocol suite was developed and refined. Along the way, the network protocols developed virtual local area networks (VLANS), virtual private network (VPN) subnets, and even so-called supernets. In theory, there is no practical limit to the number of nodes that can be connected to a TCP/IP network. Today, we are working on IP version 6, which has a potential limit in the trillions of connected nodes, all communicating together on a common backbone, the Internet. After the pure line network came hub or star networks. The hub was simply a line network in which there was a single central point to which all the nodes connected. That device was called a hub. Hubs work well for a few nodes, for example, up to 256 nodes depending on traffic. However, as the number of nodes increases, so does the number of collisions of data packets. A collision is when two data devices try to send a data packet on the same line at the same time. It is a funny thing about physics: It always works. For anyone who wondered if the data world somehow is more mysterious than the physical world, collisions prove the fact that the same rules work everywhere. As in any other kind of collision, things get broken. So when a data collision occurs, neither packet can get through intact. Neither packet gets to its destination; both must be sent again until each one is on the data bus alone to find its destination. Until then, both data devices may send the same packet repeatedly until one of them makes it, and then the other packet will have no competition for the data bus and it can find its destination too. Thus, with increasing collisions comes increasing traffic. In fact, there is a critical mass beyond which there are more requests to resend information than there can be new information being sent. That is a system crash.

This problem can be resolved by analyzing the data traffic on a typical network, which will almost always prove that most traffic across the network does not in fact have to be sent across the entire network but only to nodes[8] that are logically (and often physically) grouped together—for example, nodes within a specific building or a campus. By limiting that kind of traffic to just the nodes within that group, and making exceptions for traffic that specifically asks to go outside the group, we can vastly reduce the amount of traffic, again making more overall traffic a reality. The device that does this is a data switcher. The data switcher is capable of switching traffic only to the devices to which the data is being addressed, based on a logical group so that most traffic is unencumbered by the other traffic that does not need to go out to the overall network. Fewer connections, fewer collisions, more traffic. So a switch is a device that determines where data goes.[9] As many nodes connect together using switches, they form a local area network (LAN).

There is a higher level of restriction than that of switchers. Routers can do the same job for entire buildings and a campus, making sure that traffic that does not really need to go from Chicago to New York stays on the Chicago campus. Routers connect individual LANs into wide area networks (WANs). Routers can even be used to create logical subnetworks (subnets) that can ensure that the security system is inaccessible on the company's administrative network. A subnet is essentially a VLAN (a network within a network). Routers are also capable of creating a VPN, which is essentially a tunnel within a network or Internet connection that shields the session from prying eyes on the network or Internet. This is useful when a remote user is compelled to use the Internet for private company work. Think of it as a wormhole through which you could operate your laptop at home as though you were actually connected by hardware directly to your network at work. This is different than an Internet session that can easily be hacked. A VPN shields the communication between your laptop and your network within a force field of encryption. VLANs and VPNs are used to facilitate communications between segments of an enterprise security system across a corporation's WAN or across the Internet.

Routers also route data not just based on its intended address but also based on what kind of data it is. For example, certain types of data can be "zipped right past" other switches and ports on the network if those ports have no need to see that kind of data. This is an important principle for security systems that we will understand better as we begin to discuss unicast and multicast data types later. Digital video systems sometimes use multicast-type data in order to conserve the bandwidth of the LAN. However, many devices cannot coexist with multicast data, so a router is used to ensure that those devices never see the multicast data.

Remember the ring? Did you think it was dead with line and tree networks? Oh, not so! One critical element of enterprise security systems is that they need to be reliable, redundant, and robust. By connecting a line of switchers together and closing the two ends of the line, we get a loop or ring again. By adroit switch programming, we can configure the system such that it communicates not just one way to home but both ways around the loop. Again by adroit switch and router programming, we can configure the loop so that if one switch or node is lost, for example, if the loop is cut, the others will communicate left and right from the cut in the loop so that only the node and not the entire tree is lost in the pruning. Routers and switches can be programmed so that the loop heals itself and reports the lost node so repairs can be effected in a timely manner. I recommend designing all enterprise-class security systems as a dual-redundant self-healing loop wherever possible.

WIRELESS DIGITAL VIDEO

Conduit and wiring is expensive. It can represent up to 70% or more of the total cost of outdoor systems. However, conventional wisdom is that wired reliability is not possible in wireless systems. That is not so. If the goal is to replicate a dual-redundant self-healing wired loop, it is indeed possible and practical to do so at lower cost compared to that of conduit and wire. However, there are a few problems, which will be discussed here.

Wireless Approaches and Frequencies

There are usually many ways to do things, and that is certainly true for wireless video. Following is a list of the most common ways of transmitting video wirelessly:

- Laser: Although becoming more difficult to find, laser transmitters and receivers have several advantages over other methods. The system typically comprises a laser transmitter and receiver pair, with optical lenses and weatherproof enclosures. The system is normally one-directional, so it is not well suited for pan/tilt/zoom cameras that need control signals. Laser video transmitters are immune to radio frequency noise but are affected by heavy fog or rain or blowing objects (Fig. 6-19).
- Microwave: Microwave wireless systems can transmit either analog signals or data. Unlike laser and many radio systems, virtually all microwave systems require a license. Properly

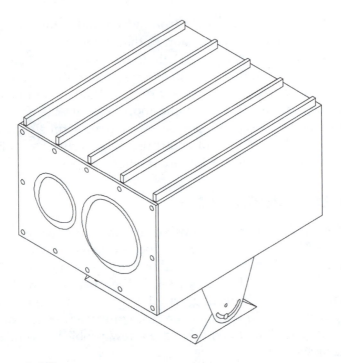

Figure 6-19 Laser communicator.

applied microwave systems can transport signals considerable distances, typically up to 20 miles. Microwave systems
can be bidirectional and require careful, permanent placement. Although temporary systems exist, those are usually
deployed by the military, not for civilian use. Microwave systems are subject to a variety of interference factors, including
fog, rain, lightning, and other microwave signals. However, when fiber is not practical and radio frequencies are a
potential problem due to other radio frequency interference,
microwave is often a sure thing (Fig. 6-20).
• Radio: Most wireless video today is transmitted over radio
waves. These can be either analog or digital. Radio-based
wireless systems are of two types, licensed and unlicensed.
It is often more reliable to use licensed systems for permanent
installations because interference is less likely.

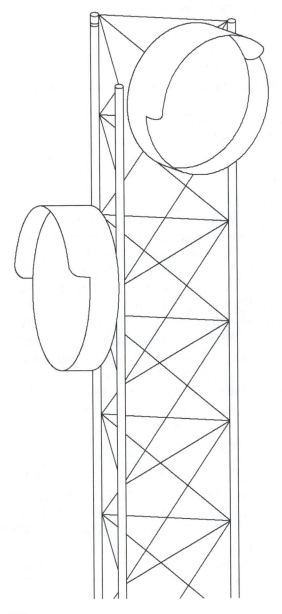

Figure 6-20 Microwave tower.

- Frequencies: The following are common frequencies for radio video transmitters/receivers:

    440 MHz (FM TV–analog)
    900 MHz (FM TV–analog and digital)
    1.2 GHz (FM TV–analog)
    2.4 GHz (FM TV–analog and 802.11 digital)
    4.9 GHz (public safety band)
    5.0–5.8 GHz (802.11 digital)
    10–24 GHz (digital)

Analog

There are very few analog transmitters and receivers available today. Most of them are in the UHF frequency band. Analog transmitter/receiver pairs suffer from radio frequency noise and environmental conditions more so than do digital systems, and their signal becomes weaker with distance, affecting their image quality. Analog radio systems directly transmit the analog PAL/NTSC video signal over the air. Most of these systems require a license if their power is more than 50 MW.

NTSC is a transmission standard named after the National Television Standards Committee, which approved it for use in the United States. It transmits a scan rate of 525 at 60 Hz and uses a video bandwidth of 4.2 MHz and an audio carrier of 4.5 MHz.

PAL stands for phase alternating line. PAL is used in many countries throughout Europe, Africa, the Middle East, South and Southeast Asia, and Asia. PAL signals scan 625 lines at 50 Hz. The video bandwidth is 5.0 MHz and the audio carrier of 5.5 MHz. Some countries use a modified PAL standard called PAL N or PAL M. PAL N has a video bandwidth of 4.2 MHz and audio carrier of 4.5 MHz. PAL M has a scan rate of 525 lines at 50 Hz, video bandwidth of 4.2 MHz, and audio carrier of 4.5 MHz.

Analog frequencies were shown previously as FM TV (see the list above).

Digital

Digital radio frequency systems transmit IP (TCP/IP or UDP/IP) signals over the air. Typically, to transmit video, either the video signal is sourced directly from an IP enabled video camera, or an analog video signal (PAL/NTSC format) is converted to UDP/IP through a video codec.

TCP/UDP

The main difference between TCP/IP and UDP/IP is that although both are IP, TCP is a method for ensuring that every packet reaches its destination. When one does not, the destination computer makes a request to the transmitting computer to resend the missing packet. This results in more traffic. For data such as video or audio, which are dynamic and constantly changing, there is no point to going back for a packet because the image will already have been displayed or the audio will have been heard. Thus, UDP/IP is used. UDP is a connectionless protocol that, like TCP, runs on top of IP networks. Unlike TCP/IP, UDP/IP provides very few error recovery services, offering instead a direct way to send and receive data over an IP network. It is used primarily for broadcasting video and audio over a network.

Frequencies

Common digital radio frequencies are 2.4, 5.0, 5.8, and 10–24 GHz. Some of these frequencies are unlicensed and others require a license. Generally, 802.11a/b/g/i does not require a license, whereas other protocols do.

Latency Problems

Digital signals insert circuit delays, called latency. Latency is normally measured in milliseconds (msec), microseconds (μsec), or nanoseconds (nsec). Cabled wire inserts zero millisecond latency. High-quality digital switch latency is measured in the microsecond range. The very best switches measure latency in nanoseconds. Latency becomes a significant problem above 150 msec. You should strive to design systems that have latency under 50 msec. Long latency times have three potential effects: First, you are not seeing the video in real time, but instead you are seeing a delay of the actual image. Second, you are not controlling a pan/tilt/zoom camera in real time. This is a major problem. Imagine trying to pan/tilt/zoom a camera to look at a license plate in a parking lot. Now imagine that each time you adjust its position, it overshoots its target because you are looking at the image later than the camera is sending it. This requires a constant adjustment until you can finally, and with much frustration, target the license plate. Following a moving target is utterly hopeless. Lastly, very long latencies (>1 sec) can on many systems cause the TCP/IP processing process to lose track of packets, resulting in the sending of many duplicate video packets or the loss of video packets. The loss of packets results in very bad or totally useless video, and the sending of additional packets can result in even slower (possibly useless) transmission that is so full of duplicate packets that no entire image can be received in a timely fashion. This is especially true of satellite transmissions. Low latency is good. The best digital wireless systems insert less than 1 msec per node. Some common system design approaches can inject up to 35 msec per node.

Satellite

Video can also be sent via satellite. There are two common methods.

Satellite Dish

Satellite dish transmission uses either a fixed or a portable satellite dish to uplink and downlink to a geosynchronous satellite. In the fall of 1945, a Royal Air Force electronics officer and member of the British Interplanetary Society, Arthur C. Clarke [the famed author of *2001: A Space Odyssey* (1968)], wrote a short article positing that if a satellite's orbit positioned directly over the equator could be configured such that it rotated at exactly the same speed as the rotation of the earth, then it would appear to "hang" motionless in orbit above a fixed position over the earth. This would allow for continuous transmissions to and from the satellite. Previous early communications satellites (Echo, Telstar, Relay, and Syncom) were positioned in low Earth orbits and could not be used for more than 20 minutes for each orbit.

Satellite video is fraught with four major problems: precise positioning, weather interference, latency delays exceeding 240 msec, and the expense of a fixed IP address on a satellite dish. The time to set up precise dish positioning can be up to $1/2$ hour, depending on skills (some people never get it). We have seen satellite latency of up to 2500 msec. That kind of latency is almost impossible to deal with.

Satellite Phone

Satellite phones can also be used to transmit video. Unlike satellite dishes, no precise positioning is required. Simply turn on the radio, connect the video camera, establish the communication, and send. Satellite phones are very expensive, as is their satellite time, but for reporters in the field and offshore oil platforms, they make a great backup to satellite dish communications.

Latency Problems

All satellite communications insert very high latency, typically more than 240 msec. This is useless for pan/tilt/zoom use, and the insert delay makes voice communications tricky. However, if you cannot get communications there any other way, it is a real blessing. For unmanned offshore oil platforms, when connected to an alarm system, the video can confirm that a fishing vessel has moored itself out 100 miles from shore and that a break-in to the platform is occurring. Combined with voice communications, those intruders can be ordered off the platform in virtual real time with an indication that the vessel number has been recorded. During high security levels, the video system allows for a virtual "guard tour" of the platform, without the need to dispatch a helicopter at a cost of thousands of dollars for each sortie.

Wireless Architectures

There are three basic wireless architectures, and they are an analog of the wired networks.

Point-to-Point

Point-to-point wireless networks are composed of two nodes, and they communicate wirelessly between the two. It is analogous to a modem connection. Wireless point-to-point connections require a line-of-sight signal or a good reflected signal.

Point–to–Multipoint

Point-to-multipoint connections are networks in which a single wireless node makes connection to several or many other wireless nodes. The single wireless node serves all the others, and all of them communicate to each other through the same single node. This is analogous to a hub or switch or router connection. Wireless point-to-multipoint connections also require line-of-sight signals or absolutely reliable reflected signals.

Wireless Mesh

Wireless mesh systems are like the Internet. That is, each node connects onto the matrix of the mesh and finds as many connections as it can. It selects a primary connection based perhaps on best signal strength or rules set for the least number of nodes between the source and destination node. If the node cannot talk directly to the destination node, then that signal will "hop" through other nodes until it finds the destination node. A wireless mesh is like the Internet. You may not know how you got to a server in Europe, but you sure can see the web page. Wireless meshes can let signals hop several times, so even if there is no line-of-sight connection available, you can almost certainly hop around that oil tank, tree, or building by jumping across several other nodes that do have line-of-sight connections to each other. A well-designed wireless mesh network will automatically and continuously search for the best available connection or shortest available path for each and every node from its source to its destination. It will do this every time, all the time, making sure that you always have a good, solid signal.

Full-Duplex Wireless Mesh

Old radio heads like me know that there are two ways of talking over the air: half-duplex and full-duplex. The difference is critical for digital video systems, and if the reader learns anything about wireless systems in the book, this is the thing to understand. In half-duplex systems, each node (transceiver) can either listen or talk but cannot do both at the same time. So when it is talking, it is not listening. When it is listening, it cannot talk. For a digital video system, that means that the bandwidth of the transceiver is effectively cut in half, not because it has in fact less bandwidth but because it is communicating bidirectionally only half the time. For a 54-GHz system, that means that it starts out of the box as a 27-GHz system. Subtract network overhead and encryption and you are left with approximately 22 or 23 GHz less available bandwidth. OK, you say, I can live with 22 GHz. However, if you understand that the purpose of wireless mesh networks is to use the mesh to retransmit video from node to node, it takes on new meaning. That loss of half of the bandwidth occurs with each retransmission. From the first node to the second bandwidth is 22 GHz minus the video signal (e.g., 2GHz), leaving 20 GHz. From the second node to the third, it is halved again from 20 to 10 GHz, and now we subtract the second video camera's signal load too. That is another 2 GHz, leaving only 8 GHz. There is not enough bandwidth left to safely add a third camera since we need to reserve at least 6 GHz of overhead for communication snafus. We are effectively out of bandwidth after only two camera nodes.

On the other hand, full-duplex wireless nodes communicate both directions (transmit and receive) all the time. That is because a full-duplex wireless mesh system uses two radios in each node (one transmitter and one receiver). By careful antenna selection, we can transmit and receive continuously at each wireless node. Considering our example again, we can communicate digital video effectively across up to 10 nodes, assuming a 2-GHz drop for each camera. (I use a standard of four hops). Another trick is antenna selection. There are basically two types of antennas for all radio systems: directional and omnidirectional. An omnidirectional antenna transmits or receives in a pattern like an apple. There is a slight pinch at the top and bottom of the pattern, but the rest of the radiation pattern is spherical, at least in the horizontal plane. Directional antennas narrow their "view" by restricting the view that its designer does not want. By "pinching" the part of the spherical radiation pattern that is unwanted, the part that is desired is lengthened, sometimes considerably. This creates "gain." Useful signals can be derived from either a line-of-sight connection or a single reflected signal. However, that reflected signal can be a problem if the receiver can see both the original and the reflected signal. Reflected signals arrive later than line-of-sight signals because they are traveling a longer distance from source to destination. All antennas suffer from a phenomenon called multipath. Multipath signals are signals that originate from the transmitting source but from at least two sources, at least one of which may be a reflected signal. There is another type of antenna that is little known (at least until now), called a multiphased omnidirectional antenna.

SECURITY COMMUNICATIONS

Security communications are the root of response. Communications involves the following categories:

- Communications between security officers and the public they serve
- Communications between security officers and other security officers
- Communications between security officers and the public via telephones
- Communications between security officers and public agencies (fire/police, etc.)

Security communications serve several purposes:

- Receiving information and direction in order to do their job
- Assisting the public with access or information
- Directing subjects to comply with established security policies
- Coordinating emergency responders

Two-Way Radios

Two-way radios are the heart of communications for any security staff. They provide the ability for security officers to communicate with each other and with other facility personnel, including management and maintenance/cleaning staff. Two-way radios are used for communications from the security console to field officers and from officer to officer in the field.

Two-way radios have varying frequencies. Common spectrum sections include the 150- and 450-MHz bands. Radios with 800 MHz are a blend of traditional two-way radio technology and computer-controlled transmitters. The system's main advantage is that radio transmitters can be shared among various departments or users with the aid of computer programming. Virtual radio groups, called "talk groups," are created in software to enable private departmental conversations. This gives the system the look and feel of one having many different "frequencies" when in fact everyone is sharing just a few. A quick reference of public and private radio frequencies can be found at http://www.bearcat1.com/freer.htm.

Cell Phones

Cell phones can provide an inexpensive means of communications, particularly cell phones with a two-way radio function. They provide in a single unit both a two-way radio and the ability to call the police directly when needed, as well as managers, etc.

Cell phones have limits, however. Before deciding on using a cell phone as a primary means of communication, it is important to conduct a test with the type of cell phone planned for use in every dark recess of the building, parking structure, stairwell, restroom, storage room, and throughout the entire facility. Otherwise, you may discover a dead spot in exactly the place where the worst possible emergency is occurring, exactly when it occurs.

Cell phones are particularly valuable for patrol officers in vehicles because of their wide geographical reach, allowing the officer to be reached both on and off the property.

Intercoms

Security intercoms enable console officers to talk to anyone near a field intercom station (typically another officer or a member of the public). Calls can usually be initiated either from the console or from the intercom field station by pressing a "call" button. Most intercoms are hands-free devices, although handsets are sometimes used. ADA (Americans with Disability Act)-compliant intercoms also provide a visual indicator that the call has been sent and acknowledged, in case the user is hearing impaired.

Other types of intercoms include call-out only stations and intercom bullhorns. Call-out stations are similar to standard intercoms but are not equipped with call buttons. The console officer always originates the call for this type. Intercom bullhorns are similar to call-out stations but are equipped with a horn that acoustically amplifies the audio so that the console officer and subject can communicate at farther distances (usually up to 100 ft). Intercom bullhorns usually also require an auxiliary amplifier in order to provide adequate power to be heard at that distance. The horn gathers the voice of the subject, although it is more difficult for the officer to hear the subject than it is for the subject to hear the officer. Bullhorns are often used only for directions to the subject and not back to the officer.

Emergency Phones

Emergency phones (also called assistance phones) are intercoms that are also equipped with flashing lights or strobes to help a responding officer find the subject who is calling and to deter a crime against that subject since the strobe calls attention to the area, making a crime of violence less probable.

Paging Systems

Paging systems are strictly for communication from the console officer to the field. Paging systems can be specific to a single paging speaker or horn or to a field of speakers and horns in order to cover a large area. Paging systems are useful for making announcements to large numbers of people simultaneously, such as to order an evacuation or to issue directions in an emergency.

ANALOG VS. DIGITAL
Analog

Intercom and voice systems historically used analog communications—that is, a microphone was connected to an amplifier and a speaker. For larger systems, a matrix switcher was used to manage one or a few console communications paths out to many field intercoms. This is called a circuit-switched network. Traditional telephone systems are also circuit-switched networks. Each circuit can carry only one communication and there must be a continuous wire connection from speaker to subject. This approach is fine for a single site, but it has drawbacks, including the fact that the wiring is of a fixed architecture. So one intercom master station wires to many field stations. If one wants to add more master stations, one must wire from master to master. There is a single point of failure at the main master where the field intercom stations are first wired. Also, when the organization wants to move the location of the main master station, much costly rewiring is necessary.

Digital

For enterprise systems, the drawbacks of circuit-switched networks present major problems. How do you maintain a circuit from New York to California? The cost of leased lines is too high, so digital intercoms are used. As digital video systems become more prevalent, it is also easier to "piggyback" voice communications on that digital path. Digital systems use packet-switched networks instead of circuit-switched networks for communications. Therefore, their path can be dynamic. If the organization wants to move its console, it only has to connect the new console to the nearest digital switch.

Digital intercoms have certain drawbacks too. For security, audio is more important than any other communication.

Dropped audio could mean a lost life. So audio communications must be configured as the priority communication in order to ensure that no communication is lost as, for example, a new screen of video cameras is loading from one guard tour to the next. This is a programming element and cannot be configured in software if it is not written into the code. Audio compression protocols commonly include the G.7xx series, including G.711, G.721, G.722, G.726, G.728, and G.729. Another common protocol is the MPEG protocol, including MP-3. These are all UDP protocols. The software designer must ensure that the audio protocol is given priority of communications over the digital and data protocols. Where this is not done, the security officer can find it difficult to talk while video is loading. This condition is unacceptable, although at the time of this writing several video software manufacturers publish software with this flaw. Their common workaround is to require an additional client workstation just for audio. This is one of those design flaws that no one would buy if they knew about it ahead of time.

Digital audio has many advantages. Additional intercom stations can be added on anywhere an extra switch port exists, dramatically reducing wired infrastructure costs. Additional switches can be added at little cost in new infrastructure. For enterprise systems, the Internet or asynchronous transfer mode networks permit communications across state and national boundaries, making possible a monitoring center in one state that monitors sites throughout the world.

Wireless Digital

Any digital communication can be configured to operate wirelessly as well as on a wired network. This enables communications to remotely located emergency phones across an endless expanse of park or parking lot. All one needs is power, and that can sometimes be obtained via solar panels and batteries. Emergency phones are an ideal application for solar panels and batteries since they draw power only when in use, except for a small amount of power for the radio frequency node. This is usually very low, typically less than 25 W for a well-designed system.

Communication System Integration

It is also possible to integrate two-way radios, cell phones, land phones, and intercoms into a consolidated communications system. Typically, there are only one or two security officers at a console, but there may be many communications systems. In the worst case I have seen, at a high-rise building in Los Angeles, there were 10 separate intercoms for elevators, 4 intercom systems for security, 4 two-way radio systems, 2 paging systems, 8 telephone lines, and cell phones. All this was (barely) manageable until an earthquake struck. Then, chaos broke loose in the security console room. Remember, that was 29 separate communications systems for a console room with one or two officers. That does not work very well.

In an ideal configuration, the systems have been coordinated such that there is no more than one of each type of system (interdiscipline coordination-instilled design flaws) and those few systems are further coordinated into a "consolidated communications system" (CCS). The CCS assembles the various communications platforms into a single piece of software that manages the communications to a single (or multiple) console officer station. Calls that cannot be taken are queued.

Queued calls go to an automated attendant that provides feedback to waiting parties. In the earthquake example, people in a stopped elevator would hear an automated message from the intercom speaker when they press the help button advising them that an earthquake has just struck the building and that there is a heavy demand on the security console officer and advising them that their call is in a queue. They would be advised to push the help button a second time if there is a medical emergency, advancing their call in the queue. In the meantime, there would be a digitized ring tone and recorded message with enough variation to keep their anxiety level low. The system could also advise them of the expected wait time.

COMMAND/COMMUNICATIONS CONSOLES

Monitoring Consoles

Consoles and workstations provide a means to instruct the security system on how to behave and interact with its environment and users, to provide a face for the security system to its human user (viewing cameras, using the intercom, responding to alarms, etc.), and to obtain system reports. There are a limited number of common implementations of these types of workstations. System size dictates the type.

Small Systems

Single-site systems are often designed with a common workstation that will provide all system services together in a single computer. The system may separate alarm/access control, video monitoring, and the intercom master station into three separate units and may commonly be designed as an analog video/intercom system rather than digital. However, this trend will change over time toward digital video and intercom as these systems become more prevalent in the smaller systems. In any event, the alarm/access control system will likely comprise field devices (card readers, locks, etc.), field device controllers, and a single computer to manage them.

System interface and automation will likely be limited to activating video cameras in response to alarms, and this interface may well be accomplished using dry contacts.

Thus, the small system will likely comprise a single computer workstation for the alarm/access control system, a video multiplexer and perhaps a pair of analog video monitors for the few video cameras, and an intercom master station to answer intercoms. These will likely be located at a lobby desk, security office, or manager's office.

Medium-Sized Systems

Medium-sized systems will typically incorporate a higher level of system integration and possibly more than one workstation or console. Medium-sized systems may well separate system functions into those that will exist on a server and those that will operate on a client workstation.

These systems may be designed as analog video/intercom or they may be digital. It is possible that the client workstations will include a separate workstation for the lobby desk or security office and another one for administration of the system by a manager.

Enterprise-Class Systems

Any enterprise-class system (multiple buildings and/or multiple sites) that is not designed initially with a digital video/digital intercom infrastructure will be a costly system to upgrade, expand, and maintain as time goes by.

These systems routinely incorporate a high level of integration to other building systems and routinely have both local and remote or centralized system monitoring and/or administration.

All enterprise-class systems are built around a client/server model and may involve many clients and many servers, including servers acting as local and/or central archivers, local and/or centralized guard workstations, and local and/or centralized administrative workstations including photo identification and identity verification workstations.

Workstation and Console Specifics

Command, Control, and Communications Consoles

The most sophisticated of all security consoles, the C3 console, is the operational heart of an enterprise-class alarm monitoring and management system. Usually having more than one console (sometimes up to a dozen), the C3 approach is the ultimate in centralized corporate oversight for safety, security, and sometimes even operational efficiency.

Incidents such as major refinery explosions can be effectively prevented if health, safety, and efficiency (HSE) monitoring is augmented centrally. This method of centralized monitoring can advise local on-site HSE personnel of unsafe practices in conflict with established corporate safety or security policies that may be occurring without the knowledge of local managers. For every employee who might complain about the intrusion of centralized authority, lives can truly be saved by avoiding unsafe industrial practices that would otherwise go unnoticed.

A C3 console normally incorporates one or more workstations, and each workstation includes a number of LCD monitors. Typically, two to four monitors display video, one displays alarm and control maps, one may display alarm/access control system activity, and an additional monitor may be used for an application package such as a report writer, spreadsheet, or word processor. On some systems, e-mail service and voice communications software may be used. C3 consoles may also have one or more large screen displays that anyone in the room can easily see. These are typically run from one of the workstations in the console. The C3 console generally also incorporates Situational Analysis Software to help the console officers understand what is being displayed in the system in the context of locations of buildings, avenues and waterways in the real world.

One consideration regarding C3 consoles (and others as well, but especially C3 consoles) is the issue of workstation processing power. Every program and process requires CPU, memory, and video card processing cycles, and there are a finite number for each individual workstation, based on its processor, clock speed, and video card. It is possible to crash a workstation that is overloaded with requests for processing cycles. That is a bad thing. So it is important to design workstations in a manner that ensures that it will not happen. The good news is that Moore's law indicates that processing power will grow by a factor of two approximately every year and a half. The bad news is that the processing power of any workstation is determined by its weakest link, which could be the processor, the video card, memory type and capacity, the operating system, or the software. There is not a single, simple formula to calculate how much processing power is required for a given application. However, there is a simple way to make a useful calculation:

- Find a machine that is roughly similar to the type of machine you intend to specify. Generally, the manufacturer of the digital video software will have several machines to select from in its lab.

- Ask the lab technician to start up the machine with only the operating system and the digital video application running (displaying no cameras at this time). Load the Task Manager and note the CPU usage in percentage of utilization.
- Now display one camera at the resolution and frame rate to be viewed. Again, look at the Task Manager and note the difference in CPU processing percentage of utilization.
- Then display 4 and then 16 cameras and note the percentage of utilization of CPU.
- Next, open a browser window on top of the video that is already open and again note the CPU utilization figures.
- Lastly, load on top of this a standard spreadsheet or word processing application and again note the CPU utilization, with all this running.

From the previous information, you can calculate how much CPU utilization will occur when the computer is fully loaded with all intended camera signals and ancillary browsers programs. This will be a real-world number that is meaningful.

The system should be designed so as not to ever exceed 60% of CPU utilization. Exceeding 60% of continuous duty will result in overheating and shortening of the life of the CPU. It may result in the inability of the computer to adequately process video, causing observably bad images and possibly crashing the computer. This condition can also occur if the image specifications are exceeded. For example, if the computer's capacity is based on the display of 32 2-CIF images at 15fps and the console user reprograms the resolution to 4-CIF and the frame rate to 30fps, these results could occur. The user must be instructed as to the design limitations of the workstation.

Important elements of any security console workstation include the processor, memory, the video card, and the quality of monitor. It is unwise to skimp on servers and workstations. They do the heavy lifting in the system. Unlike other parts of the system in which scale equals dollars (more units = more money), a significant investment in servers and workstations does not usually equal a significant increase in the overall cost of the system. It is a wise investment for the designer to recommend and for the client to make.

Ergonomics for C3 consoles are also a major consideration. The console design may comprise any of a number of configurations, including a wrap-around design in which the console is nestled into a corner or side wall or a cluster of individual workstation desks facing a large screen display or video wall at one end of the room. Special attention should be paid to the quality of lighting; keyboard, mouse, and monitor position; and the quality of chairs. All these factors have a bearing on the ability of the console officer to observe video over a period of many hours.

There has also been much discussion regarding how many cameras should be displayed on a console, and like everyone else, I have an opinion. First, let's state the various cases made. The many-is-better argument goes like this: If many cameras are displayed, then the console officer can observe the video of any camera at his pleasure. He can quickly scan all the available views and may see something that he would never observe if the cameras were not otherwise displayed. The fewer-is-better argument goes like this: Some scientific studies have shown that an officer cannot view more than approximately six images with any precision of observation over any long time period. Having more monitors may create complacency on the part of the observing officer, and in any event it is better if most video views respond to some kind of alarm or event indicator if possible. For this reason, it is better to use many cameras and fewer monitors and have the cameras triggered by alarms where possible.

I am in the second camp. However, there is a caveat. I am also an advocate of creating a series of scene views using related video cameras—for example, all the cameras on the first level of a parking structure, second level, etc. These related camera groups can be assembled to create a "virtual guard tour" that allows the console officer to "walk" the facility by sequentially selecting the groups of related cameras. Additionally, any alarms can also be programmed to select the related group of cameras, not just the single camera that is nearest to the alarm event. A superset of guard tour groups is video pursuit, which is discussed later in the book.

C3 Console Use in Public Agency Settings

C3 consoles are of particular use for mass transit facilities where the responding officer will almost always be a sworn police officer. For such installations, it is important to use the C3 console as a vetting console, staffed by civilians, not by a police dispatcher. This is to ensure that the dispatch officer is not swamped by nuisance alarms, of which there may be many in such installations.

After vetting the alarm through the C3 console, real events needing the dispatch of a sworn officer can be passed to the dispatch console for appropriate action.

A well-designed C3 console scheme should permit the civilian console officer to be able to "pass off" the event to a sworn officer at a different console simply by moving an icon representing the civilian monitor to an icon representing the sworn officer's monitor. When this is done, the video should queue at the sworn officer's monitor, sounding an alarm to direct his or her attention to the event and keeping the civilian online to hand off the audio.

Lobby Desk Consoles

Security workstations are often placed at lobby desks where the public is assisted. Here, the security designer is often requested to design the workstation into a highly aesthetic environment.

Careful coordination with the interiors architect is required in order to determine the ergonomic elements required. The architect will need to closely coordinate the design of the console with the measurements of the lobby desk security components.

Dispatch Consoles

Similar to C3 consoles, dispatch consoles also may have many workstations. In addition to the security video, alarm/access control, and intercom elements, radio dispatch will be a major element. Computer aided dispatch (CAD) software will likely be implemented, and this must also be coordinated in order to display locations of cars, personnel, and activities. The video system can be integrated with CAD software to achieve this result, and the security intercom may also be integrated with the two-way radio system, telephone system, and even cellular/radio phone system to facilitate communications. In all other respects, dispatch consoles are similar in requirements and design to C3 consoles, except that the designer is often burdened with very limited space, sometimes requiring more functions be added into a very small existing space.

Administrative Workstations

Administrative workstations facilitate the programming of cards, system software, hardware and firmware configuration changes, and the creation and reviewing of system reports. Administrative workstations are generally limited to no more than two monitors and may be combined with other duties on the security manager's or site manager's desk.

Administrative workstations are the simplest and least demanding of security workstations. As always, observe processor, memory, and video card requirements. Administrative workstations include the computer, monitors, keyboard, and mouse and report printer.

Identification Badging Consoles

Virtually every medium and large system involves photo identification badges. These are usually bonded on or printed directly onto an access credential.

Photo identification credentials typically display a photo of the credential holder, a logo of the organization or some other identifying logo, the name and department of the person, and may also display a color or pattern scheme that is an identifying feature of the person's access privileges. This function presents the human readable portion of an access credential that facilitates an organization's staff to easily identify people wearing badges, the organization or department to which they belong, and whether they are allowed unescorted access to the area in which they are found.

Photo identification systems comprise an identification badging console (workstation), a digital camera, lights, background, posing chair, and a credential printer.

Based on badging volume and the organization's human resources processes, the system may be centralized or distributed across several sites, and the credential printers may be attached to either the workstation or a network in which they are shared by several photo identification workstations.

Identity Verification Workstations

Although rare, identity verification workstations facilitate absolute verification of a credentialed person through an access portal. These are used in high-security environments such as nuclear and weapons storage facilities, research and design facilities, and other places where critical proprietary information or assets that could present harm to the public are housed.

The identity verification workstation is typically used with a revolving door, optical turnstile, or man-trap to provide a means to verify with certainty that the person holding an access credential is who he or she claims to be.

The workstation is part of the overall identity verification portal, which includes a credential reader; a movement pausing mechanism (revolving door, physical or electronic turnstile, man-trap, or in the simplest form, an electrically locked door); and a visual recognition system, usually in the form of a video camera and computer software, that displays a live image of the person next to an image retrieved from the photo identification database corresponding to the one stored for the access credential that was just presented at the portal. After making the comparison, the security officer staffing the identity verification portal verifies that the credential is valid for the portal (authorized for the portal and the date and time of use) and that the credential holder is the person who is authorized to carry the credential (the live video image of the person matches the photo ID image). After verification, the security officer manually unlocks the door using a remote electronic release, allowing the credential holder into the restricted area.

GUARD CONSOLE FUNCTIONS

Guard consoles are used to manage the security of the facility. The guard console is the aircraft control tower of the security operation. From this location, it should be possible for the console guard to keep an eye on all the major access control and intrusion events occurring in the building. Basic guard console functions include

- Vetting alarms for appropriate response
- Granting access remotely
- Video surveillance
- Video guard tours
- Video pursuit
- Building system interfaces

Vetting Alarms

Any alarm that occurs anywhere in the security system will report to the guard console. The console software should be integrated to extend its eyes, ears, and mouth into the depths of the facility, wherever an alarm occurs. The guard should receive immediate notification of the alarm and immediately be able to verify the alarm from the console. Often, the best way to do this is by the presence of a video camera near the alarm. If the alarm is verified as an intrusion, the console guard must then take some action, either dispatching an officer to respond (radio) or confronting the subject via security intercom. For this reason, good design principles indicate that, where possible, every alarm should have a camera nearby to permit alarm verification. Ideally, there should also be a field intercom station or field talk station near the camera to direct the subject away from the area of the intrusion. Additionally, the software should be configured such that for every alarm a camera is programmed to queue for display automatically, and that camera image should be recorded. For digital video systems, a pre-event record period is also recommended. That is, even if the camera is not programmed for continuous archiving, the system should be archiving every camera continuously for 2 minutes such that in the event of an alarm for which that camera may respond, that 2 minutes being recorded before the alarm becomes part of the alarm video event archive. Otherwise, it is recorded over continuously.

Granting Access Remotely

Another common function of guard consoles is the remote granting of access to authorized visitors, contractors, and vendors. Typically, one or more remote doors may facilitate such access. If there is a constant flow of people through the door, it may be appropriate to locate a guard there to facilitate authorization and access granting. However, often the flow does not warrant the cost of a full-time guard. For such cases, it is ideal if there can be configured a vestibule for access granting to include a card reader for authorized users, a camera, and an intercom to facilitate a gracious granting of access privileges. These designs take two common forms.

Finished Visitor Lobby

A finished visitor lobby may be used for remote access granting after normal business hours—for example, in a multitenant high-rise building environment. The vestibule provides a secure means of granting access without putting anyone in the building at risk, including the lobby desk guard.

Visitor vestibules can be under the control of the console guard and/or may also be under the control of a tenant via use of a building directory and intercom system. In such cases, the visitor looks up the tenant and places a call using the code next to the tenant's name. Upon answering, the tenant can enter a telephone code unlocking the inner door and permitting access into the building.

Where the control is exclusive to the console guard, the guard may also have control over the elevator system to ensure that the visitor actually goes to the floor he or she has requested and for which he or she is authorized by the tenant.

Delivery Lobby

Delivery lobbies can be created at a loading dock to reduce guard force count. In such cases, again a vestibule is created and the system is activated as an event whenever the vestibule is occupied, when the outer door is opened.

An assumption is made that the delivery person is unfamiliar with the building, so its use is in the hands of the guard, making the delivery person's knowledge level unimportant.

The guard console will display the delivery lobby camera upon opening of the outer door, and the delivery lobby intercom will be queued. The console guard will initiate a call to the delivery person asking her to whom she is making a delivery. After answering, the guard will ask the delivery person to present her drivers license and delivery company identification face up on a credential camera reader. The credential reader is a lighted box with a platen for placing the identification papers for viewing.

After recording the delivery person's identification, the guard instructs the delivery person to place her delivery papers on the platen to record the location of the package for delivery. After this is done, the guard will then enable the elevator–hall call buttons and may also direct the elevator to the proper floor if he has been given elevator floor select control on his console.[10]

Video Surveillance

Video surveillance involves the act of observing a scene or scenes and looking for specific behaviors that are improper or that may indicate the emergence or existence of improper behavior.

Common uses of video surveillance include observing the public at the entry to sports events, public transportation (train platforms, airports, etc.), and around the perimeter of secure facilities, especially those that are directly bounded by community spaces.

The video surveillance process includes the identification of areas of concern and the identification of specific cameras or groups of cameras that may be able to view those areas. If it is possible to identify schedules when security trends have occurred or may be likely to occur, that is also helpful to the process. Then, by viewing the selected images at appropriate times, it is possible to determine if improper activity is occurring.

One such application is for train platforms. Following a series of reports of intimidating behavior at a particular train platform, the use of video cameras and intercoms was found to reduce the potential for such events as the perpetrators began to understand that their behavior could be recorded and used to identify them to police. Furthermore, the act of getting on a train did not deter the police who boarded at the next station and apprehended the criminals. Word got around and the behavior was reduced dramatically.

Video Guard Tours

The use of correlated groups of video cameras programmed to be viewed as a group allows the console officer to see an entire area at once. He can then step through the spaces of the facility, each time viewing the entire area as though he were walking through a guard tour.

It is much faster to perform a virtual video guard tour than a physical guard tour, thus allowing more frequent reviews of the spaces. Additionally, since the cameras are always in place, people behaving improperly are unaware that they are being viewed by authorities until a response occurs, either by dispatched officer or by intercom intervention, either of which can be effective in deterring improper behavior.

Video guard tours are especially effective at managing very large facilities, such as public transportation facilities in which the spaces can be vast and the time to travel between areas can be significant.

Video Pursuit

The guard tour cameras can also be set up to create a "video pursuit" that will allow a console officer in an environment such as an airport or casino to follow a subject as he or she walks through the space by selecting the camera in the group into which the subject has walked. With each selection, a new group will be displayed where the new display includes the selected camera and other cameras displaying views into which the subject might walk if he or she leaves the area under display. As the subject moves from camera to camera, video pursuit keeps the subject centered in a cocoon of cameras. A corresponding display of maps will show the console officer where the subject is located by highlighting the central camera and those around it where the subject might walk.[11]

COMMUNICATIONS SYSTEMS

Security communications systems facilitate rapid information gathering, decision making, and action taking.

Security System Intercoms

Security intercoms provide a convenient way for visitors to gain information or access at remote doors. They may be used either to facilitate remote access granting or to direct the visitor to a visitor lobby. The visitor can query the console security officer by pressing a call button on the intercom, thus initiating a call. Likewise, the console security officer can also initiate a call directly from the console.

A second type of intercom is the officer-controlled security intercom. Similar to a conventional intercom station but without the call button, these are often placed next to a video camera for use in directing a subject after verifying an alarm.

The third type of security intercom is the intercom bullhorn. It is similar to the officer-controlled intercom, but has the ability to reach farther distances due to the bullhorn.

Elevator and Parking System Intercoms

Security intercoms are often located in elevators and elevator lobbies and at parking entrances.

Emergency Call Stations

A security intercom coupled with a blue strobe and emergency signage, this intercom is a welcome point of help in areas where an assault could occur, such as in parking structures and walkways on a college campus. Reports indicate that assault crimes can diminish from historical norms where emergency call stations are used.

Digital intercom systems utilize a codec from the field intercom station to the digital infrastructure. The digital video software often accommodates the communications path and can also automatically queue the intercom for use whenever the camera viewing the intercom is on screen. That can be accomplished automatically in response to an alarm.

Analog intercoms use either two-wire or four-wire field intercom stations. Four-wire intercom stations use two wires for the speaker, two for the microphone, and sometimes two for the call button, whereas two-wire intercoms use only two wires for all three functions. Four-wire intercoms can operate in full-duplex mode (simultaneous talk/listen), whereas two-wire intercoms can only operate in half-duplex mode, although this is often more advisable since it allows the console security officer to control the conversation and ensures that conversations in the console room will not be unintentionally overheard at the field intercom station.

Direct Ring-Down Intercoms

These are telephones that ring to a specific number when the receiver is lifted or the call button is pressed (hands-free version). These are commonly used in elevators and emergency call stations. Direct ring-down phones are available in both CO (central office line connection) and non-CO versions (non-CO versions create their own ring-down voltage and need only a pair of wires connected to an answering phone station set). These are frequently used for remote parking gates. Both types are also usually equipped with remote control over a dry contact relay at the ring-down station, permitting remote access through a parking gate or door.

Two-Way Radio

Two-way radio systems facilitate constant communications among a dispatcher, console security officer, security management, security guards, and building maintenance personnel.

Two-way radio systems can comprise an assembly of hand-held radios with no master station or may be equipped with a master station at the security command center. In any event, a charging station will need to be accommodated in the space planning of the security command center.

Two-way radio systems can be integrated via communications software with other communications systems to create a consolidated communications system that can integrate radio, telephone, pagers, and intercoms into a single communications platform.

Pagers

Pagers can be used to notify roving security officers of an alarm or can discretely notify an officer of a condition requiring his or her attention. Many alarm/access control systems can connect directly to a paging system transmitter for local broadcast within a building or on a campus. The systems can also be connected to a telephone dialer in order to broadcast a page across a city or the country. At a minimum, the security console can be configured to utilize paging software to key in messages independent of any other interface.

Wireless Headsets

For security consoles and lobby security desks that require the console officer to move about considerably, it is useful to equip the intercom/telephone or two-way radio with wireless headphones. These free the console officer from the common tether of a standard headset.

Wireless headsets can be connected a variety of ways depending on the manufacturer and model, including to a headphone plug, USB, or RS-232.

SUMMARY

The basics of alarm/access control systems include identification devices (card readers, keypads, and biometric systems). Keypads can be simple or complex, the most advanced of which scrambles the numbers for each use and limits the view of adjacent users. Card reader types include magnetic stripe, Wiegand, passive and active proximity, and smart cards. Many organizations use multitechnology cards, which allow the user to access various facilities, each of which may require a different card technology.

Access cards are commonly used with photo identification systems such that the access card and identification together form the credential. Photo identification cards help identify users by sight, showing what areas they have access to and displaying their photo, name, and department.

Other devices include locks, door position switches, and request to exit devices. Common electrified lock types include electrified strikes, electrified mortise locks, magnetic locks, electrified panic hardware, and specialty locks. Door and gate position switches can be either surface mounted or concealed. Other devices include door and gate operators and revolving doors and turnstiles. Access control system field elements are controlled by electronic processing boards, which include a microprocessor, memory, and field interface modules. All these devices are managed by servers and workstations.

The different subsystems of an integrated security system can be blended together into a single system. The system can also be interfaced with other systems to achieve advanced automated functions.

Early analog video systems included only cameras, cable, and monitors. As demand increased, more cameras were displayed on a few monitors using a sequential switcher. As the technology progressed, sequential switchers grew to become digital matrix switchers, and quads and multiplexers promised to display and record multiple cameras onto a single tape. Analog video was recorded by using a helical-scan spinning record head. Early recorders used 2-in. reel-to-reel tape, which was later replaced by cartridges, notably the VHS cassette.

Digital video records and transmits the video as a series of ones and zeros rather than as a voltage on a coaxial cable, as does analog video.

Digital systems transmit their information in packets. In order to truly understand digital video systems, or networks, one must fully understand how the TCP/IP protocol works. It is also important to understand how network switching and routing work. Other issues that are important to understand include both wired and wireless networks. Wired networks utilize cable, switchers, and routers. Wireless networks utilize lasers, microwave, and radio links, including land and space-based radio. Typical radio-based networks connect via point-to-point, point-to-multipoint, and with wireless mesh networks.

Security communications are the root of response. Common technologies include two-way radios, cell phones, and intercoms. Intercoms can also be related to emergency phones and paging systems.

Command and communications consoles vary greatly depending on the needs of the facility they serve. Small systems often have simple consoles, providing only basic functions. Medium-sized systems generally include some system integration elements, whereas enterprise-class systems often use extensive integration. Console types include lobby desk consoles, dispatch consoles, administrative workstations, identification badging consoles, and identity verification consoles. Guard consoles vet alarms for appropriate response, grant access remotely, conduct video surveillance and video guard tours, utilize video pursuit, and manage building system interfaces.

CHAPTER NOTES

1. A barcode is a machine-readable array of lines that due to their spacing and line width **contain a unique identity that is assigned to an asset.** Barcodes can also be in the form of patterns of dots, concentric circles, and hidden in images. Barcodes are read by optical scanners called barcode readers.
2. Biometric identification devices identify the user by some unique physical attribute, typically including fingerprints, retinas, iris patterns, hand geometry, ear patterns, and voices. Biometric algorithms can also be used to identify people by their walking gate, facial patterns, and handwriting.

3. The designer is cautioned to select intelligent video systems with great caution. Like buying a bar at retirement, the dream is often sweeter than the reality unless careful research, testing, and selection occur before the system is implemented.

4. There were a few select examples of "frame grabbers" that created digital images from analog video signals. A typical implementation included a circuit to select the horizontal and vertical synchronization pulses from the video signal, an analog-to-digital converting circuit, a color decoder circuit, memory to store the acquired image (frame buffer), and a data interface that the computer could use to control the acquisition of the video signal. Early frame grabbers had only enough memory to acquire and store a single frame, hence the name. Modern streaming video systems derive from this early technology.

5. Encryption is a process of replacing clearly written text language (clear text) with a substitute of mixed up characters (or even pixels of an image) so that the meaning of the text is concealed. The intended recipient will have a key to unlock the clear text from the garbled letters, numbers, or pixels so that the message can be read.

6. Griffiths, R. T. 11 October 2002 *From ARPANET to the World Wide Web.* –Leiden University, Leiden, The Netherlands. Available at www.let.leidenuniv.nl/history/ivh/chap2.htm.

7. Cisco Education, available at www.cisco.com/univercd/cc/td/doc/cisintwk/ito_doc/tokenrng.htm.

8. *Node* is a common term meaning a network drop—that is, a computer, printer, server, or other device that feeds data to/from the network.

9. People who are learning about network architecture are often confused by the terms *hub, switch, router,* and *firewall.* A simplified but easy way to remember these is that a hub connects nodes together, a switch determines where data goes, a router determines what kind of data goes, and a firewall blocks malicious data traffic. These devices can be combined elegantly to construct a network that sends data exactly where and to whom it should go and

denies malicious data from ever landing on the network. Modern data devices can combine the functions of switch, router, and firewall into a single device called a network gateway.

10. With thanks to Chuck Hutchinson, Senior Security Manager, Crescent Real Estate Equities, Ltd.
11. Video pursuit was invented jointly by the author and his protégé, Mr. David Skusek.

Physical Security Elements

7

Physical security is the most basic countermeasure and one of the most effective. When one of my early mentors was extolling the virtues of electronic security, I stated that I believed that physical security was more important than electronics. When my mentor challenged me to cite an example, I asked him to imagine a steel frame structure out in an empty field. On the structure would be hung video cameras, intercoms, alarm sensors, card readers, locks, etc. but without the benefit of walls, doors, etc.—just the steel frame in a field to support all these devices. I asked, "We have a complete security system. But does the security system offer any security?" Of course not, he said, and conceded the point.

Physical security is anything that prevents unauthorized access to an asset by means of a barrier, be it a wall, door, rising bollard, fence, etc. Electronic security is any element that uses electronic components to deter, detect, assess, communicate, or assist in the response to an event. There is no security without physical security. Effective integrated security system design requires a comprehensive knowledge of physical security.

BASIC PHYSICAL SECURITY

The most basic physical security is the physical architecture and landscaping of a facility. Whether it is a 20-foot-high storm wall that prevents vehicle access, a fence that deters and delays access to the property, the walls and roof that prevent or delay entry without special tools, or locked doors or windows with bars that delay offenders, these all form the basis on which the designer can build a useful integrated electronic security system. The natural and existing physical security of a facility will also define what type of electronic security measures are required to achieve adequate security. For example, imagine an atrium hotel where each hotel room door opens onto a very large open space. This arrangement will require individual electronic locks on each hotel room door to secure the patron's assets and person. On the other hand, a research and development department that is in its own building may only require a few alarm points and locks on its perimeter and access control leading from its one reception lobby.

BASIC PHYSICAL SECURITY SKILLS: KNOWLEDGE OF THE TOOLS

Each type of electronic security system has its own types of components (we will call them tools) that are used to build the system. For access control systems, the most basic tools are doors and electronic locks.

DOOR TYPES

Security door hardware has often been the bane of security system designers. There are literally hundreds of combinations of door position switches, electrified locks, electric hinges, and automated door operators and a seemingly endless combination of hardware types to perform virtually every function known to man. A solid understanding of doors and electrified door hardware is necessary in order to be competent in designing integrated security systems.

First, it is useful to understand how architects select door hardware. Architects categorize buildings by classes. A Class A building has finely finished lobbies and corridors and is filled with fine appointments. Class B buildings are suitable for receiving guests and will make a pleasant impression, but they do not have the expensive architectural features of a Class A building. Class C buildings are more serviceable for office/warehouse functions, where there is a mix of public and utility functions within the same space. Class C buildings may be provided with both utilitarian and basic public amenities. Both Class A and Class B buildings will have their finer elements in the front-of-house (public) areas, and Class C building will have these elements in the back-of-house (back corridors and loading dock) areas.

Door types are selected by the architect based on strength requirements and aesthetic factors. For example, an architect would never design hollow metal doors for the front lobby of a Class A office tower because they do not fit the design ethic of the building's lobby. Similarly, the architect would not design plate glass doors for the loading dock since they do not have the strength required to stand up to carts banging against the doors, and there is no value to being able to see through the doors; in fact, it would be a liability because it would assist criminals to surveil the building before making a simple entry by breaking the glass in the door. There are really only a few types of doors, but there are many variations of these few. Variations include door handing, door hinge types, door openers and closers, door coordinators, and some other fairly arcane variations of these. Understanding doors is the first step to access control system design competency. Door types include

- Hollow metal
- Solid core
- Glass storefront
- Herculite™

- Specialty doors, including Total Doors™, balanced doors, and historical doors

Hollow Metal Doors

Hollow metal doors are one of the most common types of doors used in commercial and industrial environments. A hollow metal door is composed of a steel frame that has steel panels laminated to both sides. The door is typically equipped with mounts for hinges and a pocket for a mortise lock.

Better hollow metal doors may also be equipped with a steel tube from the center hinge to the mortise pocket for wiring an electrified mortise lock and an electrical pocket at the top of the door for mounting a magnet for a door position switch.

Hollow metal doors are robust doors that can take a beating. Depending on door height, they may be equipped with three to five hinge mounting points. Hollow metal doors may also be furnished with a plastic laminate, wood veneer, or stainless-steel finish to achieve a desired aesthetic effect.

Hollow metal doors are often supplied with a hollow metal frame, together creating a fire-rated assembly. Fire ratings of 60, 90, and 120 minute are available.

Typical electrified locks for hollow metal doors include electrified mortise locks, magnetic locks, and electrified panic hardware. Magnetic locks may be either surface mounted or concealed, and electrified panic hardware can be applied with either surface or concealed vertical rods. Electrified panic hardware may be of any type (with mortise lock, rim type, or with vertical rods).

Hollow metal doors are very easy to use with automatic door operators. Five or seven knuckle hinges are the most common hinging methods for hollow core doors, although pivots are not uncommon. More hinges are better than fewer for any security door application.

Solid Core

Solid core doors are wooden doors that are fully filled with wood or wood composite materials, inside a frame of wood. Solid core doors are often used in commercial applications, particularly in high-rise office building corridors. These are mostly applied to tenant suite doors rather than on the main fire corridor, where hollow metal doors are more common due to their lower cost and often higher fire rating. Solid core doors are in common use for the interior doors of Class A office buildings.

Solid core doors are usually mounted into a pocket for a mortise lock unless panic hardware is planned. Such doors may also be drilled through the center of the door from the center hinge to the mortise pocket for wiring an electrified mortise lock. If a door position switch magnet is required, this will typically be drilled in the field.

Solid core doors are robust doors that can withstand heavy use. Depending on door height, they may be equipped with three to five hinge mounting points. Solid core doors may also be furnished with a fine wood laminate to achieve a desired aesthetic effect.

Solid core doors are usually mounted into either a hollow metal frame or formed aluminum frame, together forming a fire-rated assembly. Fire ratings of 60 and 90 minutes are commonly available with hollow metal frames, and 60 minute ratings are common with formed aluminum frames.

Typical electrified locks for solid core doors include electrified mortise locks, magnetic locks, and electrified panic hardware. Magnetic locks may be either surface mounted or concealed, and electrified panic hardware can be applied with either surface or concealed vertical rods. Electrified panic hardware may be of any type (with mortise lock, rim type, or with vertical rods).

Hollow metal doors are also easy to use with automatic door operators. Standard five or seven knuckle hinges are the most common hinging methods for solid core doors, although pivots are not uncommon. More hinges are better than fewer for any security door application.

Glass Storefront Doors

Glass storefront doors are common public entry doors for Class B and C commercial buildings. These doors are obvious by their aluminum frame, with a tempered glass panel. Although they do not have the aesthetic appeal of Herculite doors, storefront doors do provide light for lobbies and a more open feeling to public areas as one enters the building. It is common to see storefront doors on medical, commercial, government, office, storefront commercial spaces, and other types of buildings in which glass doors make a pleasant point of entry.

Storefront doors are reasonably robust and can stand high daily use. They are not, obviously, security doors because one can make entry by breaking the glass. Storefront doors are typically hinged with pivots rather than hinges, although hinges, including full-height hinges, are not unusual.

Typically, storefront doors are equipped with panic hardware—a pair of handles or a handle and a push bar. Common electric locks include electrified panic hardware (vertical rods are most common) and magnetic locks. A very rare version of the storefront door is actually assembled from two glass panels with an aluminum panel in the center wherein is mounted a mortise lock.

Storefront doors can be easily automated, and this is often found in grocery stores and other commercial applications. Storefront doors are almost always equipped with a mechanical dead bolt at the strike or bottom of the door.

Herculite Doors

Herculite doors are solid glass doors that are immediately recognizable by the fact that they have no metallic frame on their vertical sides. They are commonly used in Class A commercial spaces as the main lobby entrance. It is not uncommon to find Herculite doors with a steel band on the top or bottom (or both) to facilitate the mounting of security locking hardware, although this is not always so. Herculite doors are almost always equipped with a mechanical dead bolt at the bottom of the door.

Herculite doors are usually electrically locked using concealed or surface-mounted magnetic locks. When surface-mounted magnetic locks are used, this is an indication of a lack of awareness or interest on the part of the door hardware or security system designer because concealed or full-width surface locks are much more in keeping with the high aesthetics of Herculite doors.

Two other electric locking options are the use of standard electrified panic hardware with surface-mounted vertical rods and the far more elegant Blumcraft™ locks (see Electrified Specialty Locks).

Herculite doors are not well suited for automatic operators due to the point stresses on the doors, although this is sometimes done. The doors are made to be leveraged from the door handle, not the top of the door, where the constant torquing can weaken the door, and they have been known to break as a result of this. I assure you that there is little more impressive than to witness a 12-ft high Herculite door disintegrate into 10,000 bits of glass pebbles from such abuse.

Herculite doors are also unique in that there is always approximately a $1/4$-in. (1 cm) clearance between the doors. This allows for easy insertion of numerous types of objects that could trigger an infrared request-to-exit (REX) detector that might be mounted above the door on the inside. This will often cause the door to open from the outside without a card credential. Also, the opening will be recorded as a legal exit since the REX detector initiated the opening. There are three ways to prevent this:

- Move the REX detector away from the door approximately 5 ft. This is not recommended because it can cause the door not to open if people gather at the door to say goodbye, allowing enough time for the original exit sense to time out. People have panicked in such circumstances, in some cases yanking on the door's handle repeatedly until the door shattered.
- Utilize mechanical egress hardware such as electrified panic hardware or Blumcraft hardware. Blumcraft hardware has its own vulnerabilities, including use of a coat hanger to pull the exit handle.
- Use a pair of exit detectors, including a secondary motion detector sensing approach to the door and the REX detector above the door. By setting the sensitivity on a microwave motion detector such that it will only trigger when under the

presence of a human (child or adult) and not with the mere presence of a newspaper stuffed through the slot, this kind of vulnerability can be mitigated.

Specialty Doors

There are a number of doors made for unique applications.

Revolving Doors

Revolving doors are a familiar sight at airports and large department stores. They facilitate rapid movement of people in and out of the building while keeping cold winds out of the warm interior space. They can also be very useful in access control since only one person can typically use each quadrant at a time.

All manufacturers of revolving doors make card reader interlocks to facilitate the passage of only one authorized user at a time. Some interfaces are more elegant than others.

A good interlock should incorporate a pawl in the rotating mechanism that is released for one half rotation to allow passage of a person entering the door. It is important that the door's interlock is sophisticated enough to ensure that the user will not be locked into the side of the revolving door but can in fact always exit the other side.

Better interlocks are also configured to prevent the passage of more than one person and the simultaneous use of the opposite side of the door for ingress while egress is occurring under card authorization.

Revolving doors are normally access controlled both ways—that is, not just for entry or exit, but both will be under access control. The door may be operated on a schedule or may be on access control at all times.

Best practices indicate the use of a delayed egress door panel (also under access control) next to the revolving door to permit entry or exit by a handicapped user. The delayed egress function ensures that the door will not be used to bypass the revolving door, and the door's card reader will be programmed only to permit use by handicapped cardholders (Fig. 7-1).

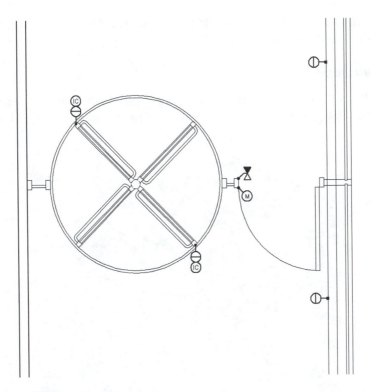

Figure 7-1 Revolving door.

Total Doors

Total Door™ is a registered trademark for a very unique type of door. Total Doors are shipped as an entire assembly, including the frame, electrified locks, and other hardware. Unique attributes of Total Doors include a full-height hinge, an integral panic hardware locking system, and a full-height locking latch assembly that operates like a full-height thumb and finger gripping the opposite door of a pair. The locking mechanism is quite secure and the doors are uniquely able to adapt to difficult frame environments, particularly where other doors might often need realignment.

Total Doors can be easily configured to operate as a biswinging pair of doors with no center stile (a very unusual configuration for any other type of door) and can be configured with automatic operators (Fig. 7-2).

Balanced Doors

Balanced doors are a relatively rare type of door that is mainly used at the main entry of a building to its lobby. These doors

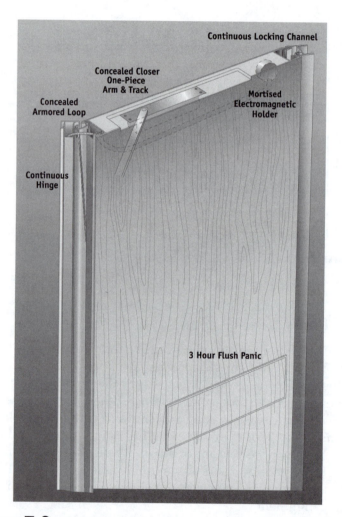

Figure 7-2 Total Door™ system. Image used with permission of Total Door.

require very little effort to open because they are balanced on articulating arms top and bottom rather than on normal hinges. Balanced door articulators are usually placed on very heavy door panels to make their operation a very light task, similar to much lighter doors on normal hinges. Balanced doors are often very ornate and make use of fine materials. Their objective is often not only an elegant function but also elegant style.

Balanced doors are very difficult to control with electrified locking hardware since they do not open and close like any other type of door. Surface-mounted magnetic locks have been used with success, whereas concealed magnetic locks have not due to the fact that balanced doors are not intended to close precisely. Due to the elegant style objective of balanced doors, full-width surface-mounted magnetic locks are a good choice.

Historical Doors

There are many types of historical doors that are both beautiful and can be very difficult to configure with access control or automatic operators. In general, historic doors have high aesthetic and historic value and should not be modified if at all possible. Historic doors are often equipped with unique and beautiful historic locks that have no comparison in modern locksets, making their use challenging.

One common type of historic door lock is the case lock. The case lock is like a mortise lock without the mortise pocket in the door. In lieu of the mortise pocket, the door is cut out where the lock sits, and the lock is fitted into the cutout and bound in place by a very tight friction fit between two oversized escutcheons that are tightened against each other, with the door and the lock fit tightly in between.

There is no modern electrified lock equivalent, and although case locks have been modified to be electrified at very great cost and with no attached warranty, there are other options. One is the use of a very unique electric strike that, instead of falling away like a normal strike, pushes the latch bolt out with a solenoid or cam. Although these strikes are difficult to find, they can easily be adapted to work with case locks.

The second most common type of historic lock is the rim lock (surface-mounted lock). Depending on the value of the door and the visual and historical aesthetics, a variety of auxiliary electrified locks can be fitted into the housing of the original rim lock.

I have encountered dozens of types of historic doors and locks, each more unique than the last. Historic doors and locks require a solid imagination and attention to detail in order to secure without destroying the value of the doors or the locks.

Security Doors

Security doors are a superset of hollow metal doors that are equipped with very robust door frames, door panels, and door hinges. Security doors are extremely robust and intended to withstand constant abuse. Security doors can be found in detention facilities, public housing facilities, and anywhere the architect or security designer wants to be assured of solid physical protection.

Security doors can be locked with mortise locks, magnetic locks, or electrified panic hardware. A good choice is to use electrified dead bolts and/or a four-point locking system to prevent frame spreading or opening the door with tools. This is a good choice for loading dock or rear perimeter doors where the burglar may have time to attack the defenses. Few burglars will continue to attack a door after realizing that it is not vulnerable to conventional methods and tactics.

Security doors should be used with high-security door frames. These combinations will typically carry 2-hour fire ratings or better.

Blast Doors

Blast doors are a type of security door that is designed to withstand severe atmospheric overpressures as well as severe attacks from physical tools. Blast doors have extremely robust door frames, panels, and hinges and are almost always configured such that the frame is interlocking with the door to prevent the intrusion of atmospheric overpressures. Blast doors are rated in atmospheres. Blast doors are commonly secured with very robust magnetic locks.

Soundproof Doors

Soundproof doors are used where noise isolation is essential, such as in recording studios, vivariums, and sometimes hospitals. Soundproof doors are typically thicker than conventional doors (2–6 in.) and are closely fitted to their door frames to ensure that no path of sound exists between the door and the frame. It is common to see plunge operators on soundproof doors, similar to those found inside walk-in freezers. Magnetic locks are a common choice to secure soundproof doors.

Door Hardware

Door hardware is the bits and pieces that hang the door in the frame and adapt it to its operating environment. Door hardware includes hinges, handles, closers, coordinators, automatic operators, locks, and the like. Very few security system designers know very much about door hardware. The best ones know a lot.

Hinges and Pivots

A hinge comprises a pair of small plates formed to fit to the door and the frame and to allow for a pin to pivot the plates and thus the door from closed to open. Hinges mount on the side of the door opposite the handle.

A pivot is a pair of assemblies that mount at the top and bottom of the door and allow the door to pivot along a vertical line created between the two devices. The bottom pivot supports the door's entire weight. It is made of two plates that swing apart like scissors around a single pinned hinge that lies just outside the door. One plate is mounted to the threshold, and the other is mounted to the bottom of the door. On the top of the door, this assembly is repeated, except that it only steadies the door in place and does not bear any weight. The bottom pivot may be configured with a door assist or door closer (sometimes a combination of the two) to make the door easier to open and close.

Full-height hinges look like piano hinges turned on their side and are formed of two full-height metallic panels with a hinge pin. Full hinges are largely immune to torquing of the door or settling of the frame. They are also less vulnerable to any attempt to remove the hinge pin. Full-height hinges are also useful for extremely high-traffic doors where normal hinges might show aging in a few years.

Handles, Levers, Push Bars, and Paddles

Handles, levers, push bars, and paddles facilitate the opening and closing of the door by pushing or pulling on the device. Handles can be used both inside and outside the door to push on or pull toward the user. Push bars are limited to the inside of the door.

Handles may be passive or attached to and designed to operate a mechanical lock. Levers are handles that turn to activate a mechanical lock. Push bars may also be passive or active, where the active bars are part of emergency egress (panic) hardware. Paddles are a small version of a panic bar, where a simple paddle is placed at the opening side of the door and, when pushed or pulled, it releases a latch bolt.

Door Closers

Door closers are pneumatic cylinders that facilitate the slow and steady closing of a door to a closed and latched condition. Door closers can be located in the threshold of the door or within the top header or on the outside of the top of the door and frame.

Door Coordinators

Door coordinators ensure that double doors close in a specific order so that the passive leaf of the pair is closed before the active leaf closes and latches into it. Door coordinators may take many forms. One common form consists of a lever that drops down slightly from the top of the frame to hold the active leaf open until the passive leaf closes, also causing the lever to lift, and thus allowing the active leaf to finish closing.

Automatic Door Operators

Automatic door operators are motorized assist units that operate articulating arms at the top of the door, facilitating the opening of the door(s). Automatic door operators must be carefully coordinated with the help of a door operator interface circuit so that the electrified locking hardware, access control system, and door operator perform a proper sequence of operations for the safety of the user and the door hardware (especially the automatic door operator):

- The card is read or the REX device initiates an open request.
- The access control system closes a dry contact linked to the door operator interface circuit.
- The door operator interface circuit sees the open request and releases the electrified door lock.
- After a proper delay (typically 250 msec) to ensure that the electrified door lock has finished its action, the door operator interface circuit will activate the automatic door operator, which then opens the door.
- When the door recloses, the door operator interface circuit senses that the door is closed and reactivates the electrified door lock, locking the door.

The sequence is ready to begin again. This sequence ensures that the automatic door operator is not attempting to operate against a locked door, which is very hard on the door hardware and can cause the automatic door operator and electrified door lock to fail prematurely. I designed one of the first commercially available door interface circuits still in use by a major automatic door operator company.

Door Ventilators

Door ventilators are louvered panels that are placed in the bottom of a door to facilitate cooling of the contents of the room (often used in telecommunications and electrical rooms). Door ventilators are potential security vulnerabilities if not secured with a reinforcing grille.

Door Frames

Many of the previously discussed door types can be fitted into a variety of the common frame types.

Hollow Metal

Hollow metal frames are among the strongest types of common frames. Hollow metal frames are formed of strong steel and have a subframe that enables them maintain their form over time and with the constant stresses of door openings.

Hollow metal frames are always equipped with hinge mounting plates and strike pockets. They can also be equipped with electrical boxes fitted for an electrical hinge, Hi-Tower lock, and concealed magnetic door position switch. The security systems designer should understand that modifying the frame to accept these types of electrified door security elements may in most cases void the door assembly's fire rating and should be avoided.

Hollow metal frames can be used with any type of door but are most commonly used with hollow metal doors and solid core doors.

Formed Aluminum Frame

Formed aluminum frames are commonly used to mount storefront doors and solid core doors. Formed aluminum frames comprise a lightweight aluminum panel formed to the specific shape of a door frame. Some manufacturers form the frame by a method of extrusion, not by bending a panel.

Formed aluminum frames can be used with hinges or pivots. These frames can be easily damaged with tools, often resulting in the removal of the door. Formed aluminum frames are inadvisable for use in high-security applications but may be used in simple access control environments. Formed aluminum frames may be fire rated with very low ratings.

Extruded Aluminum Frame

Extruded aluminum frames are typically formed as a closed box frame and are commonly used in storefront door mounting applications, next to a window wall. Extruded frames are stronger than formed aluminum frames but are not a significant delaying mechanism against a burglary attack using tools of force. Obviously, in storefront door applications, the glass door is the weakest link. Extruded aluminum frames are not often fire rated.

Wood Frame

Wood frames are sometimes used in commercial security applications, but their use is inadvisable. Unlike hollow metal frames, wood frames cannot stand up to continuous rugged use. It is not uncommon to have to reinforce wood frame hinges or replace the frames due to wear and tear. Wood frames cannot defend against any attack using tools of force, and they do not easily adapt to electrified hardware since the installation of such hardware often corrupts the structural integrity of the door frame. Wood frames are not often fire rated.

Frameless Glass Opening

Herculite doors are generally mounted into a frameless glass opening using top and bottom pivots.

High-Security Frames

A variation on hollow metal frames, the high-security frame is structurally reinforced to withstand determined attacks with tools of force.

Blast Frames

Blast frames are highly reinforced frames intended for use with blast doors.

Soundproof Frames

Soundproof frames can be made from either hollow metal or wood (usually wood) and are designed with gaskets to hold the door in the frame in a manner that does not allow sound to travel between the door and the frame.

Pedestrian Gates

Pedestrian gates are openings in fences or buildings that are not intended to defend against weather.

Chain-Link Gate

The most common type of pedestrian gate is in the form of a bent-tube frame covered with chain-link fabric. Common locks include magnetic locks, electrified panic hardware, and electrified mortise locks. Special care must be taken to ensure a free path of egress from the protected area and that an intruder cannot improperly release the electrified lock from the outside. This is often accomplished by creating a physical barrier other than the fence fabric, such as a woven steel mesh, through which the outsider cannot reach the unlocking mechanism. Chain-link gates are simple and adequate for low-security applications.

Estate-Type Gate

Estate-type gates are made of wrought-iron frames and fabric and have a higher aesthetic appeal than chain-link gates. Locking mechanisms and precautions are the same as for chain-link gates. Their use is also indicated for low-security environments.

Reinforced Frame Gate

Reinforced frame gates are made of heavy-gauge tempered steel frames and a reinforced steel fabric. Their use is appropriate for high-security and high physical abuse environments, including public housing and public transportation systems. Common lock types include high-security magnetic locks, high-security electrified mortise locks, and robust electrified panic hardware.

Occupancy Ratings

Architectural occupancy ratings determine the kind of doors that must be used, the widths of corridors, the types of door frames, and appropriate door hardware. This is a complete study unto itself, and the implications are serious if mistakes are made.

Complicating this, each community adopts its own standards, making for a maddening array of requirements even within a close geographical area. A qualified architect or fire code official should always be consulted for questions of occupancy; however, there are certain rules that seem universal:

- Fire exit doors should always swing outward so as not to allow the buildup of people trying to flee a building during a fire. Although it is common to see inward-swinging doors in commercial spaces in certain countries, regardless of what local codes permit, I do not recommend swinging exit doors inward except for residential property applications.
- Fire exit doors should always be equipped with door hardware allowing for free mechanical egress. It is unwise to rely on electronic systems to facilitate egress from a building during an emergency, and this practice violates code in most jurisdictions.
- For delayed egress doors, a fire alarm override should be configured that immediately opens the door in the event of a fire alarm in the building.

ELECTRIFIED LOCKS

Common Electrified Locks

Electrified Mortise Locks

Arguably the most common type of electrified security lock is the electrified mortise lock. Manufactured by a large number of companies, this lock is the mainstay of basic electrified security programs throughout the world. A mortise lock is a lock that is placed into a pocket (mortise) in the door, giving it additional strength compared to other types of locks. The electrified mortise lock is a standard mortise lock with a solenoid-activated pawl within the lock that places a barrier to turning the lock from the outside. Typically, the inside handle is always free to turn, making egress possible at any time with no special knowledge. The solenoid is tripped to unlock the lock, allowing the outer handle to turn (Fig. 7-3).

Figure 7-3   Electrified mortise lock. Image used with permission of Security Door Controls.

Magnetic Locks

The second most common type of electrified lock is the electromagnetic lock, commonly called a magnetic lock. Basically formed by mounting an electromagnet to the door frame and an armature mounted to the door, the magnetic lock is available in two basic versions, plate locks and shear locks. The plate lock is the simplest and most reliable, placing the locking elements on the outside of the door such that the armature approaches the magnetic in a face-to-face fashion (Fig. 7-4).

A variation on the magnetic lock designed for high-aesthetic environments is the magnetic shear lock. This places the magnetic in the top of the door frame facing down, and the armature is mortised into the top of the door. The magnet draws the armature up to lock the door, and when released, the armature falls back into the top of the door, allowing the door to open. Magnetic shear locks should be used with caution

Figure 7-4 Electromagnetic lock. Image used with permission of Security Door Controls.

because they have been known to experience mechanical failure, usually related to door misalignment. The result nonetheless is often that the door cannot be opened when the lock fails. It is inadvisable to use magnetic shear locks in any path of fire egress and especially on single doors in the path of egress where the failure of the lock could result in the inability of people to exit in a fire. I try to avoid the use of magnetic shear locks unless the door in question is not a fire exit door, absolutely nothing else will work, and the door is not the only exit from the area (Fig. 7-5).

Magnetic locks are often equipped with contact sense circuits that can detect when the armature is in contact with the

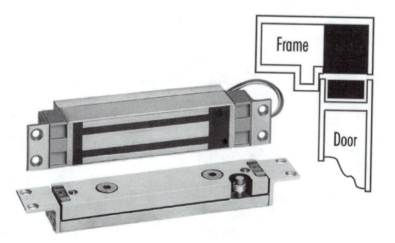

Figure 7-5 Magnetic shear lock. Image used with permission of Security Door Controls.

lock and that the lock is energized. This is an effective door position switch when used in a configuration in which it can be ensured that the door will always be locked when it is closed. If the door may be closed but not locked, some of these circuits will not indicate a door closure, possibly causing a hold-open alarm since most alarm/access control panels assume that the lock and door position switches are two separate devices and function separately.

Although magnetic locks are very reliable, caution should be taken in their application to ensure that a secondary method of releasing the door is always available, usually in the form of a push button marked "Push to Exit" in language acceptable to the local fire authority. We also typically design them for use with one of several types of exiting devices.

REX Infrared Sensor

Positioned above the door, this sensor detects the presence of a person near the door handle. The REX detector is normally wired to the exit sense input of the access control panel, which releases the lock, bypasses the door alarm, and logs the event (Fig. 7-6).

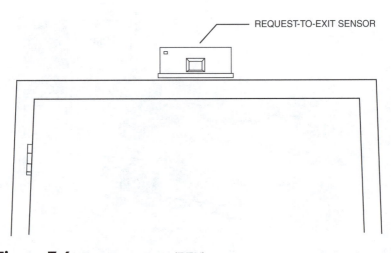

Figure 7-6 Request-to-exit (REX) sensor.

Push to Exit Button

An exit button is commonly placed near the exit door in a manner acceptable to the local fire authority. The push to exit button should be wired such that two circuits are activated. The first circuit would trigger the exit sense input on the alarm/access control panel, while the second would create a hardware interrupt directly to the power of the magnetic lock, thus ensuring that the lock will be unlocked regardless of the condition of any electronics (Fig. 7-7).

Panic Bar

A panic bar can also be used as an exit switch even if it does not mechanically release the door. The use of a panic bar is a familiar visual indicator of emergency exit. Panic bar switches are usually also equipped with not only an adjacent push to exit push button but also a button under the panic bar to bypass the switch in the panic bar in the event of the failure of the panic bar switch. Some panic bar switches are mechanical and some

Figure 7-7 Exit push button. Image used with permission of Convergint, Inc.

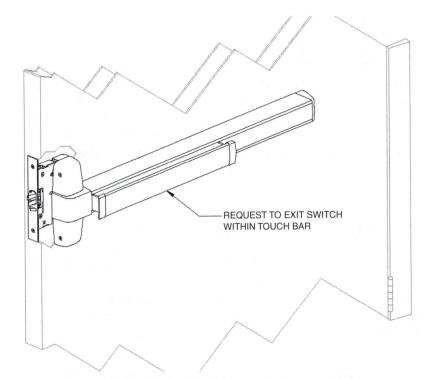

REQUEST TO EXIT SWITCH
WITHIN TOUCH BAR

Figure 7-8 Panic bar exit switch.

sense contact with skin. The type that senses contact with skin is not appropriate where people requiring exit may be wearing gloves, use an object they may be carrying to open the door, etc. I prefer the mechanical switch type for this reason (Fig. 7-8).

Delayed Egress Hardware

Delayed egress hardware combines a magnetic lock with a panic bar exit sensor and adds a countdown timer, audio annunciator, visual countdown indicator, and alarm signal. These configurations solve a very common conflict between fire egress needs and security needs. This problem had not been solved for many years until the development of this ingenious hardware. These locks are commonly used in schools and in back-of-house[1] areas where the law requires a fire exit door but where the organization does not want to encourage the use of that door for anything other than an emergency. The door locking system requires marking in accordance with acceptable rules of the local fire authority and functions as follows:

- The person requiring exit approaches the door and pushes on the panic bar.
- An alarm sounds and a countdown timer commences, typically 10 to 15 seconds, adjustable. Typically, a numeric indicator on the magnetic lock shows the time remaining. The alarm is continuous during the countdown.
- On some systems, an audible countdown announcement accompanies the numeric indicator on the magnetic lock.
- On many systems, it is required to continue to push on the panic bar during the countdown period.

Each fire authority has special rules affecting how delayed egress hardware is implemented. Often, a variance to code is required for their use (Fig. 7-9).

Fire Authority Approval

Be certain to know, understand, and comply with all local fire authority regulations for the state, county, and city where the installation is being considered. Each municipality may have

Figure 7-9 Delayed egress lock. Image used with permission of Security Door Controls.

different and sometimes perplexing rules, especially as concerns elevator lobbies and the use of magnetic locks. We have, for example, seen fire authorities require delayed egress hardware on a single leaf door adjacent to a revolving door that was not in the path of egress where by normal logic it should not have been required.

Fire Alarm Interface

In all cases, it is recommended to interface magnetic locks or any other type of lock that does not provide free mechanical egress to the fire alarm system such that those locks unlock automatically in the event of activation of a smoke detector, fire pull station, or sprinkler activation on the floor of the lock and the floors above and below the floor of the lock. We encourage a test key for the interface. In many communities, it is advisable simply to dump power to all magnetic locks in the building upon any fire alarm condition (Fig. 7-10).

This presents an interesting challenge: How do we secure the building when anyone can simply pull a fire alarm and unlock a protected office suite? This question indicates why careful consideration of the types of locks is appropriate, and why it is important to explain these considerations to the client so that he or she can make an informed decision.

Man-Trap Door Assemblies

A man-trap is a sequence of two doors under interlocking access control, separated by a small vestibule. (Man-trap is a term you do not want to use with fire code officials, by the way; call it a vestibule.) The purpose of a mantrap is to ensure that only authorized people are entering a restricted access space. Be advised that man–traps are not legal in some jurisdictions.

Typically, the man-trap includes a normal card or keypad reader on the outside door and a biometric credential reader on the inner door. This sequence of dual credentialing and dual doors helps ensure that no one can force their way into a space or simply tailgate behind a valid user as the normal entry door closes behind him or her.

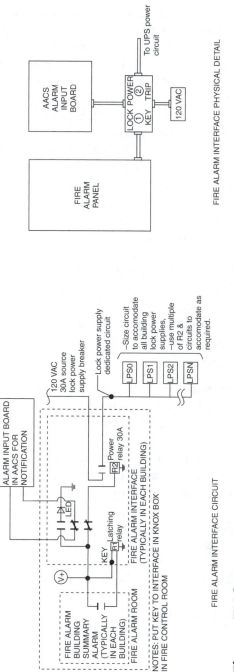

Figure 7-10 Fire alarm lock interface.

Man-traps have an interlocking circuit so that both doors cannot open at the same time, ensuring security through a sequential entry or exit through the two doors.

Man-traps normally involve hollow metal doors, and the security designer must take life safety into consideration. Normally, an interlock circuit ensures that both doors cannot open at the same time, and there should always be a fire alarm override to ensure egress in the event of a life safety condition. This may be acceptable in many communities, although a variance is almost always required for a man-trap interlocking vestibule. Where the normal method is not acceptable, the designer may suggest using delayed egress hardware on the doors, which is only activated if someone attempts to open one door while the other is open. Again, a fire alarm interlock is always appropriate.

Man-trap assemblies are available commercially or can be custom fabricated with interlocking relays. The manufactured variety offer some liability protection for the designer, architect, and building owner compared to the custom fabricated type, although they are often more expensive to acquire.

Electrified Strikes

Electrified strikes used to be the mainstay of electrified locks. They are in fact not a lock at all but, rather, a means of releasing a door latch remotely. Electrified strikes replace the conventional door strike into which a typical door latch closes.

Unlike a conventional door strike, which requires that the door latch be retracted in order for it to open, the electric strike unlocks the door by simply folding back to release the door latch as the user pulls the door open. It springs back instantly as the door latch clears the strike so that it is ready to receive the latch as the door closes again.

There are various types of electric strikes, but they all operate the same. They are classified into two broad categories, high security and low security, depending on the strength of the latch release pawl inside the strike.

Strikes also come in both fail-safe and fail-secure types. In the fail-safe type, power is required to energize the strike, thus locking the door. In the fail-secure type, power is required to release the strike, thus the door is always locked from the outside. In all cases, the door can be released from the inside with no special knowledge.

Electrified Panic Hardware

Electrified panic hardware is an ideal hardware to use anywhere that normal panic hardware would be used (i.e., in the path of egress). Electrified panic hardware simply combines a mechanical panic bar that will always allow exit in any circumstances, with no special knowledge, with some form of electrified lock. Several common electrified lock types are used with electrified panic hardware.

Electrified Rim Lock

The electrified rim type lock combines a electrified retracting deadlocking latch bolt with a rim-mounted strike plate. This configuration is very reliable and is commonly used in back-of-house areas where aesthetics are not so important (Fig. 7-11).

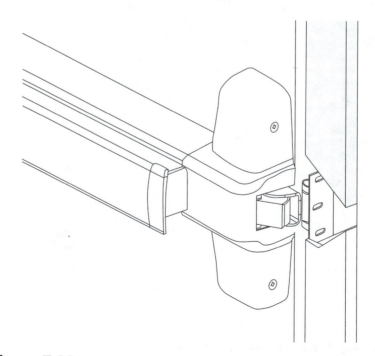

Figure 7-11 Rim panic hardware.

Electrified Mortise Lock

Mechanical panic hardware is combined with an electrified mortise lock to create a very secure, panic exit friendly and aesthetic locking system. The system includes a panic bar on the inside of the door and a normal mortise door handle on the outside of the door. Pushing on the panic bar causes a cam to rotate the mortise handle release as though a handle were used inside (Fig. 7-12).

Solenoid-Released Vertical Rods

For high-traffic doors, especially in double-door pairs, and where reliable locking is required, it is common to use vertical rods to lock the doors at the top and bottom rather than at the strike. Several manufacturers make both concealed and exposed vertical rod electrified panic hardware that can reliably

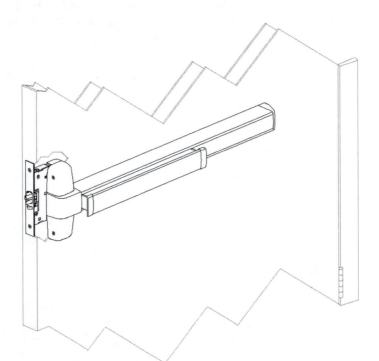

Figure 7-12 Mortise panic hardware.

fit this need. Vertical rods latch into top and bottom strike plates upon returning from an open condition. Pushing on the panic bar retracts the vertical rods, allowing the door to open freely. When electrified, a solenoid releases a pawl that allows the outer door handle to rotate on some models. On others, a high-energy solenoid retracts the vertical rods completely without any outside assistance. This application is especially useful when coupled with automatic door hardware to open the door for handicapped or for the convenience of the public. For higher aesthetic installations, the vertical rods can be concealed within the door, making a very pleasing visual presentation (Fig. 7-13).

Magnetic Lock

Although some designers use a signal switch inside mechanical panic hardware to release a magnetic lock on the door, I do not recommend the use of this approach. Any electric failure of the circuitry could result in a failure of a fire exit door to open. If this combination is used, it should be wired such that the panic bar signal switch directly interrupts the power to the magnetic lock as well as a separate circuit to trigger the request to exit on the alarm/access control panel. These configurations are problematic because many alarm/access control systems do not react quickly enough to the request to exit to avoid an alarm when the door opens before the system has sent a door unlock signal. This sequence can take up to 500 msec on many systems. By then, the person is entering the open doorway, so an alarm always occurs with each opening. This does not make for happy clients.

Specialty Door Hardware

Specialty door hardware includes both locks that fit unusual needs and other hardware to perform special functions.

Monitor Strikes

A monitor strike is a switch located inside the strike pocket of a latching door lock, such as a mortise lock. The purpose of the monitor strike is to indicate with certainty not only that the door

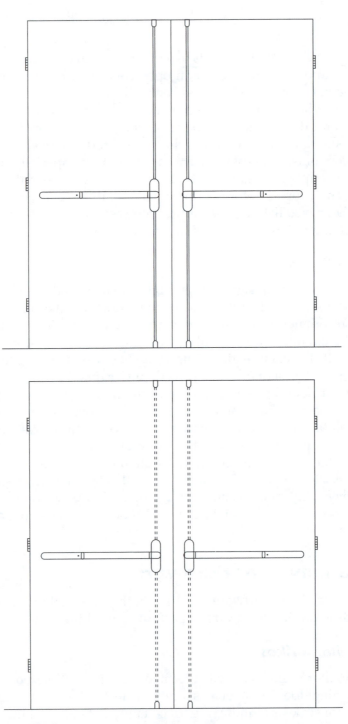

Figure 7-13 Vertical rod panic hardware.

is closed but also that the latch bolt is secure in the strike pocket. Monitor strikes can also be used in the pocket of a dead bolt to positively ensure that the dead bolt is thrown and locked.

Blumcraft Hardware

Blumcraft locks are specifically made for Herculite doors. Herculite doors are frameless solid glass doors. They may be equipped with a top rail, a bottom rail, or both, but they are obvious by their lack of side frames, having only exposed $1/2$-, $5/8$-, or $3/4$-in. glass. Herculite doors are used in main lobbies and other areas where the owner wants to make an impression of style and elegance. These doors are notoriously difficult to lock or automate, and the normal locking mechanisms appear quite industrial looking against this highly elegant door. The Blumcraft lock uses a beautifully crafted articulating push bar that latches at the top of the door into a strike pocket, much like a normal latch bolt (only at the top of the door instead of at the side). Normal exiting is accomplished by pushing on the articulating push bar, which withdraws the latch and allows the door to open. For remote release or release by a card reader or REX device, the articulating arm latch bolt is coupled with an electric strike at the top of the door to release the latch and remotely open the door. The result is a stylish and beautiful door that can be remotely operated or operated by an access control system (Fig. 7-14).

Hi-Tower Locks

HiTower locks were developed to accommodate the needs of securing fire stairwell doors in compliance with local, state, and national codes and doing so in a fashion that will not violate the fire rating of the stairwell door assembly.

I was once called to assist a building manager of a 31-story high-rise office building in San Francisco; he had given the job of electrifying the stairwell doors to the lowest bidder, whose number was significantly lower than the next lowest bidder. The unfortunate security contractor was not familiar with fire code and had commenced to cut electric strikes into the door frames of 8 of the 35 floors of the building when the fire inspector

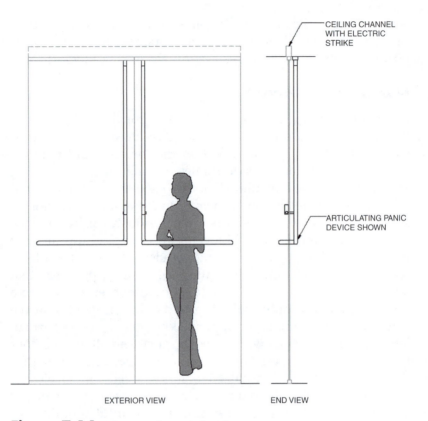

CEILING CHANNEL
WITH ELECTRIC
STRIKE

ARTICULATING PANIC
DEVICE SHOWN

EXTERIOR VIEW   END VIEW

Figure 7-14 Blumcraft panic hardware.

happened to be in the building and noticed this. The fire inspector sought out the building manager, advising him that this practice destroyed the fire integrity of the fire stairwell 2-hour door assemblies and violated the law, rendering the building's certificate of occupancy void on the spot.

HiTower locks get around this problem by placing the lock in the door frame within a rated electrical enclosure that replaces the existing strike pocket, and this lock activates a mechanical release within a specially modified mortise lock that exactly replaces the original mortise lock. The lock is fire rated, and virtually every fire authority accepts it. A variance is typically required.

High-Security Locks

A few manufacturers make very high-security locks that can be electrified.

High-Abuse Tolerant Locks

Securatech makes a lock that was created for the New York public housing market where door hardware abuse was prevalent. The lock has several unusual characteristics. It is an electrified mortise lock that is equipped with an extremely robust mechanism and two unique features: It has a break-away clutch handle that simply turns freely when struck sharply, and it can be equipped with an electrified dead bolt. These locks can be expected to last the life of the building (Fig. 7-15).

Electrified Dead Bolts

There are several locks on the market that supply electrified dead bolts. These are typically electrified mortise locks, although there are a few cases of simple electrified dead bolts. Typically, the dead bolt is triggered separately from the latch bolt on its own circuit. The lock is typically configured with an internal pawl that releases to allow the person exiting to turn the handle. When the inside handle is turned, it releases both the latch bolt and the dead bolt. The lock relatches automatically when the door closes, but the dead bolt must be re-engaged each time the door closes. This requires either a manual activation of the dead bolt or an electric activation of it, which can be configured by a monitor strike switch to lock the dead bolt after the door is closed and latched (Fig. 7-16).

One manufacturer makes an electrified dead bolt that relocks automatically with each door closure, having its own built-in monitor strike. In the past, a prevalent type of electrified dead bolt was a configuration that was mounted at the top of the door. These locks were available in either concealed or surface-mount types. This lock involved a dead bolt that was propelled down from the frame into a receiving pocket. Both the dead bolt and the receiving pocket were equipped with repelling magnets. When power was released, the dead bolt was propelled

Figure 7-15 High-abuse electrified lock. Image used with permission of Securitech Group.

back up by magnetic repulsion. There have been some reports of problems with shifting of the door frame over time, causing a binding of this type of dead bolt. This type of dead bolt has fallen out of favor due to this fact and is no longer permitted on occupied spaces in some municipalities, where its use is limited to storerooms.

Four-Point Locks

Four-point locks are very secure compared to typical locks. Four-point locks are secured at the hinge side, at the latch side, and top and bottom. This application is useful on doors that are likely to be attacked with tools such as a frame spreader. At least

Figure 7-16 Electrified dead bolt. Image used with permission of Securitech Group.

one manufacturer makes these locks in an electrified version (Fig. 7-17).

Locks to Avoid

Electrified Cylinder Locks

Cylinder locks are very weak and cannot withstand even modest breaching attempts. These locks were electrified in order

Figure 7-17 Four-point electrified lock. Image used with permission of Securitech Group.

to facilitate remote access through a door under light duty in extremely low-threat areas, such as at a doctor's office. Electrified cylinder locks will not stand up to continuous duty or a solid kick.

Lightweight Strikes

A few electric strikes are strong enough to be considered security devices, but most should not be relied on for high-security environments. Unfortunately, most electric strikes are not rated for their strength, making it difficult to determine whether or not one should rely on them to resist a forced attack. Any strike that does not list its physical strength should be assumed to be incapable of resisting a forced attack.

One of the favorable attributes of electric strikes is that they do not draw power except when they unlock. This makes them suitable for environments in which power availability is a concern.

CONCERNS ABOUT SPECIAL KNOWLEDGE

Wherever possible, I prefer to design locking systems that require no special knowledge to operate and that have free mechanical egress (not relying on electronics to unlock the door to exit). This is consistent with the basic principles of free egress outlined in the National Fire Protection Association (NFPA) Section 101, which has been adopted by most states and municipalities throughout the United States. Similar codes and regulations apply in virtually every country. It is inadvisable, and usually illegal, to design locking systems that require special knowledge or the ability to read signage in order to exit a fire egress space. We advance that it is inadvisable almost anywhere.[2]

SUMMARY

There is no security without physical security. Effective access control design requires a comprehensive knowledge of physical security. Understanding door types is basic to designing access control. Door types include hollow metal, solid core, glass storefront, and Herculite doors and also specialized doors, including Total Doors, balanced doors, and historical doors. Other specialty doors include revolving doors, security doors, blast doors, and soundproof doors.

Door hardware is the bits and pieces that hang the door in the frame and adapt it to its operating environment. These include hinges and pivots, handles, levers, push bars and paddles, door closers and door coordinators, and automatic door operators. Door frame types include hollow metal, formed aluminum, extruded aluminum, wood, and frameless glass openings. Specialty frames include high-security frames and blast and soundproof frames.

Pedestrian gates are openings in fences and buildings that are not intended to defend against the weather. Pedestrian gates include chain-link gates, estate-type gates, and reinforced frame gates.

Occupancy ratings determine what kind of doors must be used, the widths of corridors, the types of door frames, and appropriate door hardware.

Common electrified locks include electrified mortise locks, magnetic locks, strikes, and electrified panic hardware. Push to exit buttons or panic bar switches should be used with all magnetic locks, in addition to any other automatic unlocking exit method. All electrified locks should use an interface to the building's fire alarm system to ensure that locks are unlocked automatically in the event of a fire in the building, thus ensuring free egress. Delayed egress hardware provides for securing an exit door against improper use while ensuring that it is available for exit during an emergency. For all electrified locks, fire authority approval is required. Local codes vary, so the designer should know the local interpretation of national and state codes and any local codes. Electrified panic hardware ensures that high-volume exit doors can function in an emergency while providing access control. Specialty door hardware includes monitor strikes, Blumcraft hardware, and HiTower locks. Other specialty locks include high-security locks, such as high-abuse locks, electrified dead bolts, and four-point electrified locks. Locks to avoid include electrified cylinder locks and lightweight strikes. NFPA Section 101 is the primary reference for life safety regulations and should be known by all security system designers. It is a good rule of thumb to design electrified locks for use with no special knowledge and free mechanical egress.

CHAPTER NOTES

1. Back-of-house/front-of-house are architectural terms that indicate whether the area is part of the public space or behind the public space. The term back-of-house derives from the hospitality industry, where it indicated the area used by servers and maintenance personnel. More generally, back-of-house indicates any unfinished area (e.g., fire stairwells and back corridors), and front-of-house indicates finished areas.
2. NFPA Section 101 is the basic life safety code in use in the United States. A copy is available from many booksellers and should be in the possession of any security designer. I encourage a thorough knowledge of this code as a basic element of any design skill set.

8

The Security Design Process

ESTABLISH ELECTRONIC SECURITY PROGRAM OBJECTIVES

Electronic security in general is a subset of the overall security countermeasures that should be implemented for any organization. In my opinion, electronics should be the last element to be implemented. Yes, you heard me right, the last. That statement is coming from a person who has made a nearly lifelong career out of designing electronic security systems. There is a hierarchy to security countermeasures, and it should start with policies and procedures, then physical and network security, security awareness training, operational security programs, and, finally, electronic security. It does no good to have cameras and card readers if the building is not locked at night. Ridiculous, you say? You can point to any 10 high-rise or corporate buildings that are more than 20 years old, and I assure you that on average more than 90% of those buildings have no record of who held the master keys to the building going back 10 years, let alone the life of the building. A master key gives the holder access to virtually every asset in the building. Master keys leave no trace of who used them, and many building electronic security systems are not monitored 24 hours a day and do not have useful cameras on every door. Even with cameras, the master key holder can conceal his or her identity from them. Electronics is the high priest of false security. So first, as a designer, do no harm. Advise the owner to secure the building with strong physical security. Next, how many organizations run effective background checks of their employees, contractors, and vendors (and their contractors' employees)? Second principle: Do not let criminals into the building. Please—advise the owner. So the foundation is to establish and prioritize overall security objectives.

DEFINE COUNTERMEASURES

There are three categories of countermeasures:

- High tech: electronic security systems, information technology security, telephone system security, etc.
- Low tech: locks, barriers, landscaping, lighting, signage, etc.
- No tech: policies and procedures, security programs, security awareness training, guard programs, bomb and drug dogs, etc.

ESTABLISH SECURITY POLICIES RELATED TO ELECTRONIC SYSTEMS

Every security countermeasure should help fulfill a specific security policy. I am suspicious of any countermeasure whose purpose cannot be found in established security policy. This indicates that either the countermeasure was not well thought out or the security policies were not. In either case, additional consideration is indicated.

ESTABLISH THE BUDGET

The security budget has three dimensions: countermeasure determination, prioritization, and phasing.

Countermeasures Determination

Appropriate countermeasure selection is a process that involves the following steps, which are from the American Petroleum Institute/National Petrochemical and Refiners Association (API/NPRA) methodology. This methodology is one of the most complete and straightforward to use, and it allows for a financial and risk calculation that is most thorough as well as allowing for stakeholder input into the process[1]:

- Define the assets to be protected and characterize the facility where they are located. Facility characterization includes a compete description of the environment, including the physical environment, security environment, and operational environment. Determine the criticality of each major asset and the consequences of the loss of the asset. Consequences can be measured in loss of life or injury, loss of monetary value, environmental damage, and loss of business or business continuity.
- Perform a threat analysis. Define both the potential threat actors and the threat vectors (methods and tactics that the threat actors may use to gain entry or stage an attack). Threat actors may include terrorists, activists, and criminals. Criminals may be either economic criminals or violent criminals, such as those who cause workplace violence. Rank the threat actors' motivation, history, and capabilities. Rank the threats by their ability to harm the assets using the previous criteria.
- Review the basic vulnerabilities of all the protected assets to the types of attacks common to the declared threat actors.
- Evaluate the existing and natural countermeasures that are already in place or in the existing design of the building or its site. For example, does a storm levy make vehicle entry more difficult? Is existing lighting a deterrent? The difference is the remaining vulnerabilities to protect.

- Determine the likelihood of attack:

  - Determine the probable value of each of the assets to the probable threat actors (asset target value calculation).
  - Likelihood = threat ranking × asset attractiveness × remaining vulnerabilities.

- Calculate the risk of attack: Risk = consequences × likelihood.
- Determine additional countermeasures needed to fill the remaining gap in vulnerabilities prioritized by the risk calculation previously (Fig. 8-1).

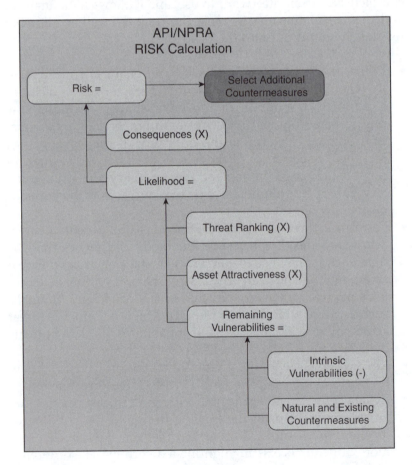

Figure 8-1   API/NPRA risk calculation.

- Determine from what resources the additional countermeasures can be sourced.

Prioritization

Priority should be given to protecting life first, then the environment and business continuity, and, finally, financial stability. Using this method, a clear picture can be presented to the client as to what actions should be taken, in what order, at what cost, and with what return on investment.

The designer can categorize each countermeasure by its ability to address life saving, mission preservation, and/or financial preservation (i.e., consequence reduction).

Countermeasures can also be categorized by high-tech, low-tech, and no-tech, which can affect from which budget the cost will be paid and under whose management the implementation and operation will occur.

Lastly, countermeasures can be categorized as either preventative or mitigating in nature. Preventative countermeasures either have a deterrent effect or can impede the ability of a threat actor in the act of an attack. Mitigating measures limit the resulting damage or consequences of the attack that does occur.

Finally, the cost of each countermeasure can be calculated.

Countermeasure Effectiveness

It is also useful to summarize the total categories for each countermeasure in spreadsheet fashion. For example, Which countermeasures affect the most threat vectors? Which are both preventative and mitigating? Which have the most benefit to life saving and consequence reduction?

Phasing

Many security projects must be phased for implementation. Using the prioritization method described previously and particularly if a summarization of countermeasure effectiveness has been calculated, a case can be made and easily understood as to which countermeasures should be programmed in which order. These can be phased as budget becomes available over a period of time as is appropriate to the organization's budget program.

PHASES OF THE DESIGN AND CONSTRUCTION PROJECT

The following phases apply whether the project is being designed by a consultant for bid by contractors or directly by a designer employed by a contractor resulting from a negotiated bid with the owner, without the use of a consultant. Regardless, the steps will be the same, although they may more fluid and less formal if there is no consultant involved.

The Predesign Phase

The predesign phase includes a risk assessment and coordination with the architect to get physical security elements included into the architectural program. This work requires close coordination between the security department, the project manager, and the architect.

Schematic Phase

The schematic phase is that portion of the project in which the designer writes on paper the purpose of the project and the means by which he or she will fulfill that purpose. This will result in a basis for design document that describes in written terms what measures should be taken to meet the needs of the project and what it is likely to cost in rough numbers. The schematic phase may also include one or more simple drawings that illustrate the design concepts.

Design Development Phase

Following approval of the concepts and budget expressed in the schematic phase, the designer will be released to develop the design to a point at which the owner can see on plans where devices will be placed to achieve the design. This visualization often results in slight adjustments before the design is finalized. It may be necessary to add cameras or sensors or to re-route the infrastructure in a way that is more accessible or that fulfills some other project requirement. The owner also often makes other project adjustments that will affect the security system design slightly, including such things as the configuration or location of a lobby security desk or security monitoring center.

Contract Documents Phase

Once the design has been visualized and accepted through the design development phase, the designer will be released to complete the design. This will involve selecting the exact equipment that best fits the needs of each location (e.g., camera configurations and mounting) and routing the conduit, calculating the size of conduit and boxes, specifying products and installation practices, and the like. The resulting design will be complete enough for bid estimators to prepare a bid and for contractors to build from. There is usually some adjustment to the finished design necessary to meet the needs of the specific brand and model of equipment that the contractor intends to use, but the concepts of the contract documents package will be made sufficiently clear to get the job done. The contract document package will include both drawings and specifications.

Bidding/Negotiation Phase

Very often, if the designer is a consultant, he may be asked to participate in the review of bids based on his design. He will likely receive requests for clarification or information by bidding contractors and will review bids by contractors. He will be asked to provide the owner with a recommendation.

This is a very important phase. The success of the project and thus the designer's long-term business reputation depends on the quality of the contractor selected and how well that contractor executes the intent of the owner and the consultant.

There are several guides to whether or not a specific contractor is a good choice for the project. These may include the following factors:

- Is the contractor licensed as a security contractor in the geography to be served? Beware: Sometimes specific security contracting licenses are required in certain geographic regions. Sometimes a license may be required for each of several sites where work will be done. The consultant should know this ahead of time. (Again, know your codes.)
- Is the contractor financially able to complete the project? Is the contractor large enough to complete the work or is this project too large for him? Is there any pending litigation that could place his firm (and thus this project completion) in jeopardy? How is the contractor's credit? Is he able to get products delivered on credit or must he ask for a large advance? Can he float the final retainer until he completes the project through the residual work punch list?
- What is the contractor's reputation for work quality? The reference checks will verify this.
- What is the contractor's reputation for project management? Have past clients expressed concern over poor work flow or schedule compliance? Was the contractor able to complete past projects on time, or did the projects drag on for months with little "pick-up" items that never seemed to get finished?
- Is the contractor able to complete the engineering requirements for the work? Does he have one or more engineers on staff or some arrangement with a stringer engineer who works when there is work to do? This is often a deciding factor.

It is my experience that contractors who place little emphasis on engineering often cannot finish the project on time and to the client's satisfaction. Additionally, I have observed a direct correlation between engineering skills and installation skills. If there is a slipshod attitude toward engineering, it seems to follow that there is also less concern toward a consistent application of high-quality installation practices. This makes sense because every installation decision is really an engineering decision—where and how to hang a camera, what type of relays or software to use to coordinate system communications, etc.

These decisions will either be made by a single qualified engineer who has the whole big picture of the project in his mind, or they will be made by a bunch of guys in the field with screwdrivers in their hands. Trust me, you cannot buy a more expensive engineer than a guy with a screwdriver.

The result of the screwdriver approach is that the field technician arrives at the work site and begins work on the fourth floor, which is his designated work area. He then discovers that he needs a certain part. He must stop work, go get the part, stand in line, pay for it, return, find a parking spot, get his tools, and return to install the part. Hours are lost each time this happens. Also, while he is making these decisions, his counterpart on the seventh floor is undergoing the same process, duplicating the lost time and, unfortunately, he has decided on a different approach with different parts for his solution. So now the system has different solutions for the same problem on different floors—lots of lost time, delays, and late projects incorrectly built to multiple design standards compared to when a single coordinated approach is used.

- What do the contractor's past clients think about his performance during the warranty period and after? Is he considered responsive or lethargic? Is he proactive or does he only come when there is a problem? Does he have parts in stock or does he always have to order them, with an attendant delay in completing the repairs?

The following are the key elements in the bid review:

Reply to Request for Information Form

This form has a place to recap the question and for each answer. The answer should refer to the drawings and/or specifications by page, article, and paragraph or should point to an addendum if the answer cannot be found in the published construction documents.

Reference Checking Form

There should be one reference check form for each bidder.

Bid Analysis Form

The bid analysis form provides room for an overall review of the contractor's qualifications:

- Financial qualifications
- Engineering skills
- Project management skills
- Installation practices
- Warranty experience
- Conformance to specification requirements
- Conformance to bid standards
- Price
- Ranking with and without price as a factor

A Note on Bid Analysis

The bid documents generally provide significant latitude for bidders to adapt specific systems they represent to the project concepts illustrated in the drawings and specifications. Remember, the drawings and specifications do not (or should not) illustrate preference to a particular brand and model of security system equipment but should instead illustrate the intended system architecture and imply their functions. As such, different bidders may forward varying interpretations of the project concept in their bid, and this may result in varying manufacturers, models, and even quantities of equipment from one bidder to the next to fulfill the intent of the contract drawings and specifications.

The bid review is not the time to determine absolute compliance to the specifications since these normal variations in the bidding bill of quantities are to be expected, and the implications of the variations cannot be known until the shop and field drawings are submitted, where the intent of the use of each proposed component is illustrated in place in the system design.

That will occur both during the shop and field drawings and during final acceptance. A good specification also requires compliance corrections throughout the warranty period if the system is found not to fulfill a specified function during the warranty period.

No one should assume that minor variations in product models and quantities during the bid should be considered abnormal.

Construction Review Phase

After the project is awarded to the contractor, the designer will review the contractor's work if he is a consultant, or he will be responsible to customize the design if he works for the contractor.

Usually, a shop and field drawing set will be ordered that identifies the exact count and type of each product for each assembly on the project. The drawings will include a comprehensive set of plans; single-line (block) diagrams; schematics; and assembly, wiring, and system interfacing details. The consultant will review these and specify changes where the design is out of conformance with the construction drawings and specifications. The contractor's designer will make the required changes and resubmit. The shop and field drawing submittal will also include a complete bill of quantities and copies of data sheets of proposed equipment.

Then the construction begins. The designer may or may not be assigned as the project manager. The project must be built on the project schedule, and each milestone must be met. As the project nears completion, the system must be tested and commissioned. Testing involves checking to determine that each part of the system operates and communicates to the reporting console(s). Commissioning involves customizing the system operation to meet the specific needs of the project. This involves setting operating system and software configurations, setting time zones and schedules, setting access level permissions and zones, etc. Chapter 19 is dedicated to project commissioning and finalization.

SUMMARY

The security design process begins with the establishment of electronic security program objectives. Establish security policies related to electronic systems, and establish budgets. Budgets have three dimensions—countermeasure determination, prioritization, and phasing. Countermeasures determination includes defining the assets of the facility, performing a threat analysis, reviewing the basic vulnerabilities of all of the protected assets to the types of attacks under consideration, evaluating the existing and natural countermeasures, determining the likelihood of an attack, calculating the risk (risk = consequences × likelihood), and determining what additional countermeasures may be required to fill the gap in vulnerabilities.

Prioritization should be given to protecting life first, then the environment and business continuity, and, finally, financial stability. All countermeasures should be phased if there is inadequate budget for total implementation.

Phases of the design project include the predesign phase, the schematic phase, the design development phase, and the construction documents phase. These are followed by the bidding phase and the construction review phase.

CHAPTER NOTE

1. Although I am conversant and skilled in many methodologies, the API/NPRA methodology is often preferred because its results are complete, easy for any client to grasp, and it can be universally applied to any environment, not just the petrochemical environment. Software tools exist to assist in this calculation, although a tool can be easily created using any database or spreadsheet program.

9

Preliminary Design Process Steps

BASIS FOR DESIGN

The Basis for Design is a document that sketches out in simple terms the objectives and proposed methods and budget for the security system. Typically, the Basis for Design will include a goals statement that outlines the objectives of the electronic security program and how it will interact with the security force to support its operational mission.

The system should be described as a whole system and each of its subsystem components. For example, the enterprise security system, the enterprise security system monitoring center, and a typical site, where each site is described for its subsystems (i.e., alarm/access control system, digital video system, security intercom system, etc.) and system interfaces to other related systems.

Finally, the budget for the system will be outlined in an attachment so that the cost can be separated from the operational aspects for internal organizational discussion.

RESEARCH

Next, the designer will begin researching what products to use for the installation. Research is not specification. That is, research is information gathering about what requirements need to be met. Research may include a variety of areas: for example,

- What access card and access control system technology is appropriate to specify? Is a standard already in use? Is it satisfactory? What about a photo ID system? What requirements are appropriate for its use?
- What digital video and network architecture needs to be specified?
- What existing systems need to be integrated, including existing intercoms, access control systems, video systems, elevators, parking systems, building automation, alarms, and other monitoring locations?
- What are the architectural considerations? Is a lobby desk being designed? What equipment needs to go in it? What are the ergonomic issues?

There are endless possibilities for research. It is important to begin making a list of questions to answer, clearing the list with the client, and getting answers to the questions. This will often involve interviews with key stakeholders within the client's organization. A separate schedule is appropriate for those meetings to facilitate coordination. Sometimes, outside stakeholders are involved, including community leaders and public agencies.

DEVELOPING DRAWING AND SPECIFICATION RESOURCES

Surveys

Once the objectives of the system are defined and agreed on by the client, it will be necessary to survey the property to determine what types of devices to specify and how to coordinate their interface to the environment, the buildings, other systems, and users.

Camera Placements and Fields of View

The security policies and the Basis for Design will define the objectives for the video system. From that, camera placements will derive. The designer should walk the property and buildings to look for conditions that comply with the video requirements for the security policies and Basis for Design and, upon finding them, note the proper locations for the cameras on drawings. It is also important to note what policy the camera serves so if a question arises or budget issues evolve, the position of the camera can be defended or prioritized downward to a later phase.

Each camera placement should be defined in notation as to its type, resolution, color/monochrome, enclosure, lens type, auto/manual iris, infrared supplemental illumination, mounting and aesthetic requirements, and whether it is to be a fixed camera or equipped with a pan/tilt/zoom feature.

Access Control and Alarm Placements

Similarly, locations of proposed access control points should be determined based on compliance to stated security policy and in conformance with the Basis for Design.

Vehicular Access Control

Access provisions should be considered for visitor and employee/contractor/vendor vehicles and special cases, including close-in parking access for handicapped people and pregnant women. Although traffic flow is a separate discipline and can easily require its own book to describe, access control measures for each class of vehicle should be considered. This will include both card and intercom access control and appropriate barrier types. Additionally, traffic flow may dictate that lanes change direction by time of day (bidirectional lanes). All this will dictate appropriate parking control hardware, signage, directional instruction signage (red/green lights or text), and placement of equipment and signage.

Public Access to the Buildings

The building should be surveyed for access control and alarm points for both appropriate public entrances and back-of-house entrances and exits, including the loading dock and any other similar portals.

Public entrances may be configured for after-hours access and/or to lock automatically after hours. Signage may be necessary to direct the public to an appropriate entrance, and the use of intercoms may be indicated to help visitors find the correct entry.

Access beyond the Public Lobby

After September 11, 2001, it became commonplace to screen the public at the main lobby of the building rather than to allow the public to roam freely on upper floors without proper vetting at the front lobby. This may require the use of a visitor badging system and possibly electronic turnstiles to control public movement beyond the main lobby. Electronic turnstiles should be coordinated with the placement of the lobby desk to ensure that the lobby desk security officer has a good view of the electronic turnstiles in case anyone needs assistance or attempts to circumvent them. It is common for visitors new to the building not to realize that a visitor badge is required to enter the elevator lobby (Fig. 9-1).

Access within Semipublic Spaces

Semipublic spaces include the elevator lobby, if it is beyond the electronic turnstiles, and certainly upper floor public corridors.

Figure 9-1 Optical turnstiles with paddle barriers. Image used with permission of Smarter Security Systems.

Semipublic access can often be controlled by either floor-by-floor elevator control or control of elevator lobby doors. Both methods have their advantages and limitations.

Floor-by-floor elevator control helps ensure that users have access credentials to enter the floor in question from a given elevator. However, this is by no means guaranteed since anyone can get off on any floor when the elevator doors open.

A somewhat more secure means is access control of the doors on the elevator lobby. In nearly every case, this will require a code variance unless there is a fire stairwell within the elevator lobby. This method is still not entirely certain to prevent unauthorized people from entering the floor since they can accompany an authorized user through the door.

Access to High-Security Areas

For buildings with high-value assets to protect, including proprietary information assets, it is often advisable to utilize access control readers, sometimes coupled with a secondary access control credential such as biometric readers or keypads used on doors along semipublic hallways. These are often used on server rooms, research and development labs, and executive office suites. Some organizations make heavy use of access control doors along semipublic corridors to help ensure that unauthorized people do not enter private office areas.

Emergency Egress

At all times and in all areas, fire egress safety must be observed. All fire exit doors must be configured for free mechanical egress, and some of those doors are also appropriate for access control measures. These fall into two broad classes—a fire stairwell is used as an example:

- Access control from the stairwell side is required to prevent entry from one floor to another.
- The stairwell is off-limits except in an emergency to prevent private conversations, such as in a research and development area.

In the first case, it is common to place an access control reader within the stairwell, using a HiTower lock on the stairwell door with a variance from the fire authority. It is common for the authority to require every fifth floor to be unlocked, although most authorities will accept an intercom to a 24-hour staffed desk with a door release and a fire alarm override as a substitute for this requirement. Local authorities have differing opinions on this, and their preferences must be observed.

In the second case, a variance is required. Security policy and architectural design go hand-in-hand, each one affecting the other. Sometimes it is necessary to reconfigure a space architecturally in order to meet both the security and the egress requirements.

Positive Access Control

Positive access control is a principle of access control in which the desired goal is to ensure that every person must check in and out through an access control portal to enter or leave a space. This can be accomplished by man-traps (not popular with fire authorities), revolving doors, and electronic turnstiles equipped with mechanical paddles. In each case, the user must both check in and check out of the area through an access control portal and cannot "tailgate" through with another user, as can be done through an elevator, a door, or an electronic turnstile not equipped with mechanical paddles.

Environment

Physical

The designer should survey and note the physical environment. Will certain devices require weather resistance? Is lightning a problem in this region? Is power reliable or has it been known to brown-out, create overvoltage conditions, or spike? Are driving wind, rain, salt air, extreme heat, or other harsh conditions a factor? How about space limitations for the server, for the console, or for lobby desk? For each device, it is important to note the ceiling and wall surfaces and determine if any additional ceiling access panels may be required.

Operational

Are there any unique or significant operational conditions found in the survey? What are the hours of operation? Is the security staff employee staff or are they contract guards? What is their training level? These kinds of factors can affect decisions on software and training requirements in the specifications.

Security

Security environmental factors should have already been outlined in the risk analysis. Where the client does not wish for a risk analysis to be performed, or where one is not available to the designer, it is important to get a clear understanding in broad terms as to what assets are being protected, against what threats, and what is the history of security events. A review of crime statistics is usually indicated.

Door Survey

For every door that will receive security hardware and for every perimeter door to the building or to a defined secure area, a survey spreadsheet should include notations as to the door type, frame type, fire rating, and security rating.

For each alarmed or access controlled door, the survey form should include information regarding the type of access control and alarm hardware to be mounted on the door and information about its location, whether or not there will be an intercom associated with the door, and other relevant factors.

Codes and Regulations

It is obviously imperative for the designer to observe all applicable codes and regulations. These may include NFPA Section 101 (life safety), MARSEC, and ISPS codes for water-based facilities, and Class 1, Division 1 and Class 1, Division 2 requirements for environments with flammable or explosive environments. There may also be numerous other codes and regulations. It is advisable to get to know the local building code enforcement agencies and fire authorities.

Safety

Safety of the systems is paramount. NFPA Section 101 is the basic guideline for safety on access control systems. The designer should know it intimately.

Power Locations

The survey should also note where power is required and from where it can be sourced and whether or not additional power is required over that already available.

Gathering Resources

After the survey, it will be obvious that some additional information may be needed. This may include determination as to whether or not any variances are required and the need for interdiscipline coordination between related construction trades.

A list of coordination items should be prepared, along with the names of people with whom coordination should occur and a schedule for completion of coordination.

COORDINATING INTERFACES TO OTHER SYSTEMS

I recommend preparing a folder for each related trade and placing the coordination materials in each folder for preparation and, finally, presentation at an appropriate meeting. When coordination is presented to other trades, it should include relevant drawings or sketches and a descriptive narrative of the interface and proposed language for inclusion in the specifications of all related trades. If the proposed specification text is presented in third-person language, it can be used verbatim in both affected trades, ensuring that both are working to the same exact language. Along with a requirement in both specifications for acceptance of the interface as a condition for acceptance of either trade, this process motivates contractors who might otherwise view the interface as a last-minute annoyance to view it instead as a path to a final paycheck. This process changes the dynamic of the interface from one of "If it doesn't work, talk to that guy" to one of "Let's work together to make this work for the client." The following interfaces are normal to encounter.

Building Shell and Core and Interiors Architects

This will commonly involve ceiling access panels, aesthetic issues, coordination of lines of sight for video cameras, fire code questions, door finishes, and other aesthetic and code issues. The architects will also have their own preference on when and how to issue addenda and bulletins,[1] when and how to "cloud" drawing changes,[2] etc.

Specifications Consultant

The specifications consultant will determine what specification format will be required for the project. Typically, this will be the Construction Specifications Institute format, although others may apply. Another common format in Europe and the Middle East is the FIDIC format.

Door Hardware Consultant/Contractor

The door hardware consultant or contractor will provide information on what door types, frame types, fire rating, and door hardware will be used. The security designer will provide access control requirements to the door hardware consultant or contractor. This may include a sequence of operation for vestibule doors and other security operational requirements. Additionally, aesthetic and electrical considerations will be discussed.

My practice is that the door locks, electric hinges, and door position switches are furnished and installed by the door hardware contractor, and the card readers, request-to-exit devices, and wiring are provided by the security contractor.[3] The door hardware contractor will hand over the door hardware to the security contractor, and the whole assembly is warranted by the security contractor.

Electrical Consultant/Contractor

Since electronic security systems work on electricity, it follows that it is a good idea to coordinate their electrical requirements. I am an advocate of low-voltage systems design. I use as few high-voltage connections as possible, so virtually every device is powered by low voltage, and the power supplies for that are centralized in just a few locations. Nonetheless, certain devices beg for a high-voltage connection. These may include parapet-mounted or pole-mounted pan/tilt/zoom video cameras, parking gates, and doors with certain types of electrified panic hardware.

The electrical load for these should be calculated along with any uninterruptible power supplies, battery chargers, etc. When this information is provided to the electrical consultant or contractor, the security designer should request a list of electrical panel and breaker assignments for each circuit so identified.

HVAC/Building Automation Consultant/Contractor

There are a variety of possible coordination factors for the HVAC/building automation consultant or contractor, including (1) coordination of fire stairwell pressurization with the fire alarm system and access control system and (2) lighting systems that are coordinated to light the way into the user's office suite from the parking structure. Interfacing the irrigation system to the perimeter intrusion detection system is also an effective deterrent for intruders on the property. The list of interfaces with building automation systems can be nearly endless.

Landscape Architect/Contractor

The landscape architect and contractor can assist in the coordination of perimeter intrusion detection systems, irrigation systems, vehicle barriers, underground conduit, and the like.

Parking Consultant/Contractor

The security designer will coordinate parking controls, parking access control system pedestals, underground conduit, and overhead vehicle access control tag readers.

Elevator/Escalator Consultant/Contractors

Coordination with the elevator consultant or contractor involves a variety of factors, including coordination for access control, video, and voice communications.

There are two types of access control systems for elevators, hall call button control and floor-by-floor access control. Placing a card reader at the hall call buttons in the elevator lobby effectively secures the elevator by prohibiting its use except for people holding an access credential. This method is useful in areas where an elevator is designated for specific individuals only or where it is desirable to limit the use of the elevator during certain hours, such as at night. Also, hall call card readers are generally much less expensive to implement due to the fact that only one contact is required (to enable the hall call buttons, such as to their ground circuit), whereas floor-by-floor control requires a more elaborate interface.

There are a variety of floor-by-floor elevator control systems. The basic objective of floor-by-floor access control is to use a card reader within designated elevator cars to permit credentialed access to only the floors for which that credential is authorized. This involves several elements:

- A card reader in the elevator car.
- Some kind of control interface to the elevator control system that enables and disables the elevator occupant's ability to select certain floor buttons.
- Optionally, the elevator control system may also record which of several floor buttons the occupant has selected among those several buttons for which he or she may be authorized to select.

In the simplest kind of access control interface, the access control reader is located on the surface of the elevator's swing return panel (the panel on which the elevator floor select switches are located). Care should be taken to ensure that handicapped users can reach both the card reader and the floor select buttons. The card reader may also be mounted behind the swing return or side panel. This is a more aesthetic installation, concealing the card reader. In such installations, it is desirable to provide a visual indicator to knowledgeable users as to where to present their access card (where the access card reader is located). This is often achieved by placing an icon of the building or organization in that location or sometimes simply a dot or location marked by a pattern or color change from the background surface. If the concealed card reader is to be located behind the elevator's swing return, then a glass or Plexiglas™ panel should be installed in the surface of the swing return in order to provide a radio frequency (RF)-friendly path between the card reader and the credential. It is common to mark this panel with the building or organization's logo as an indicator of where to present the credential.

The other end of the elevator connection is the circuitry or interface that provides the actual floor-by-floor control. There are three common methods for this. By far the most common today is a software interface between the alarm/access control system and the elevator controller. This can be accommodated in a variety of ways, most typically with a RS-232 or Ethernet interface between the two systems. Commonly, the interface may occur between the elevator controller and the alarm/access control system elevator control system panel, but the connection may also be between the elevator controller and the alarm/access control system host computer or host server. Some systems can accommodate Ethernet interfaces. The software interface may be a database exchange, such as SQL, the passing of an ASCII string from the alarm/access control panel/server to the elevator controller, or an XML or API interface. Usually, choices exist, and the dialog between the security system designer and the elevator consultant/contractor will establish the options and preferences.

Another interface that works with older elevator controllers establishes a dry contact connection between the elevator controller and the alarm/access control system controller. This will typically require one dry contact for each floor for each elevator controlled, plus usually an extra contact to place the system in free or access control mode. The additional contact can be eliminated on some systems if the floor control contacts are used for both purposes; that is, free access is enabled simply by energizing all contacts to all floors. This interface facilitates placing the elevator on free access during daytime business hours and on access control mode after hours, weekends, and holidays. For both of these cases, the relays are typically placed in or near the elevator control room, which can be in the penthouse upstairs or in the basement depending on whether the elevator is a traction type (controls upstairs) or a hydraulic type (controls downstairs). A recommended practice is to place the alarm/access control electronics in a room near but not in the elevator control room and an interface terminal cabinet inside the elevator control room. This ensures that maintenance on the alarm/access control panel can be accommodated without necessitating an untrained person to enter the dangerous elevator control room, where an errant tie or pants cuff can be lethal.

A very old method of interface that is rarely used today is to use dry contacts directly in the circuit of the floor select buttons on the elevator car. This requires that a alarm/access control system controller or relay board must be on the elevator car, not in or near the elevator control room.

Communication between the elevator devices and the alarm/access control system is typically over the elevator traveling cable. This may be either a ribbon or a bundled cable, depending on the elevator's manufacturer and model. Another method is to use a wireless transmitter or laser in the elevator hoistway. This may be a good solution if no extra traveling cables exist. There are a few manufacturers that make appropriate wireless devices. A data format converter may be required.

One common problem with elevator access control systems is that elevator power is notoriously dirty, with lots of voltage fluctuations, spikes, and inductive surges. A separate uninterruptible power supply for the elevator access control electronics (both on the car and in or near the elevator control room) is often a good idea in order to ensure a reliable system. Alternatively, very good AC surge suppression and DC power filtering is appropriate.

Elevator Video Cameras

Increasingly, it is common to place a video camera within the elevator. This presents both aesthetic and technical issues. Aesthetically, there are three common approaches to elevator video cameras: corner-mount cameras, mini-dome cameras, and concealed cameras. Whereas corner-mount and mini-dome camera mounting is straightforward, concealed cameras can be a challenge. There are no hard and fast rules for concealing cameras. The environment and elevator car design dictate the installation. Keep in mind that camera location is typically dictated by a desire to view the face of the person entering the car, and it is also helpful to view what floor button has been pressed or, if available, a display of what floor the user departs. This can often be done by ensuring that the camera can view the floor label when the door opens. Typical concealed camera mounting locations include the rear ceiling corner, the rear wall near the ceiling, and the swing return, which can view the face of the person pressing a floor button, although this will not ensure a good view of the person if he or she asks someone near the buttons to press the desired floor.

Connection to the camera may be by coax, twisted pair using the traveling cable or by RF or laser. If the camera is digital or uses a codec, 802.11 is a very good choice. Again, clean power is very important.

Elevator intercoms are dictated by law in virtually every municipality. However, the elevator intercom can be either a direct ring-down phone or an intercom, and either can be interfaced to the main security intercom, especially a digital intercom.

A direct ring-down phone is a telephone that is connected directly to a central office telephone line (this may be shared with other elevator phones in the building) and rings a dedicated telephone number when the receiver is lifted or a call/help button is pressed. Depending on the specifications, it may be possible to have the phone provide either a digital or a voice announcement of its location by building and car number upon initiating the call and before connecting the calling party to the answering party. There are two ways to interface these phones. One method is to have it ring directly into a dedicated phone in the security command center. Another is to convert the ring-down signal into a digital call (VoIP) that rings into the digital intercom.

An intercom approach usually requires the use of an approved intercom system. The elevator manufacturer will have already received Underwriters Laboratories approval on an intercom for its elevators. It is costly and time-consuming to get approval for another system, and they will not welcome this option. The security system designer will have to determine how to adapt the approved elevator intercom to one being designed for the security control room. Here is a tip: Make the interface from the elevator intercom master station, not to the car. Typically, the elevator intercom master station has some provision for remote monitoring (the local elevator installer will probably not be aware of this; you may have to talk to the factory to get this information). That is often the best place to effect the interface.

Another option is to leave the approved system in the car and add a second system that is actuated in parallel to the main system. This allows for the security office to use a single system throughout the facility and leave the officially approved elevator intercom master station in the corner of the security command center, unused but available. This is the least desirable option.

All these decisions must be made in consultation with the client, the elevator consultant/contractor, and, sometimes, a code official.

Elevator Alarms

We do not normally think of alarms in elevators, but in certain circumstances it is advisable to do so, such as for public housing or in areas where damage has occurred.

Any elevator alarm may result in one or both of the following actions:

- Open a hands-free talk channel between the elevator and the guard
- Allow the guard to return the elevator to the lobby, where the offender can be apprehended

In an elevator that was suffering vandalism by knife to a fabric rear wall, I designed a thin foam insert with foil on the front and rear, connected to the inputs of an alarm board. This was placed just behind the replacement fabric. When a knife slit the elevator wall fabric, it also made a contact on the foil of the foam fabric backing, recording the video for posterity, causing an alarm at the lobby desk, and sending the perpetrator to the lobby for arrest.

Remote Elevator Control

Remote elevator control is recommended for any elevator over which close control is required, such as in an apartment building, corporate penthouse, or freight elevator. An elevator control panel should be provided for a lobby desk security guard for such cases, along with floor-by-floor control for tenants and authorized users. This allows the guard to direct the visitor to a specific elevator and then select the correct floor for the visitor, sending him or her to the selected floor without any control by the visitor.

Telecommunications Consultant/Contractor

Telephones may be located at the security command center, lobby console, guard station, security manager's office, and parking security office, and hands-free stations may be located at parking entries and remote doors, etc. The security force may use its own internal telephone system in lieu of an intercom system, or it may use a system that is a subset of the larger facility telephone system.

The security system designer should make a spreadsheet identifying what type of telephone receiver is required at each location; the number of outside lines available; the number of station sets; and whether or not they are to be handset, headphone equipped, hands-free, etc. Some may have direct access to outside lines, and in some locations a direct central office line may be required in case of power failure affecting the private automatic branch exchange (PABX). Certain phones may have direct inward dialing, whereas others may go through the PABX or automated attendant. It is best not to leave these details to the telecommunications consultant or contractor, even in consultation with the client, because they may not be sensitive to or aware of any special operational needs of the security force that may affect the design of the telephone system.

Additionally, on enterprise security systems, the telephone system may be integrated with the two-way radios, intercoms, cell phones, etc. using specialized software with which the telephone vendor or consultant may not be familiar. Such software is generally not off-the-shelf but may require the assistance of a specialized communications integration consultant to develop it or to customize an off-the-shelf package. Customizable, off-the-shelf packages have been offered by Motorola, Plantronics, and others.

Information Technology Consultant/Contractor/Information Technology Department Director/Manager

Increasingly, security systems are themselves information technology (IT) systems, making a high-level of knowledge of IT systems a fundamental requirement for a security designer. In any event, the IT department and the organization's IT consultant and vendor will be very interested in the issues that the security designer is addressing.

Is the security system using any part of the organization's existing or planned IT infrastructure? How are those interfaces defined? What data are being exchanged or what data paths, switches, routers, or servers are being shared? Will the security system server be housed within the organization's existing or planned server room? Who will maintain the servers, mass storage, the operating systems, the connections to other systems, and the security system software? Does the organization have any specific standards as to brand/models of servers, workstations, switches, routers, etc.? Does the organization have standards about system scalability, and how is that addressed in the selection of switches, servers, mass storage, etc.?

Be assured that the organization's IT department or vendor will have something to say about some or all of these issues. Be advised that it may be difficult to arrange for a meeting early on in the project. IT departments and especially vendors are well-known for having disruptive last-minute input on such subjects. Best practices indicate an early discussion of these items. If none can be arranged, it is highly recommended to publish a memo to the client's project manager requesting the meeting and, failing that occurrence, to publish a memo outlining the direction of the IT-related decisions so that it can be circulated, reviewed, and approved. The memo should include a date by which review must occur and language stating that cost increases and schedule changes could result if review occurs later. If a last-minute meeting then occurs, the designer should come prepared with the request for the meeting and the memo outlining the decisions requesting review. When the IT department or vendor inserts their last-minute dictates, the security system designer will not be placed "on the spot" to make the changes on an impossible schedule, and the client will understand any extra costs related to the changes.

LAYOUT DEVICES IN RESPONSE TO ELECTRONIC SECURITY SYSTEM OBJECTIVES AND BUDGET

As stated previously, every electronic security device location should be defendable by a reference to a published security policy. I recommend that the spreadsheet defining device locations and attributes should also have a column referring to specific security policies. If budget cuts are imposed, it will be easier to cut equipment based on the priority of the policy it serves. Budget cuts should be placed on those countermeasures that address the lowest risks first.

Access Control System Placements

Card readers should be placed in a manner that easily facilitates travel through the door or portal—that is, typically on the side of the door with the handle and near the door handle. Where the door serves many users with carts, and where such doors are operated by automatic operators such as in a hospital or maintenance corridor, the card reader may be placed far enough back from the door to conveniently present the access credential while the user is behind the cart.

Push to exit buttons should be placed on the exit side of the door in a location that is intuitive to users for its purpose. Signage lettering should be of a contrasting color to its background and of a size dictated by local code or $3/4$ in. high if there is no relevant code.

Keypads should be placed similar to card readers and in a manner that, if possible, obscures the key code being entered.

Biometric readers should be placed similar to card readers and in a manner suitable for their environment. For example, voice recognition systems are not appropriate for high-noise environments, facial recognition systems require certain lighting conditions in order to work reliably, and fingerprint systems and hand geometry may work less well in high dust and dirt environments.

Alarm/access control controllers should be placed in a clean, dry environment (avoid janitor closets) and should be powered from a dedicated circuit, not from a plug pack into an electrical outlet. Such placements permit interruption of the power, whereas power within a conduit is more difficult to interrupt. Ideally, the alarm/access control electronics should be installed in a larger custom-fabricated "security terminal cabinet" that would also house the power supply, terminals, and other sensitive electronics. This method is always appropriate in outdoor environments.

For outdoor equipment, the selection should include sensitivity to weather and extremes of heat or cold. Where appropriate, include heaters and air-conditioning or ventilation in the design. Best practices indicate the use of an uninterruptible power supply in outdoor enclosures to help ensure power continuity.

Camera Placements

Cameras should always be placed where they will have an unobstructed field of view of the desired scene and where they will not be subject to vandalism or environmental damage.

The security system designer should carefully consider what level of detail is desired in the view and what additional surrounding activity is desirable to view or record. Sometimes, this creates a conflict that dictates the use of more than one camera for a particular view. For example, if a proprietor wants to see the details of the face of a person entering a building but also wants to see the type of car that the person parked in front of the building, this may require two separate cameras.

It is common for security system designers to exhibit a preference for either pan/tilt/zoom or fixed cameras. However, each has its distinct advantages and limitations. Pan/tilt/zoom cameras can provide precise close-up views or wide-angle views in virtually any direction, whereas a fixed camera has a set field of view at all times. However, pan/tilt/zoom cameras cannot view areas opposite where they are pointed, so activity can occur outside the field of view that could be important but unavailable later. Pan/tilt/zoom cameras are more expensive than fixed cameras and often require additional high-voltage power, complicating and adding cost to their installation. Sometimes, it is better to apply several fixed cameras in lieu of a single pan/tilt/zoom camera, and sometimes it is better to have the pan/tilt/zoom camera due to its flexibility of view.

There is also a camera that has unique attributes of both pan/tilt/zoom and fixed cameras. It is a single-megapixel camera equipped with a fish-eye lens that is pointed into a specially formed mirror that, when coupled with appropriate software, results in an infinite number of possible views, even from the recorded image. This can provide the security manager or director with the ability to pan, tilt, and zoom in history, which pan/tilt/zoom cameras cannot do. The trade-off, however, is that megapixel cameras consume much digital storage space, making storage of their images somewhat costly.

Another application of megapixel cameras is on towers on large sites, coupled with a very long zoom lens and a pan/tilt mount. Because of the stunning resolution of megapixel cameras, a single camera can often be used to view a large area from a single very high tower with a commanding view of the entire site that would normally require up to seven lower resolution cameras from several towers. This approach can result in considerable cost savings in towers, cameras, power connections, and RF transmitting equipment, making the additional cost of storage quite attractive.

Intercom Field Station Placements

Field intercom stations should be placed where they are accessible to the user and where the user can clearly hear the console security officer and vice versa. Factors for consideration include the height of the intercom station. For example, handicapped-accessible stations should be mounted at 30 in. above grade or above the finished floor, whereas intercoms intended for use by drivers in vehicles should be mounted at a height that accommodates the intended vehicles and their occupants. That could mean that two intercoms are needed if the range includes sports cars and four-wheel-drive SUVs. Certain environments absolutely dictate two intercoms, such as entries accommodating both cars and semi-tractor/trailers.

There are two types of intercom systems, half-duplex and full-duplex. Half-duplex intercoms allow the console guard to control the conversation by pressing a push-to-talk switch, whereas full-duplex intercoms allow for free communications from both sides continuously. A variation on the half-duplex model is a Vox (voice-activated) function, in which the half-duplex control is yielded to whoever is talking, typically with preference to the calling party (the person at the field intercom station). Outdoor intercoms should almost always be configured for half-duplex, push-to-talk operation, where the console operator controls the conversation. This will prevent a high noise level at the field intercom station from locking the conversation in the Vox circuit of the intercom system, which will try to keep the field intercom channel open in response to the background noise.

Note that in areas where people have a right to expect privacy, it is unwise for the designer to configure the system for open-microphone operations. The designer should know that there is legal precedent for this.

SELECT REQUIRED DEVICES

Define Functional Needs

Following the selection of device locations, attention should be paid to functional needs and environmental needs. For each device in the security system, a list of desirable and undesirable functions can be defined. It is often useful to spreadsheet these issues, particularly where a novice designer is involved, in order to have more intuitive insight into the process of selection not only of the appropriate devices but also of their configuration. For every selection, both intended and unintended functions result. It is highly useful to have insight into the unintended (and sometimes undesirable) functions as well as those that are intended.

Define Environmental Needs

For each device, it is also useful to spreadsheet the environmental requirements that the device should meet—outdoor, cold, heat, chemical, salt air, inconsistent power, etc. After using this exercise for a few to a dozen projects, the process may become intuitive, and the spreadsheet approach can be discontinued.

From the spreadsheet, a clear picture will emerge that may reduce the types and numbers of different devices for each application. Often, it is possible to find a single device that can meet the needs of several to many applications. The client will often appreciate that there are fewer types of equipment used, even if there is a slight cost delta to achieve this. The cost delta will be paid for many times over as the system ages and it requires only a few rather than many different types of components to replace parts.

Define Communications Means

Each system element communicates as part of the larger security system. Increasingly, security systems are being digitized, and a single communications infrastructure is emerging. Soon, virtually every component may communicate via TCP/IP. In the interim, various systems may have their own communications needs, which may include RS-485, RS-232, analog, POTS ("plain old telephone system"), proprietary cabling and protocol schemes, and dry contact.

It is important to remember that for many installations, the system wired infrastructure can represent up to 40% of the cost of the entire system. In outdoor systems, that percentage increases to nearly 80%. So it pays to shop around for alternatives to wired infrastructures, especially where several different wiring schemes and thus cabling types are required to accommodate the systems.

In typical systems, it is likely that there will be one scheme for the alarm/access control system, a second for the video system, a third for voice communications, etc. Thus, this would result in three separate sets of cables or fibers in the ground or in the conduit of the building. Reducing that to a single TCP/IP infrastructure can save tens of thousands of dollars.

ANALOG VS. DIGITAL VIDEO AND AUDIO SYSTEMS

For very large systems the choice is simple. Analog systems design for any multisite system is no longer the best choice for the client. For any single-site system, there are several key decision factors.

The Decision Tree

Scalability

Will the system ever likely need to connect with any other systems in any other buildings? If so, a digital system is quite possibly the better choice. Even if the connection will only be to another building on the same campus, a digital infrastructure makes a lot of sense.

Digital infrastructures for video and intercom facilitate connections across vast spaces, literally worldwide, almost as easily as within a single building. Unlike analog systems, a digital infrastructure can easily scale up to a larger system, often without additional infrastructure costs. Digital system infrastructure is typically in increments of a factor of 10 (100, 1000, and 10,000 Mbps). By observing the 45% capacity rule, systems can normally be expanded considerably without the need for additional infrastructure wiring.

When necessary, additional cascading switches can be added to accommodate additional cameras and intercoms. Best practices indicate that the system should be designed with considerable additional capacity within the primary switches, in terms of both port counts and throughput availability. The additional cost for such capacity is modest, and the additional capacity provides years of expansion capability.

Longevity

The entire security industry is moving toward digital video and intercom systems, some manufacturers more quickly than others. With each major step forward in technology, there is a phasing of introduction to certain kinds of users:

- Product introduction: The new product development is innovative and is tried by early adopters—people who are eager to try anything new in technology. These people are the test bed for the refining of new technology. Often during this stage, product quality and sophistication are spotty. During this stage, the product is often "not ready for prime-time."
- Growth stage: The product is promoted to a mass market. Quality and sophistication improve, and the product moves into general acceptance. The product client base begins to see distinct advantages over the product category it may be replacing.
- Product maturity: The product is generally accepted, the product it replaces is becoming more difficult to find and maintain, and the older technology is not well regarded.
- Product decline: The product is now older, and newer technologies are vying to replace it.

Currently, digital video systems have moved from product introduction to the growth stage. Major manufacturers begin to introduce the product line to fight off competition from the companies that pioneered the product.

Digital intercom systems are still in the product introduction stage, although at least one digital video system has a viable digital intercom system integrated into its product line partly in response to the author's project specifications and the specifications of other forward-looking consultants. Other manufacturers are following.

As clients are awakening to the advantages of digital video and intercom systems, analog video and intercom systems are moving into decline. This decline will accelerate, and consultants and contractors who do not understand or install digital video and intercom systems will be at a distinct disadvantage in the marketplace as clients begin to ask for them more often. Within the next few years, digital video and intercom systems will most likely be the prevalent form of security technology.

Cost

As with each new technology, cost is a consideration. Digital video and intercom systems were somewhat pricy in the beginning, but the cost will decline as more competitors enter the marketplace, vying for each client's dollar. Obvious cost benefits to digital systems include the ability to scale its infrastructure for growth.

Functions

Digital systems evolve primarily with software and firmware upgrades. The nature of digital systems is that legacy components are virtually always supported for many years after their introduction. Regarding edge devices (cameras, intercoms, and codecs), these will likely always be supported since they connect by Ethernet, transport their signals by TCP/IP, and use standard compression protocols.

There is a historical precedence toward making products proprietary rather than truly open architecture. This is an outgrowth of what I call the "metal-bending mentality." In the early days of the industry, all functions were contained in hardware, and manufacturers could ensure a continuous flow of income from their client base by designing their systems specifically not to interface with other equipment. Although the digital world is inherently one of standardized interfaces and protocols, the security industry has characteristically attempted to customize digital hardware and protocols. Some manufacturers' standard protocol offering is for an interface to a slightly modified protocol; for example, instead of using a pure MPEG signal, the manufacturer might modify the MPEG packet slightly, making codecs offered by them compatible only with their software and thus ensuring that the client will be loyal in scaling the system. This is probably not a good practice for the industry to adapt because it inhibits the growth of the industry over the long term and arguably creates more animosity than genuine loyalty over a period of years.

CHAPTER NOTES

1. Addenda are changes to the specifications and drawings that are issued after the package is issued for bid but generally before the award of a contract. Bulletins are changes to the drawings and specifications that are issued after the contract is awarded.
2. Changes in drawings are often identified by placing a "cloud" or "balloon" around the area containing the change to draw the attention of the contractor(s) to the change. It helps quicken the process since the contractor does not have to review the entire drawing set looking for changes.
3. In my specification, the word "provide" means to furnish, install, place into operation, test, and warrant the device.

10

Getting Down to the Actual Design

MACROLEVEL DESIGN: THE PIECES OF THE BIG PICTURE

The Big Picture and the Fabric

The security system designer has an obligation to provide drawings that, when taken together, provide the following three views of the security system for the bidder, installer, maintenance technician, and the designer who will some years later expand or modify the system:

- How the system devices relate to the building and site
- How the system devices relate to the conduit system
- How the system devices relate to other system devices

Plans

Plans and physical details provide the first two views. They show how the security devices relate to the building and site and to the conduit system.

Floor plans and site plans are sometimes called "maps" by the uninitiated. A plan view is any drawing that illustrates a view of the area looking down on it from above. For ceilings, the term is *reflected ceiling plan*, based on the idea of placing a mirror on the floor of the building and viewing the ceiling by looking up at it from the mirror on the floor, thus making it possible to see the underside of the ceiling by looking down on it. Site plans are plans that show the locations of buildings and structures on a property, whereas floor plans show the areas within the building, including its walls, doors, windows, and often fixtures.

Floor plans are normally created by the architect and adapted for use by other consultants. When working on projects in which an architect is involved, including both new construction and renovation projects, it is almost always possible to obtain "architectural backgrounds" in the form of CAD files.

The security designer will need to obtain the CAD files in a form usable both to him and to others (typically AutoCAD files). It is advisable for the security designer or his CAD staff to modify the architect's backgrounds to a 50% screen (gray line in lieu of black line) form. This will ensure that the security designer's work will stand out compared to the architectural background, making the system devices and conduits easy to identify versus the building and site.

The designer will use a standardized set of device symbols to represent security devices, including card readers, cameras, door locks, request-to-exit devices, door position switches, alarm devices, security terminal cabinets, conduit pull-boxes, power supplies, and switches. These will be shown on the plans to identify where they should be installed. Each device will require a note identifying its intended mounting height and special mounting provisions. For example, does the device require reinforcement to ensure that it does not fall during an earthquake? For wall-mounted devices, it is advisable to utilize a symbol that will identify their exact intended locations on the wall. This can be done by creating symbols that have "mounting tags" with a point or dot to indicate the exact mounting location in the plan. For every device type on every plan, it is important to illustrate a mounting detail of that device (see Physical Details). A detail call-out is needed for each unique device on each plan, referring the reader to the appropriate physical detail. It is common to combine detail call-outs and notes together on a single leader pointer, pointing to the device, which minimizes drawing clutter.

Floor and site plans show not only security system devices but also the conduits that connect them together. Typically, conduit types are shown with varying line types to designate the type of conduit. Conduit types include

- Nonflexible conduits, including rigid (steel), aluminum, and Schedule 40 and 80 (PVC plastic)
- Flexible conduit
- Waterproof conduit
- Armored cables (cables that are enclosed in flexible conduit)

Conduit may also be identified by line types to signify existing and new conduit runs or runs in ceilings, walls, or under floors and within concrete pours.

Conduit installation practices should be identified by reference to code or designated standard. These may include requirements for bushed chase nipple ends on conduits to eliminate the possibility of sharp edges (burrs) from ripping through cable insulation and for 200-pound test pull strings to be placed within empty conduits to facilitate the pulling of cables through the conduit. The security designer may also want to require that conduits be marked with a conduit number corresponding to a conduit number on the plan.

A drawing convention is to show conduit paths as conceptual paths only and allow the field installer to make final determination as to the appropriate actual path of the conduit. This is because there may be obstructions that are encountered in actual practice that may not be known to the designer. However, it is incumbent upon the designer to attempt to show a practical path. I once saw a conduit drawing that illustrated a conduit path across the fifth floor from one side of the building to the other side right through a 10-story open atrium. I have also seen a conduit illustrated from the upper floor of one building to the upper floor of another nearby building. I wonder if there really is a conduit somewhere in the sky between two buildings.

Each conduit shown on the plan should include a projected size (this might change in the shop and field drawing submittal based on the requirements of a specific system vs. the one planned by the consultant). It is also important to note the size and type of each pull-box into which conduits connect.

Note that conduits terminate to any of several devices, including j-boxes (similar to light switch or electrical outlet boxes), pull-boxes (boxes through which wire is pulled but where no terminations should be made), terminal or junction boxes (where wire terminations may be made but not where powered equipment would be located), and equipment cabinets (where powered equipment will be located). All locations where cable terminations and connections occur should be accessible, and they should never be located above a ceiling space unless an access panel is provided.

Risers

A riser is a drawing that illustrates another view of the relationship of the devices to the conduit system, specifically the conduits that rise from floor to floor (hence the term riser diagram). The riser diagram also usually illustrates power drop points, including information about the source panel and breaker for each power drop. Although some security system designers like to illustrate all system conduit on the riser diagram, which can be useful, it is generally recommended to show only the vertical conduits and the major laterals leading to power drops and major equipment rooms, not every lateral conduit. This is recommended to keep the drawing simple and to maintain accuracy between the conduits shown on the floor plan and those shown on the riser diagram. If all conduits are shown on both plans, it is likely that somewhere there may be a mistake, especially when a minor change occurs in the design that ends up being shown on one plan but not the other.

Radio Frequency Communications Paths

Radio frequency (RF) communications paths are just as important to show as conduit paths. When showing RF communications paths, it is advisable to show them as line-of-sight paths and Fresnel signal paths. The line-of-sight path is the clear path directly between a transmitting and receiving antenna. The Fresnel signal path defines the outer boundary of the signal that is sensitive to moisture and multipath reflections. It is also a good idea to show the intended direction of communications toward the "home" RF node.

Single-Line Diagrams

Single-line diagrams offer the third view—that is, the relationship of the security devices to other security devices. Single-line diagrams represent the signal flow path, not the conduit or wiring path. Although these may often be the same, the conduit drawing illustrates the physical relationship, whereas the single-line diagram illustrates the electrical or signal relationship.

The single-line diagram for each system should illustrate the major devices that either signal, process a signal, or make the results of that signal available to a security professional to use in securing the facility. For a video system, this includes the cameras, pan/tilt drives, receiver/drivers, codecs, digital switches, servers, and workstations. For an alarm/access control system, it includes edge devices (card readers, electrified locks, door position switches, request-to-exit devices, gates, gate operators, loop detectors, alarm origination devices, etc.), alarm/access control system controllers (data-gathering panels), switches, servers, and workstations. For security intercom systems, it may include field intercom stations, bullhorns, digital switches, and workstations.

Each single-line diagram should include power pickup points and system interconnections to other systems.

For example, if a digital switcher is being shared between all three systems, it can be shown on one with match points to its connections on other systems, or it can be shown on all three systems using the same switcher device nomenclature (e.g., SW-2), with a note that it is indeed the same switcher. Usually, when the exact device is shown on two or more drawings, it is shown in black lines on one and gray lines on the others, with a detail call-out referring the observer to the first drawing. It is also important to note switcher input numbers in order to ensure that there are no duplications.

Title Sheet

The title sheet is a drawing that precedes all of the others. It should include the following:

- The project and system title in large bold letters; for example, "Mega Corp—Integrated Security System."
- A list of the symbols used throughout the drawings. This may include default sizes, mounting heights, a place for remarks, etc.
- A list of abbreviations used throughout the drawings—not device abbreviations (these are listed under the device schedule) but other abbreviations, such as "NIC: Not in Contract." Try to make the list exhaustive. It is extremely frustrating for readers to find an abbreviation that is intuitive to the security designer but nobody else can figure it out.
- A set of general notes that apply throughout all the drawings (e.g., notes about conduit and power requirements and environmental requirements for typical devices).
- A device schedule listing device abbreviations (e.g., IC—field intercom).
- A cable schedule listing all the cable types used throughout the drawings.
- A drawing list including drawing numbers and drawing sheet titles. It is useful on large drawing packages to further break these down by drawing type and sometimes location specifics on multisite drawing packages.

Title Block

The title block is the standard border of each drawing in the drawing package. Its form may be dictated by the client or architect, but it should include the following:

- A border delineating the drawing boundaries
- Sector identifiers for plans (e.g., row/column markers to help people on the telephone refer to a specific device by its location in drawing sector "C-6")
- The name of the project and system
- The name of the specific drawing (e.g., "Riser Diagram/Fifth Floor Plan")
- The drawing number
- The initials of the designer, engineer, draftsman, reviewer, etc.
- The date of the original drawing issue
- The name of the original drawing issue (e.g., "Construction Document Issue" or "Issued for Pricing")
- The revision number (delta number), date, and revision issue name (e.g., Addendum #4)
- The names of the client, architect, major engineers, and the security design firm

Specifications Overview

Together with the drawings, the specifications provide a complete picture of what is expected of the installing contractor. In court, specifications usually rule the day, taking precedence over drawings in case of a dispute.

The most common form of specifications used in the United States is the Construction Specifications Institute (CSI) format. Other forms are used in different areas of the world; for example, FIDIC is standard in much of Europe and the Middle East. This book uses the CSI specification as an example as to form, but the principles explained here will apply to any form.

Specifications explain in text form the intent of the specifier as to how the system should function, what products to use, what installation practices to use, among other information.

CSI specifications are laid out in three sections:

- Section 1: Description of the Work
- Section 2: Products
- Section 3: Installation Practices

Specification Sections

For more than 40 years, CSI specifications have been broken out into divisions under the MasterFormat™ Edition: Numbers and Titles. Each division's section is further broken down into three sections. Each section is then broken down into articles, paragraphs, and descending subparagraphs.

In 2004, CSI conducted the first major restructuring of the specifications sections in many years. For many years, all security system systems and subsystems were specified under the Electrical Section, Division 16.

In 1995, there was a failed attempt to encourage specifiers to write security system specifications (and also other low-voltage systems) under Division 17. Then, an adjustment to the MasterFormat Edition: Numbers and Titles occurred in 2001. Both of these were designed to attempt to bring order to an increasingly chaotic use of division numbers resulting from the fact that there was an insufficient number of divisions available to accommodate all of the emerging new building technologies.

The 2004 edition places security systems under Division 28. Division numbers have been assigned for some of the subsystems of integrated security systems, including alarm, access control, and video systems.

The idea of CSI specification divisions is to provide a separate specification division for each construction discipline so that the contractor building that work will be working under his or her own division number. However, CSI has failed to address integrated security systems, which is a single system composed of numerous subsystems. Some argue that security system specifications should be written as a compilation of numerous individual divisions, for each subsystem, so that those sections can be contracted separately to different contractors (one contract for the access control system, another for the video system, etc.). It is my most emphatic position that to implement a contract for an integrated security system in this fashion is the absolute definition of chaos. This approach virtually always ends in tears. Integrated security systems are supposed to be integrated. Breaking the specification for an integrated security system out into its subsections implies encouragement and consent for breaking the contract up into its constituent elements. This is exactly what designers do not want to happen. In every case in which I have seen an integrated system contracted among various security contractors, one for each subsystem, the owner has been dissatisfied with the result and so have the contractors and the consultant. This is the opposite of industry best practices. If there were a category for industry worst practices, this would be it.

Virtually every responsible designer, project manager, and client agrees that the success of an integrated security system requires a single point of responsibility—one contractor who is ultimately responsible for the results of the construction effort. I recommend placing integrated security systems under Division 28 under one of its unassigned divisions, such as 28 50 00. Under CSI, users are free to assign unused MasterFormat numbers and titles for subjects unaddressed by the published numbers and titles. Per the MasterFormat Application Guide, page 5,

> The above conventions were followed to provide space between the assigned numbers for flexibility in the assignment of user-defined titles and numbers. However, the user does *not* need to follow the above conventions and is free to use any appropriate number in the assignment of new numbers for new titles, *providing*:
>
> > The title does not already have an assigned number
> > The number has not already been assigned to another title
> > It is not within a division that has been designated as reserved for future expansion

CSI also recommends that you follow MasterFormat title practice when creating titles for specification sections. Again, quoting from the Application Guide,

> Some titles have been revised slightly to use terminology to more consistently reflect that MasterFormat is classifying work results rather than products. For example,

03200 Concrete Reinforcement is now 03 20 00 Concrete Reinforcing; 05210 Steel Joists is now 05 21 00 Steel Joist Framing; and 09910 Paints is now 09 91 00 Painting. In other cases where the work result title is the same as the product, the titles have remained the same. For example, 06160 Sheathing remains 06 16 00 Sheathing; 08380 Traffic Doors remains 08 38 00 Traffic Doors; and 12350 Specialty Casework remains 12 35 00 Specialty Casework.

Specifications Section 1: Description of the Work

Develop language for each of the following articles and paragraphs.

Articles in Section 1
Introduction
Scope of Work
Precedence
Bid Information
Related Work by Others
System Descriptions
Submittals
Services
Definitions

Introduction

The introduction should contain a description of the project (where, what, new or retrofit, etc.) and a general description of the deliverables (specifications, drawings, addenda, and bulletins).

Scope of Work

Systems

List each of the systems that are part of this scope of work. These systems will be described in detail later in the specifications under Systems Descriptions.

Submittals

Bid Submittal

Describe the bid process (if not otherwise described in the overall architectural bid documents). Describe any bid forms and the bid analysis process (how bids will be judged).

- Base bid: What is required in the base bid?
- Alternate bids: What types of alternate bids are acceptable?
- Required alternate bids: List any required alternate bids.
- Optional alternate bids: Describe what type of optional alternate bids are acceptable and what are not acceptable. If a conforming base bid is required before any alternate bids will be considered, state it here (I usually require a conforming base bid to prevent apples and oranges bids). I encourage alternate bids that either improve system performance over that specified or reduce system costs while operating equal to that specified. As a result, there are often some great ideas put forward by bidders.
- Renewable annual maintenance agreement: I believe that it is always wise to request a renewable annual maintenance agreement to begin after completion of the warranty period. The owner will never get a better price on a maintenance contract than at the time of competitive bid. The terms should be roughly equal to the warranty terms.
- Shop and field drawings submittal: Describe required shop and field drawings in detail as listed elsewhere in this book.
- Record documents: Describe what as-built documentation will be required of the bidder.

Services

Interdiscipline Coordination

The coordination of the security system with other building construction elements (construction disciplines) is one of the most important factors in whether or not the system will succeed as an integrated system.

There is no discipline in construction that interfaces with as many other building disciplines as does security.

Security systems interface with electrical, architectural, elevators, doors, parking systems, HVAC systems, concrete, signage, landscaping, civil, structural, plumbing, HSE (health, safety, and environment), human resources, fuel delivery, food delivery, mail-room design, x-ray, etc. What other building system has so many interfaces with other disciplines? None that I know of.

Interdiscipline coordination is the single most important differentiator between a novice and a master designer. Designers who are good at interdiscipline coordination have projects that work well and are installed smoothly. Contractors are pleased because the road map for coordination is clear and unambiguous, making the schedule more predictable and the job more profitable for the contractors. Such consultants are valued by clients, architects, engineers, contractors, and end users.

Following are the keys to successful interdiscipline coordination:

- As the basis for design is being crafted, outline the required coordination to other systems and between subsystems of the security system.
- Define the objectives, functions, and attributes of each coordination element for each system. Send this information to each consultant or engineer who will be affected, and copy the architect, project manager, and client. Receive consensus on the process. Advise that precise specification language usable by all will soon follow.
- Draft third-person specification language that can be used in the specifications of both the security system and the other building discipline specifications, such that both contractors will be working to the same language. The language should explain the purpose and objectives of the interface, how it should function, and what needs to be done to make it work by both contractors.
- Make that language available to each consultant or engineer for whom an interface is to be affected. Provide a copy of the language in a separate folder or envelope (or e-mail) for each discipline, and copy the project manager, architect, and client.

- Provide an additional paragraph for insertion in all of the affected specification sections, including the security section, that states that neither of these systems will be accepted until this interface works in its entirety. This language is the key to the success of the interface. It changes the political dynamic such that the contractors are compelled to work together to achieve acceptance of their own systems. Pointing the finger at the other contractor only holds up their own final payment. It clears the way for the contractors to work it out, not shout it out.
- Follow-up after issuance of the specification language to ensure that the language is suitable for all specifiers, the architect, project manager, and the client.

This approach is very rare in the construction industry, but it is appreciated everywhere it is used and will build your reputation as a thorough, competent designer.

Project Engineering and Provisioning

This article outlines the assigned process for engineering and procuring products for the project.

The responsibility to engineer the project is clearly defined. The contractor is responsible for refining the conceptual drawings by the initial project designer to a fully engineered set of buildable drawings. The key difference between these is that bid drawings must be designed so that any qualified contractor can bid a variety of different manufacturers' products. The bid drawings must be general enough to allow that flexibility.

Shop and field drawings are very specific, right down to which wire numbers and what wire colors land on which terminal strips on what devices (by brand and model). That level of specificity is not possible in bid drawings, but it is a must for construction. All of the shop and field engineering responsibilities are outlined here (not the specifics of the submittals, just the responsibility for it). The other information in this article provides a complete description of how to procure items for the project. Shop and field drawing approvals are required before ordering. Verbal directions should not be followed, only written changes. The purchase schedule is described. Finally, if there is a financial obligation, such as compensating the owner for loss of use of the system due to incorrect purchasing, that should also be in this article.

Project Planning and Management

Security contractors have not over the years developed a reputation for good project management. Yes, there are a few who manage projects competently, but project management has not been high on the list of priorities for many integrators and security contractors. That is a shame—for the contractors, for their clients, and for the industry. It results in poor system quality, late delivery, and failing profits.

Project management is all about the process of delivering high-quality projects on time. It is not in the contractor's best interest to have poor project management. It is false economy to think that money will be saved by pinching on project management. Let me be clear: Every day that a project is late, the money for the labor after that day comes right out of the bottom line for the contractor. Those are lost profits. It almost always adds up to more than would have been paid to manage the project competently.

I sometimes ask contractor project managers what the completion date is for the project or some important phase of its construction. It is astonishing, but they rarely know. I assure you that any project manager who does not know the completion date will not meet it. All project managers should have and use project schedule tools (Gantt charts, etc.) that help them know and maintain the project schedule. It seems that there is never enough time to finish everything one has to do. I am fond of saying that "Friday means there are only two more working days till Monday." In order to finish what is really important, instead of just what is urgent, one must observe the project schedule.

Time Management

There are time bandits out there who will steal your valuable time for their own purposes or just to occupy themselves around the water cooler. How do you determine what is the highest priority and what activities should be ranked low on the list

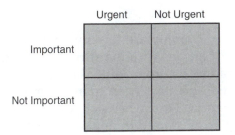

Figure 10-1 Urgent/important matrix.

of priorities? Write down the chart shown in Figure 10-1 on a piece of paper or whiteboard. Now classify all of the activities for the job into one of the four fields. You will note that those which are urgent and important and those which are not urgent and not important require little decision making about what to do. The challenge lies in those tasks that are urgent but not important and those that are not urgent but are important. Focus on the not urgent but important tasks and the project will go much smoother.[1]

Good project management involves the following elements, which should be spelled out in the specifications:

- Determine the goals, deliverables, and scope of the project. Identify the boundaries and relationships to other project participants.
- Plan the project. Create a work breakdown structure and understand project controls.
- Provide the personnel and material resources to complete the project by the completion date in conformance with the specifications. Schedule materials and manpower in order to meet the published project schedule.
- Safeguard delivered equipment until it is installed.
- Coordinate the work of this project with the work of other trades.
- Schedule each major milestone in the work of the project.
- Ensure project schedule compliance and take corrective action when the schedule is not maintained.
- Close out the project in accordance with the specifications.

Training

The objectives of training are to familiarize the operators and maintenance technicians with the attributes, programming, and software operating environment. The owner's administrator, supervisors, and operators need training on those three levels of system operation. The owner's or contractor's installers and maintenance personnel need training on how to install, commission, and maintain the system. The specifications should require evidence of training for all these.

The level of training depends on the project. For small projects, a few hours of owner's personnel training may be adequate. For enterprise systems, my specifications require separate training for each level of owner's personnel. The training sessions are recorded with audio and screen image recording software. The recorded screen and audio is edited down to essential discussion and screen shots, and a DVD is produced for each level for later training sessions.

For all projects, the contractor should be required to certify manufacturer's training for the personnel who are installing, commissioning, and maintaining the system.

Testing

Include language stating that system testing is a basic service. Testing will be discussed in detail later in the specification, under Section 3: Execution.

Warranty

In the security industry, warranties are a contentious issue. I specify minimum acceptable warranty language that must be included by the integrator in their warranty. The language indicates that any other language in the warranty that is in conflict with the language I provide is contractually void.

The warranty section should require a warranty of a given time period (typically 1 year).

The purpose of the warranty should be stated:

- To repair any malfunction or system installation deficiency during the warranty period.
- To cover the cost of correcting any installation deficiency.

- State when the warranty will begin and end.
- Discuss the issue of transferability of the warranty to other parties (not allowed by me in my specification).
- Indicate how the warranty must be transmitted. For example, if a substitute warranty is signed for by the owner, that warranty is void under the specifications and the signature is unenforceable.
- Indicate that the contractor must register all equipment of this work with the manufacturers in the name of the owner.
- Discuss any rules for subcontracting warranty repair work.
- Discuss how emergency and non-emergency repairs are to be handled.
- List hours of service.
- Discuss how chronic problems with the system are to be handled.

Precedence

This article is not typically used in new construction projects because its elements are normally included in Division 0, General Provisions. This article instructs the installer as to the order or precedence of documents and what to do if any conflict occurs during the project. Change orders, language for training, submittals, screens, etc. are all included in this article.

System Descriptions

I describe the total integrated system and each sub-system that makes it up by using four distinct methods to describe each element of the overall system.

Purpose

- What is the purpose of the system or subsystem?
- What does the owner expect to receive as a benefit for his or her investment?

Environment

What is the environment in which the system operates?

- What is the physical environment? Is the system indoors or outdoors? Is it operating in a harsh environment, such as an

offshore oil platform, or in desert conditions that can reach
140 degrees, or in the Arctic, where temperatures might be
well below zero?
- What is the security environment? What threats is the system
helping to defend against? What assets are under protection?
- What is the operational environment? Is the system operated
by trained employed staff or by contract guards who might
have a high turnover?

Functions

What functions do we want each part of each subsystem to perform? List every desired function here. If it is not listed, it is not
a specification requirement, and the system becomes acceptable
without that function. This is where poor specifiers often get bit-
ten for "extra services" by the contractor. If you do not ask for it,
you cannot expect to get it.

Attributes

What physical attributes must the system have in order to perform the functions that are specified? Do not mistake this for
a product or installation specification. This describes the general configuration of the hardware architecture of the system
elements, not the specific products to be used. You might be
unpleasantly surprised to discover that the contractor's idea of
how the system should be configured is dramatically different
from your design concept. State the design concept clearly so
that there will be no misunderstanding.

Systems may include the following:

Integrated Security System Overview

Provide an overview of what the entire system is, what subsystems it has, and what the overall system should do.

Monitoring and Control System

Usually one of the systems will provide the Graphical User Interface to operate the other systems. List all of the components of

the system, including field components, infrastructure components, and server/workstation and software components.

Alarm/Access Control System

Describe the alarm/access control system in its entirety. List all of the components of the system, including field components, infrastructure components, and server/workstation and software components.

Under functions, describe how alarms should work, identification, grouping, scheduling, and operation. Describe alarm types and how alarmed state actions should be handled when they occur.

Describe output control functions, including basic output controls, global I/O functions, data inputs and outputs, and interfaces to central station alarm receivers and panels.

Describe access control functions, including basic principles, credentials, time zones, daylight savings time, schedules and holidays, access levels and access groups, and temporary and permanent access levels. Discuss user types, user functions, and advanced access control system functions such as first card unlock, two-man rule, global anti-passback, global occupancy rule, mustering, guard tours, and card formats. Describe operator functions, including functions for administrators, supervisors, and operators. Explain ID credentialing functions and photo ID functions. List visitor management functions and monitoring and control functions, including alarm monitoring and access control monitoring. Make reference to other appropriate sections, such as the monitoring and control sub-system. Describe operator controls, including remote access granting, etc. List database and reporting functions. Finally, list archiving functions.

Digital or Analog Video System

List all of the components of the video system, including field components, infrastructure and server/workstation components, and software components.

Under functions, list each function of each component that is required. Remember, if it is not specified, it is not required.

- What does the system do? How does it do it?
- What display functions will the system perform, including alarm response, video guard tours, video pursuit, and surveillance?
- How will the console operate?
- How will the system relate to other subsystems and other building systems, such as lights and parking?

Security Intercom System

Describe the field, infrastructure, and server/workstation components of the system.

Describe how the system works in detail for users, lobby desks, and console operators.

Describe how the system interfaces and interoperates with other related systems, including call logging and event spawning (video call-ups, etc.)

Describe the type of intercom systems and their applications, including access assistance IC stations, emergency phones, elevator intercoms, suspicious subject interview intercoms, and intercom bullhorns.

Interfaces between Subsystems

List every interface between every system that is part of this integrated security system, installed by the security system contractor.

- What systems are interfaced together and to perform what functions?
- How do the interfaces work and how are they connected?

Interfaces to Systems by Other Contractors

List every interface to every system by other contractors.

- What systems are interfaced together and to perform what functions?
- How do the interfaces work and how are they connected?

System Infrastructure

Describe the overall system infrastructure, including TCP/IP building, intrabuilding, and enterprise architectures.

- RS-485 elements
- Video coax elements
- Intercom audio wiring elements
- Spare parts

Describe what type of spares are required, how many of what, and how they are to be handed over to the client.

Submittals

Bid Submittal

State the obligation to provide all listed submittals, including

- Base bid
- Alternate bids
- Renewable annual maintenance agreement

Shop and Field Submittal

Describe the submittal components:

Shop and field drawings: Identify all of the required elements, typically including a title sheet, schedules of circuits and equipment, floor plans, reflected ceiling plans, physical mounting details, single-line diagrams, schematic diagrams, and wiring diagrams.

Manufacturers data sheets: Data sheets of each major product.

Bill of quantities: A list of all products by location or system.

Record drawing submittal: The record drawings or "as-builts" as they are known in the industry are a record of how the system was actually built, not just how it was designed. In other respects, they echo the shop and field drawings.

Definitions: List all of the words that have special meaning in the specifications.

Specifications Section 2

Introduction: Section 2 lists acceptable products. Describe how the contractor can submit alternates. List each specified product for each of the subsystems in detail. There are three acceptable ways to do this:

- List each product by its description in detail, never mentioning any brand or model.
- List a number of acceptable brands and models.
- List a single brand and model that bidders can use as a benchmark against which other acceptable alternates can be submitted. If this method is used, those products should be widely available by a range of possible bidders.

List acceptable components for general components, including terminal strips, racks, and relays.

System Infrastructure

In this section, list all of the switches, router, firewall, fiber-optic media converters, RS-485/RS-232 media converters, etc.

Monitoring and Control System

In this section, list the servers and workstations, external storage media, operating systems, microphones and speakers, footswitches, and any other console devices, such as monitor mounts, desks, and ergonomic chairs. Do not list application programs except as they relate to the management of the computers. Application programs should be listed under the systems they serve.

Digital Video System

The digital video system section should list any cameras, lenses, mounts, enclosures, codecs, application software, and other DVS items.

Voice Communications System

List any field intercom stations and interface devices, intercom master stations, switches, and software.

Alarm/Access Control System

List all access control devices, including

- Card readers and cards
- Photo ID equipment (digital camera, lamp, background, badge holders, badge printers, clips, lanyards, etc.)
- Electrified door locks
- Door position switches
- Request-to-exit devices

> Infrared
> Electrified panic hardware
> Push buttons, etc.

- Motion alarms
- Other alarms
- Output control devices
- Access control software
- Perimeter detection system: software, hardware, cable, attaching devices, interface devices
- Miscellaneous products
- Spare parts

Specifications Section 3

Section 3 describes how the system is to be constructed, tested, and accepted, including the following:

- Work to be performed immediately upon award of contract

> Project familiarization and mobilization
> Preliminary interdiscipline coordination
> Permits and inspections
> Shop and field drawings submittal

- Work to be performed at the contractor's shop

  Console and rack fabrication
  Head-end testing
  Other preparatory information

- Work to be performed at the project site:

  Mounting devices
  Pulling wire
  Power coordination
  Product delivery, storage, and handling
  Safeguards and protections
  Safety barriers
  Protection
  Device installation, terminations, and adjustments
  Final interdiscipline coordination
  Grounding and powering procedures

I recommend the use of hospital-grade grounding and powering practices. This involves the use of a single ground bar at the main electrical panel to the building, with all grounds of this system going back to that ground bar without splices.

The designer should create text to describe exactly what kind of grounding practices are acceptable. Shielding should be described. Requirements to document power and ground, panels, and breakers should be explained.

Wire and Cable Installation Practices

This section should include

- Conduit and wire pulling practices
- Wire lacing and dressing standards
- Prohibitions against class mixing
- Wire tagging
- Other standards and practices as appropriate

Commissioning: System Setup and Configurations

- Final hardware configurations and testing
- Camera focusing, etc.

- Perimeter alarm balancing, etc.
- Wireless node configurations, balancing, etc.
- Setting up operating systems and domains
- User authorizations
- System configurations
- Application program loading and configurations
- Enterprise system configurations

System Testing: Testing Overview

- Test equipment requirements
- Preliminary checks and testing requirements

Acceptance Testing

After the system is tested by the contractor to his or her satisfaction, acceptance testing begins.

- State the scope of the required tests
- Test scheduling readiness and documentations
- Wireless testing
- Infrastructure testing
- System testing
- Remedial correction of testing observations

Project Completion

- Notice of Completion

MICROLEVEL DESIGN: THE THREADS THAT KNIT TOGETHER THE PIECES OF THE BIG PICTURE

Schedules

For contract drawings (issued for bid), schedules (spreadsheets) should be illustrated in the drawing set to assist the bidding contractors in understanding the system sufficiently to bid. For shop and field drawings (drawings by the installing contractor), schedules should be provided in the drawing set to assist the installers in understanding the system sufficiently to install it correctly and with the minimum amount of field decision time. The shop and field schedules should also provide all the information necessary for the purchasing department to acquire all needed materials.

Construction Drawings: Device Schedules by System

System Infrastructure

The system infrastructure schedule outlines in spreadsheet form all of the system infrastructure elements, including switches, routers, fiber optic communications nodes, uninterruptible power supplies, and the like. Any device that connects system elements together or supports their stable and safe operation should be listed. At a minimum, spreadsheet fields should include the site, building, location, floor, area, device by category number of ports, and remarks.

Control and Monitoring System

The control and monitoring system is designated as a separate system on larger security systems and may be included as part of a subsystem or smaller system. This system may include servers and workstations, video monitors, radios, headphones, keypads, mice, and the like, plus a remarks field. At a minimum, spreadsheet fields should include the site, building, location, floor, area, device by category, device specifications (if relevant for bid), and the like.

Alarm/Access Control System

The alarm/access control system schedule should include credential readers, locks, request-to-exit devices, door position switches, alarm points, output controls, alarm/access control system panels, parking gate controllers, etc. and remarks. At a minimum, the spreadsheet should include site, building, floor, area, devices by category, and remarks.

Digital or Analog Video System

The video system schedules should include cameras, lenses, pan/tilt drives, enclosures, codecs (multiplexers, quad units, and matrix switches, if analog), video keyboards, and the like. At a minimum, the spreadsheet should include site, building, floor, area, devices by category, and remarks.

Security Intercom System

The security intercom system schedule may be on its own table or might be included as part of the video system, if so equipped. The schedule should include field intercom stations, security intercom stations, intercom bullhorns, amplifiers, microphones, headphones, intercom master stations, and matrix switches (if analog). At a minimum, the spreadsheet should be formatted as discussed previously.

System Interfaces

System interfaces may be on its own schedule or could be implemented into the others. System interfaces should include the connection points between systems and the functions to be performed.

Power

Power schedules should include the high-voltage power drops locations and the devices served at each location. Some designers prefer to include low-voltage power supplies in this schedule. The spreadsheet should be formatted as discussed previously.

Cable

A system cable spreadsheet should include the cable types, brand, model of cable, and the outside diameter and rating of the cable [voltage class of insulation, indoor, plenum (above ceiling) rated, direct burial rated, etc.]

Conduit and Fill

Some designers place conduit and fill schedules on each floor, site, or ceiling plan in the construction drawing package. This made good sense in the old days when virtually every system utilized very similar system wiring architecture. However, as system architectures become more diverse, it can in fact be confusing to the bidders to dictate a specific wiring scheme when the products they prefer to submit use another. For many systems, I now leave conduit and fill schedules to the shop and field drawing set, to be submitted by the contractor who is awarded the project. Conduit and fill schedules, if shown on the construction drawing set, should include the conduit number for each conduit shown on that specific plan, its size, and the types and numbers of wires to be in each conduit (the fill).

General Network Device Configuration Schedules

Network device configurations should be illustrated conceptually on a configuration schedule. The configuration schedule should have two parts or be shown as three schedules (hardware configuration, firmware/software configuration, and user access configurations). The schedule should include all the basic requirements the security system designer intends for the system to operate under as a prerequisite to its stable and safe operation. These may include disabling unused switcher ports, access classes and permissions, etc.

Shop and Field Drawings

In addition to the schedules identified previously for construction drawing packages, shop and field drawings should also include conduit and fill schedules as described previously, if not included in the construction drawing package.

Device Wiring Schedules

A device wiring schedule (also called "run sheet") will list the exact input and output connections from and to every device in the security system. These are typically done by cabinet, rack, or console assembly. Each schedule will show all of the devices for that assembly, its connection point, and the connection by connector type and wiring type. This will be correlated to its source or destination assembly, device, and wiring point. A good practice is to show this assembly in the center of the spreadsheet and the source points to the left and destination points to the right of the schedule.

Configuration Schedules

System configuration schedules should include the exact desired configuration for each programmable device. Configurations may be shown for hardware devices, firmware or software devices, and users by class.

Physical Details

Physical details are drawings that identify all of the mounting and installation requirements for each device. These may include mounting height, positioning, structural mounting requirements, conduit and box connections, and the like.

System Interfacing Details

System interfacing details illustrate connections between systems that are necessary to create integration functions. These should usually also include a brief sequence of operation of theory of operation, not in conflict with the description provided in the specifications. Interfacing details should be provided from and to other systems being interfaced, possibly including elevators, parking, building automation, PABX, VoIP, radio, lighting, signage, concrete, and landscape.

Revised Construction Budget

Following completion of the construction drawing package, it is common to make a final revision to the construction budget.

Complete Specification

The complete specification provided as part of the construction drawing package must include all of the system requirements, fleshing out the outline provided in the design development issue.

Review Drawings, Specifications, and Prioritized Budgets

Following submission of the final construction documents package, the client may perform a final review. This may also include an interdiscipline coordination review. The client will return the package with final comments.

Revise after Review

Following receipt of the final comments, the designer will perform final corrections and issue the package for bid through proper project management channels.

SUMMARY

Preliminary (schematic phase) design work includes the Basis for Design, research drawing and specification resources, and preliminary budgeting. The Basis for Design explains what the system should be, from an interpretation of implementation of security policies. Drawing resources include security system device placements and types, access control zones, a study of codes and regulations, safety issues, and power source locations. A list of interdiscipline coordination issues should be developed. System technology goals should be decided.

The big picture of design includes three views:

- How the system devices relate to the building and site
- How the system devices relate to the conduit system
- How the system devices relate to other system devices

Plans, risers, and physical details provide the first two views. Single-line diagrams provide the third.

Specifications provide the description and legal requirements for carrying out the construction work. Specifications are in three sections:

- Section 1 includes system descriptions and contractual requirements.
- Section 2 describes acceptable products.
- Section 3 describes acceptable installation practices.

CHAPTER NOTE

1. Government of Great Britain: www.improvementnetwork. gov.uk/imp/aio/11282.

Special Design Sections

11

Information Technology Systems Infrastructure

INTRODUCTION

This may be one of the most important sections in the book. The designer who does not thoroughly understand TCP/IP is at a severe disadvantage in design, in construction management, and in system commissioning. The designer is at the mercy of installers and physics, both of which can harm him or her. Not understanding TCP/IP is like not being able to read or write. This is not a comprehensive tome on TCP/IP. I suggest that the reader buy several other books on the subject. This description is intended for the novice designer.

BASICS OF TCP/IP AND SIGNAL COMMUNICATIONS

TCP/IP is the basic protocol of digital systems. From the understanding of that protocol, all knowledge about digital systems flows.

How TCP/IP Works

The purpose of TCP/IP is to guide information from one place to another on a digital network. In the beginning, when computers were owned only by the government, military, universities, and really big business (banks and insurance companies), computers were not networked. Universities and the military held discussions on how to network their machines. The first network, called ARPANET, was developed in 1969 using Network Control Protocol, an early predecessor to TCP/IP. Although this permitted limited communications, several problems were evident, mainly that computers could only talk to other computers of the same manufacturer using the same operating system and software. This was not good since the whole idea was to allow communication, not to limit it. After several iterations, TCP/IP evolved. I will not go into the entire long story; you can look that up on Google under "TCP/IP history." TCP/IP is really two separate protocols. TCP stands for Transport Control Protocol, and IP stands for Internet Protocol. TCP was developed in 1974 by Kahn and Cerf and was introduced in 1977 for cross-network connections. TCP was faster, easier to use, and less expensive to implement. It also ensured that lost packets would be recovered, providing quality of service to network communications. In 1978, IP was added to handle routing of messages in a more reliable fashion. TCP communications were encapsulated within IP packets to ensure that they were routed correctly. On the receiving end, the TCP packets were unpacked from their IP capsules. Experts quickly realized that TCP/IP could be used for virtually any communication medium, including wire, radio, fiber, laser, and other means. By 1983, ARPANET was totally converted to TCP/IP, and it became known as the Internet.

TCP/IP Operates on OSI Levels 3 (IP) and 4 (TCP)

One of the basic functions of networking involves the process of layering communications. Like making a sandwich, one cannot begin by spreading mayonnaise on one's hand. You have to put it on bread. Then you add the meat, lettuce, pickles, etc. and finally a last layer of bread. Network communications are like that. In order to send a packet of video, audio, or data, one must build up a series of layers. At the other end, those layers are taken off until the packet is ready for viewing or listening. There are seven layers to the OSI (Open Systems Interconnection) reference model. Each layer adds a protocol. Dick Lewis (Lewis Technology)[1] uses an example of James Bond to describe how the seven layers work (Fig. 11-1). The following is his description:

> James Bond meets Number One on the seventh floor of the spy headquarters building. Number One gives Bond a secret message that must get through to the U.S. embassy across town.
>
> Bond proceeds to the sixth floor, where the message is translated into an intermediary language, encrypted, and miniaturized.
>
> Bond takes the elevator to the fifth floor, where security checks the message to be sure it is all there and puts some

7 Layers of the OSI Model					
Layer #	Layer	Functions	Methods	Transmit	Receive
7	Application	Communication Partners Identified, Quality of Service Identified, User Authentication, Data Syntax	E-Mail, Network Software, Telnet, FTP	⬇	⬆
6	Presentation	Encryption	Encryption Software	⬇	⬆
5	Session	Establishes & Terminates Network Sessions between Devices & Software Requests	CPU Process	⬇	⬆
4	Transport	Error Recovery & Flow Control	CPU Process	⬇	⬆
3	Network	Switching and Routing, Network Addressing, Error Handling, Congestion Control and Packet Sequencing	Switcher, Router	⬇	⬆
2	Data link	Data Packets encoded/decoded into bits.	Media Access Control (MAC) & Logical Link Control (LLC)	⬇	⬆
1	Physical	Electrical, light or radio bit stream	Cables, Cards, Ethernet, RS-232, ATM, 802.11a/b/g	⬇	⬆

Figure 11-1   OSI layers.

checkpoints in the message so his counterpart at the U.S. end can be sure he's got the whole message.

On the fourth floor, the message is analyzed to see if it can be combined with some other small messages that need to go to the U.S. end. Also, if the message was very large it might be broken into several small packages so other spies can take it and have it reassembled on the other end.

The third floor personnel check the address on the message and determine who the addressee is and advise Bond of the fastest route to the embassy.

On the second floor, the message is put into a special courier pouch (packet). It contains the message, the sender, and destination ID. It also warns the recipient if other pieces are still coming.

Bond proceeds to the first floor, where Q has prepared the Aston Martin for the trip to the embassy.

Bond departs for the U.S. embassy with the secret packet in hand. On the other end, the process is reversed. Bond proceeds from floor to floor, where the message is decoded.

The U.S. ambassador is very grateful the message got through safely.

"Bond, please tell Number One I'll be glad to meet him for dinner tonight."

The important point to understand is that in any network today, each packet is encapsulated (enclosed) seven times and, when received, is decapsulated seven times. Each encapsulation involves checking and packaging to make the trip a sure and safe one for the data. Each decapsulation reverses that process:

- Data begins its trip at layer 7, the application layer—software program, Microsoft Word™, etc.
- It is passed down to layer 6, the presentation layer, which adds data compression, encryption, and other similar manipulations of the data.
- It is then passed down to layer 5, the session layer. This provides a mechanism for managing the dialog between

the two computers, including starting and stopping the communications and what to do if there is a crash.

- From there, it goes to layer 4, the transport layer (TCP). This layer ensures reliable communications between the machines. The packet changes from data to segments in the TCP layer.
- Down to layer 3, the network layer (IP), where error control and routing functions are described. The segments are combined or broken up into defined-sized packets at the IP layer. Routers are layer 3 devices.
- Down to layer 2, the data link layer, where functional and procedural means to transfer data between network entities and detection and correction of errors that could occur on the lowest layer take place. It is on this layer that the addressing of exact physical machines, each with their own media access control (MAC) address, is found. Each digital device attached to any network has its own unique MAC address, allowing sure identification that the device is authorized for connection to the communication or network. Network switches are layer 2 devices.
- Finally, down to layer 1, the physical layer, including cable, voltages, hubs, repeaters, and connectors.

TCP/UDP/RTP

One of the major advantages of TCP/IP is that it is able to fix bad communications. It does this by keeping track of packet lists for a given communication. Andrew G. Blank, author of *TCP/IP Foundations*,[2] uses a wonderful illustration of a children's soccer team at a pizza parlor with an attached game arcade:

> Let's say that I take my son's soccer team to an arcade and restaurant for a team party. I have the whole team outside the arcade. My task is to get the team to the other side of the arcade, to my wife who is waiting for them in the restaurant. In this analogy, the team represents the complete file on one host, and each child represents a data packet. One of my goals is to lose as few of the kids as possible.

While we are standing outside, it is easy to put the team in order; all the children are wearing numbered jerseys. I tell the kids that we will meet on the other side of the arcade in a restaurant for pizza and that they should all move as fast as possible through the arcade and to the restaurant.

After I open the door and say "Go," the kids enter one at a time. Entering the arcade one at a time represents the fragmenting and sending of the file. Just as each of the kids has a numbered jersey, each packet has a number so that the receiving host can put the data back together.

Now picture a dozen 6-year-olds moving through the arcade. Some of the children will take a short route; others will take a long route. Possibly, they'll all take the same route, though it is much more likely that they will all take different routes. Some will get hung up at certain spots, but others will move through faster. My wife is in the restaurant waiting to receive the team. As they start arriving at the restaurant, she can reassemble the children (packets) in the correct order because they all have a number on their backs. If any are missing, she will wait just a bit for the stragglers and then send back a message that she is missing part of the team (file).

After I receive a message that she is missing a child (a packet), I can resend the missing part. I do not need to resend the entire team (all the packets), just the missing child (packet or packets).

Please note, however, that I would not go look for the lost child; I would just put the same numbered jersey on a clone of the lost child and send him into the arcade to find the restaurant.

TCP is designed to reconstruct lost packets so that an entire communication is intact. This is very important for files such as employee records, word processing files, and spreadsheets, where a missing packet can cause the whole file to be unreadable.

UDP

For video and audio, another protocol is required. TCP can cause problems with audio and video files because its attempt to resend lost packets results in portions of the communication occurring out of place and therefore in the wrong sequence, making the video or audio communication intelligible. The human eye and ear are very good about rebuilding lost portions of communications. Imagine a restaurant in which you are overhearing a conversation at an adjacent table. You may not be able to hear the entire conversation—not every word because of the noise from others talking—but you can still follow what is being said.

Instead, what we need is a protocol that will send the data without error correction and without attempting to resend lost packets. That protocol is User Datagram Protocol (UDP). UDP is called a connectionless protocol because it does not attempt to fix bad packets. It simply sends them out and hopes they arrive. The transmitting device has no way of knowing whether they do or not.

UDP and its partner, Real-Time Protocol (RTP), work together to ensure that a constant stream of data (hence the term "streaming data") is supplied for a receiving program to view or hear. RTP is used for audio and video. Typically, RTP runs on top of the UDP protocol.

As an industry default, all network data is called TCP/IP data, whether it is TCP/UDP or RTP. It is kind of like calling any tissue Kleenex™ or any copier a Xerox™ machine. It is not accurate; it is just that everyone does it.

Another important set of protocols that security designers will need to know about are unicast and multicast protocols. These are discussed in detail later in this chapter.

TCP/IP Address Schemes

Each network device has a network card that connects that device to the network. The network interface card (NIC) has a MAC address and a TCP/IP address to identify itself to the network. The MAC address is hardware assigned at the factory when the device is manufactured. It can never be changed. The TCP/IP address is assignable, and it defines where in the network hierarchy the device is located. TCP/IP addresses are used to ensure that communications errors do not occur and that the address represents the logical location on the network where the device resides. TCP/IP addresses are like postal addresses, which identify where a house is on what street, in what neighborhood, in what city, in what state, and in what country. MAC addresses are like the name of the person who resides in the house. The MAC address will change if one replaces a computer with another, but the TCP/IP address can stay the same on the network for the user of the computer so that all messages to that user, worldwide, do not need a new MAC address in order to reach him or her.

There are two versions of TCP/IP addresses, known as IPv4 and IPv6. IP version 4 was the original version under which the whole Internet worked until it was determined that the number of available addresses would soon run out. So a larger array of numbers was defined, called IP version 6. IPv6 can accommodate a very large (virtually infinite) number of connected devices.

In IPv4, addresses are broken down into what is called decimal notation for the convenience of the user. Remember, each address is actually a series of binary data (ones and zeros), but they are grouped together in a fashion that is much easier to understand. Four groups are combined together, separated by decimals. Each group (byte) can be a number from 0 to 255 (a total of 256 numbers). This is an 8-bit value. A typical address can be from 0.0.0.0 to 255.255.255.255. IPv4 provides for in excess of 4 billion unique addresses. IPv6 replaces the 8-bit value with a 12-bit value. (0.0.0.0 to 4095.4095.4095.4095). The IPv6 address range can be represented by a 3 with 39 zeros after it. It is a large number. IPv4 is still adequate for today's networks, but IPv6 is coming.

Briefly, the first one or two bytes of data, depending on the class of the network, generally will indicate the number of the network. The third byte indicates the number of the subnet and the fourth byte indicates the host (device) number on the network. The host cannot be either 0 or 255. An address of all zeros is not used because when a machine is booted that does not have a hardware address assigned to it, it provides 0.0.0.0 as it addresses until it receives its assignment. This would occur for machines that are remote booted (started up) or for those that boot dynamically using the Dynamic Host Configuration Protocol (DHCP). The part of the IP address that defines the network is called the network ID, and the latter part of the IP address is called the host ID.

Regarding the use of automatic or manual device addressing, we recommend manual addressing for security systems. DHCP incurs the possibility of security breaches that are not present with static addressing.

NETWORKING DEVICES

Security system digital networks are composed of five main types of network devices.

Edge Devices

Edge devices include digital video cameras, digital intercoms, and codecs. These are the devices that for the most part initiate the signals that the rest of the system processes. One exception to this is that codecs can also be used to decode digital signals and turn them back into analog signals for viewing of digital video signals or listening to digital audio signals. The most common use of the decoding codec is for security intercoms, where an analog intercom module is a must in order to hear and speak from the console.

Communications Media

Digital signals are communicated either along cable or wirelessly. The most common type of wired infrastructure is an Ethernet cabling scheme. Although other types exist (ring topology, etc.), none are prevalent. Ethernet is a wired scheme that allows many devices to compete for attention on the network. It is designed to handle collisions that occur when two or more devices want to talk simultaneously.

Devices contend for attention and are granted permission to speak while all other devices listen. Contention can slow a network, reducing its throughput. A network can be segmented by switches and routers to reduce contention and regain efficiency.

Ethernet is defined under IEEE[3] Standard 802.3. Ethernet classes vary by speed, with the slowest being 10Base-T [10 megabits per second (Mbps)]. Fast Ethernet is called 100Base-T and operates at 100 Mbps. Gigabit or 1000Base-T operates at 1 gigabit per second (Gbps). Wiring distances depend on wire type and speed. Ethernet is wired using unshielded twisted pair (UTP) four-pair wiring on RJ-45 connectors. Category 5 or 5e (Category 5 Enhanced) wiring is used for 10Base-T, 100Base-T, and 1000Base-T (up to 328 ft). Category 6 wire is useful for 1000Base-T runs up to 328 ft. For 1000Base-T connections, all four pairs are used, whereas for 100Base-T connections, only two pairs of wires are used.[4]

Category 5, 5E, and 6 cables use four pairs, where the colors are

- Pair 1—white/blue
- Pair 2—white/orange
- Pair 3—white/green
- Pair 4—white/brown

The second most common type of wired infrastructure is fiber optic. These come in two types, single mode and multimode. When told that the difference between the two is the number of signals they can carry, newbies often think that the single mode will carry one and the multimode will carry more. In fact, just the opposite is true.

Single-mode fiber is based on a laser, whereas multimode may use either a laser or a light emitting diode (LED) for a signal source (Fig. 11-2). Multimode fiber is typically plastic, whereas single-mode fiber is made of glass. Multimode fiber has a large cross-sectional area relative to the wavelength of the light being transmitted through it, typically either 50 or 62.5 μm (micron) fiber diameter compared to 1.3 μm for 1300-nm modulated light frequency. Accordingly, multimode bounces the light off the inside of the fiber (Fig. 11-3). As the light bounces off the walls of the fiber, it takes many different paths to the other end, which can result in multiple signals at the other end. The result is a softening or rounding of the square digital signal. Over distance, the signal becomes more difficult to read at the receiver—thus the

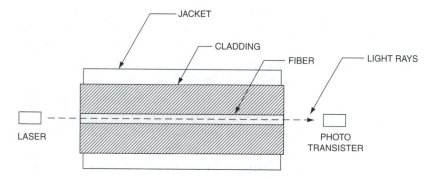

Figure 11-2 Single-mode fiber.

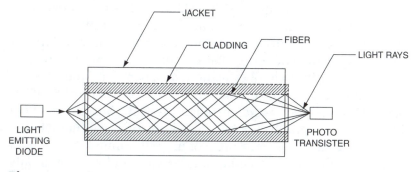

Figure 11-3 Multimode fiber.

limited distance of multimode fiber. Distance is also a factor of bandwidth. You can use multimode at longer distances with less speed. Fast Ethernet (100 Mbps) can travel farther than gigabit Ethernet (1000 Mbps). Check the manufacturer's specification sheets both for the fiber and for the transceivers you intend to use for exact limits based on speed.

Single-mode fiber is made of glass, and it pipes the laser directly down the middle of the glass tube like a waveguide.[5] This is because single-mode fiber has a small cross-sectional area (8 or 9 μm) relative to the frequency of the light being transmitted through it (1.3 μm at 1300 nm). The laser can carry multiple signals on its carrier.

The most commonly used frequencies are 1550, 1310, and 850 nm. The 1550 and 1310 nm frequencies are very common to single-mode fiber, and 850 nm is most commonly used in multimode fiber. The 1310 and 1550 nm frequencies are exclusively transmitted using lasers, and the 850-nm frequency is exclusively transmitted using LEDs. By using multiple frequencies (1310 and 1550 nm), it is possible to transmit and receive bidirectionally over a single fiber. Although this is not a common practice, some transceivers can accommodate two frequencies on a single fiber, especially with single-mode fiber. Typically, 1300 nm is used to send and 1550 nm is used to receive at one end and vice versa at the other end. More commonly, bidirectional communication is accommodated by using two separate fibers on the same frequency. No standard has been developed for multiple frequencies on a single fiber on multimode cable, but at least one security fiber-optic company has developed a fiber-optic media converter that can both transmit and receive on a single multimode fiber using two separate frequencies.[6]

Manufacturers have long since surpassed the IEEE 802.3z standard in terms of the distances served. Multimode fiber distances are typically limited to 1640 ft for fast Ethernet connections. Gigabit speeds are commonly limited to 1000 ft. Single-mode fiber distance limitations vary and can commonly be 43–62 miles with economical equipment;[7] much farther distances are possible (up to 500 miles) with more sophisticated media converters.[8] With commonly available equipment, it is possible to achieve distances of up to 93 miles with either single-mode or multimode at 100Base-T speeds and 75 miles at 1000Base-T speeds.[9]

Lastly, single-mode transceivers and fiber are more costly than their comparable multimode equivalents. The cost delta can be vast. Use multimode for shorter distances (e.g., on a campus) or where cost is a factor. However, the cost delta can sometimes be worth it is there is available single-mode fiber in the ground on a campus and the only cost to mount up the system is that of the transceivers.

Gigabit switches and routers are usually supplied with either single- or multimode fiber ports. This is the preferred connectivity method over the use of separate transceivers.

TCP/IP signals can also be communicated via radio, microwave, or laser. The most common type of radio communication network is in the 802.11 band. 802.11 is available in two major categories, backhaul or client service. The backhaul type is delivered by 802.11a, whereas client services are often provided by 802.11b/g/i. 802.11a makes available 10 channels, and with the correct antennas one can use all 10 channels in the same airspace. 802.11b/g/i are very similar but differ by the bandwidth provided and the level of security implemented. 802.11b provides 11Mbps maximum, whereas 802.11g/i provide 54 Mbps. It is possible to find 802.11g devices that provide 108 Mbps. These are full-duplex devices that use a separate transmitter and receiver to double the bandwidth. This function is very common in 802.11a, which also provides 54 Mbps per available channel. 802.11b/g/i have 13 available channels, but cross-traffic is a problem. Do not plan to use more than 6 channels in a single airspace.

NETWORK INFRASTRUCTURE DEVICES

Network infrastructure devices comprise those devices that facilitate the movement of data along the communications media. Digital cameras and codecs connect to a digital switch in order to get on the network.

Hubs

The most basic type of network device is a hub. A hub is simply a device with Ethernet connectors that connects all devices together in parallel with no processing. A few hubs have power supplies and provide LEDs to indicate port activity, but do not confuse this with active electronics. Hubs are dumb. Hubs have no ability to control the collisions that naturally occur in Ethernet environments, so when too many devices are connected together on a hub, the network throughput suffers due to delays caused by the collisions. It is inadvisable to use a hub for all but the simplest networks (less than eight devices). Hubs offer no security services. Hubs are OSI level 1 devices. Hubs connect devices.

Switches

A switch is a smart hub. Unlike a hub that presents each signal to all connected devices, a switch is able to read the TCP/IP packet header and direct the signal to the appropriate port(s). Switches are OSI level 2 devices. Switches control where data may go.

Routers

Routers are one step up from switches. In addition to directing the traffic of individual ports, they can in fact make decisions about data that is being presented to them and can decide if that data belongs on that section of the network. Routers can create subnets of the greater network. This allows functions and devices to be segmented into logical groups. Subnets reduce the overall amount of network traffic, making the network operate more efficiently. Subnets can be used to separate different sites, campuses, and buildings and are sometimes even used to separate edge devices from client workstations. Routers control what data may go.

Firewalls

Firewalls are used with routers to deny inappropriate data traffic from another network. Firewalls can be configured in either hardware or software. Security systems that are connected to any other network should be connected through a firewall. Otherwise, a security system is not secure and, thus, the facility will not be secure. Firewalls deny malicious data.

Intrusion Detection Systems

Intrusion detection systems (IDSs) can also be either hardware or software devices. IDSs continuously monitor the traffic into and out of the network to detect any unauthorized attempt to gain access to the network. The IDS will warn the network administrator of the attempt and provide insight into how the attack attempt was executed in order to adjust the firewall to limit future attempts using that method. IDSs warn the system administrator about attempts to probe the network or insert malicious data.

SERVERS

Servers process and store data for use by workstations. For security systems, there are several possible types of servers. These may be combined on a single machine or may be distributed across several physical servers.

Directory Service Server

The directory service is an index for all workstations to use to find the data for which they are searching. It tells them where to find the correct camera, intercom, or archive stream. Additional functions may include Internet information services (IISs), domain name service (DNS), and other network management services.

Archive Service

The archive server stores data for future reference.

Program Service

The program service allows programs to reside on the server rather than on the workstation. This is not recommended because the few dollars saved result in a slower system.

FTP or HTTP Service

This is very useful for remote monitoring and retrieval of data from a remote site to a central monitoring station, for example, or for a manager to "look in" on a site.

E-Mail Service

Servers can send or manage e-mail.

Broadcast Service

Servers can broadcast alerts or alarms to pagers, cell phones, loudspeakers, printers, etc.

Workstations

Workstations provide a human interface to the network. Work-stations can be either single purpose or multiuse, serving other types of programs and other networks. For large sites, it is often best to use single-purpose machines on a dedicated network. Workstations can support many video monitors in order to display digital video, alarm/access control, intercom, report and analysis software, browser, etc. We often design systems that have up to six monitors per workstation. It is also possible to operate more than one workstation with a single keyboard and mouse in order to support more functions than a single work-station can handle. This is often necessary for systems that do not prioritize intercom audio over video.

Printers

Printers can be connected either to a workstation or directly to the network, where they can serve multiple workstations.

Mass Storage

Digital video systems can store a lot of data—much more data than any other type of system. It is not unusual for us to design systems with many terabytes of video storage. This amount of storage cannot be contained in a single server or workstation. There are two ways of extending the storage: network attached storage (NAS) and storage area networks (SANs). The names are so similar that they can be confusing, but the differences are extensive.

NAS units include a processor and many disk or tape drives (or a combination of both). They are typically configured to "look" like a disk drive to the system, and they connect directly to the network, just like a server or a workstation. This means that a large volume of data traffic is on the network to feed the NAS.

A SAN is on its own network in order to separate the vast amount of traffic it generates away from the common network. This is a good idea, even for small systems. SANs can be created easily by adding a second network interface card (NIC) to the archive server and connecting the SAN to that NIC.

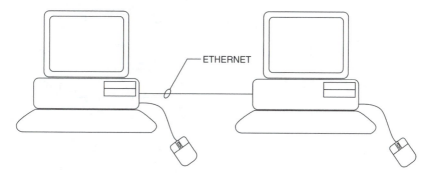

Figure 11-4 Simple network.

NETWORK ARCHITECTURE

Simple Networks

The simplest networks connect two devices together on a cable (Fig. 11-4). Basic networks connect several devices together on a single switch. This creates a local area network (LAN) (Fig. 11-5). From there, tree architecture is common. There may be a single workstation/server (one computer serving both purposes) that is connected through one or more switches to a number of cameras, intercoms, codecs, access control panels, etc. (Fig. 11-6).

Advanced Network Architecture

Backhaul Networks

Beyond simple tree architecture, as network size grows, it is common to create a backhaul network and a client network. This can be achieved in its simplest form with gigabit switches. A simple gigabit switch is equipped with a number of fast Ethernet (100 Mbps) ports to connect edge devices, such as cameras, codecs, intercoms, or access control panels, and a backhaul connection that supports gigabit (100 Mbps) speeds. The result looks like an organization chart in which the server/workstation is at the top on the gigabit backhaul network and the edge

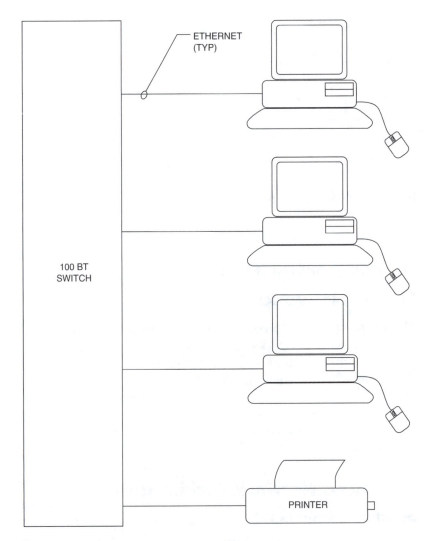

Figure 11-5 Switch connected network.

devices (clients) are on the 100 Mbps ports of the switches (Fig. 11-7).

Subnets

A subnet is basically virtual LAN (VLAN) that is a logical sub-set of the overall LAN. Subnets are used for several reasons, the

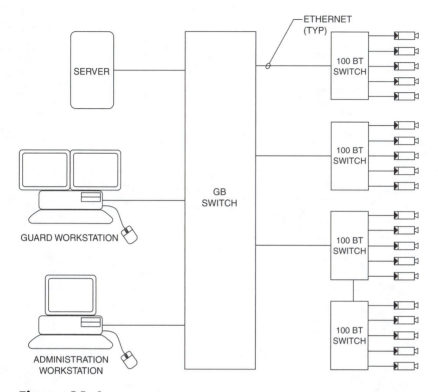

Figure 11-6 Simple tree network.

most common of which are to limit network bandwidth to manageable levels or to minimize traffic that is not appropriate for certain devices, such as segregating buildings on a campus.

Subnets to Limit Network Traffic

As network bandwidth increases, it can task the switches to a point at which they begin to drop packets. I recommend that you do not pipe more than 45% of the rated bandwidth of any device because the rated bandwidths are based on normal network traffic, not streaming data such as video. Stay under 45% and you will not usually experience problems. A VLAN is created by joining two or more networks by routers. Typically, routers are placed on the backhaul network, and they in turn

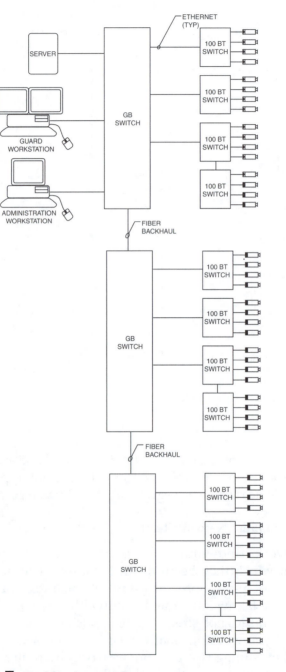

Figure 11-7 Backhaul network.

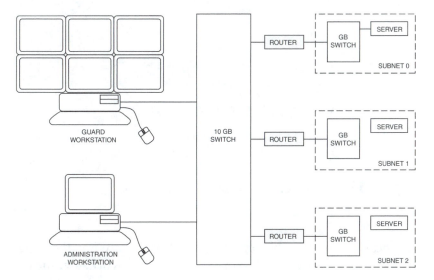

Figure 11-8 Subnet for limiting network traffic.

may have their own backhaul networks that serve many edge devices. Architected thus, no single subnet will have too much traffic on it (Fig. 11-8).

Subnets to Segregate Network Traffic

When a security system serves many buildings on a campus, it is not useful to have the traffic of one building on the network of others. So each building can be joined to the main backhaul network through a router such that its traffic is limited only to data that are relevant to that building alone (Fig. 11-9).

The security system could be placed on the larger organization's network as a subnet. Subnets can be integrated onto a larger network in a way that would seem by their physical connections to be blending the two networks, whereas in fact they operate as completely segregated networks, totally isolated from each other by routers and firewalls. Be advised that enterprise security systems using large amounts of digital video can tax the bandwidth of virtually any organization's business network architecture to the breaking point. It is often advisable to

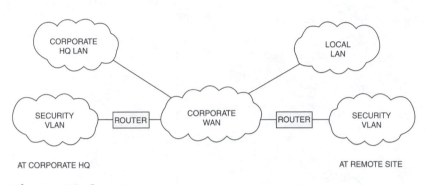

Figure 11-9 Subnet to segregate network traffic.

physically segregate the networks. Additionally, when the security system is placed on the organization's network, significant additional effort is required to secure the security system network from the organization's network, which will never likely be as secure as the security system network, notwithstanding the assertions of the organization's information technology department (Fig. 11-10).

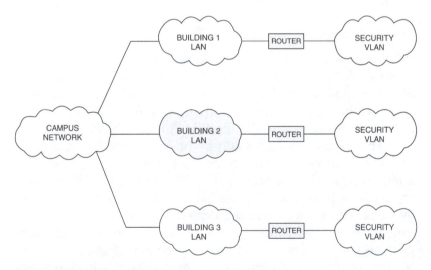

Figure 11-10 Subnet used to blend networks.

VLANs

VLANs are global subnets. Like a subnet, a VLAN segregates a data channel for a specific purpose or group. Unlike a subnet, which is a hierarchical daughter of a physical LAN, a VLAN can coexist across the mother LAN as a VLAN as though there were two separate sets of hardware infrastructure. It does this by operating on a dedicated port to which only the VLAN has privileges. Therefore, cameras, intercoms, and access control system controllers can be plugged into the same managed switch with workstations and printers of the organization's business LAN, and when the security devices' ports are dedicated to a security VLAN, those devices will not be apparent or accessible to the users or the LAN. This is one of the best methods for sharing networks between security and business units.

NETWORK CONFIGURATIONS

A network is composed of a series of TCP/IP devices connected together. There are a variety of ways to do this, and each has its own advantages and limitations.

Peer-to-Peer

The most basic network is a stand-alone peer-to-peer network. Peer-to-peer networks are created by connecting each device together through a hub or switch. Each computer, codec, or access control panel is equal in the eyes of the switch. This is adequate for very small networks (Fig. 11-11).

Client/Server Configuration

As network sizes expand, a client/server configuration is preferred. Major processing is performed in one or more servers, and the human interface is accommodated with client devices or workstations (Fig. 11-12). Cameras, intercoms, access control readers, locks, door position switches, request-to-exit devices, alarm triggering devices, etc. are all human interface devices, as are guard and lobby workstations, intercom master stations, etc.

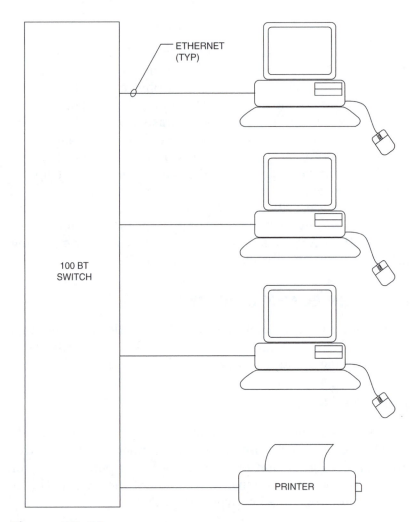

Figure 11-11   Peer-to-peer network.

Typically, the human interface devices are connected to processing devices that interface to the network via TCP/IP connection,
usually Ethernet. These may include codecs and alarm/access
control panels.

On larger networks, it is common to use multiple servers.
Commonly, there will be multiple archive servers. It is also common to use a second set of servers as a backup to the primary

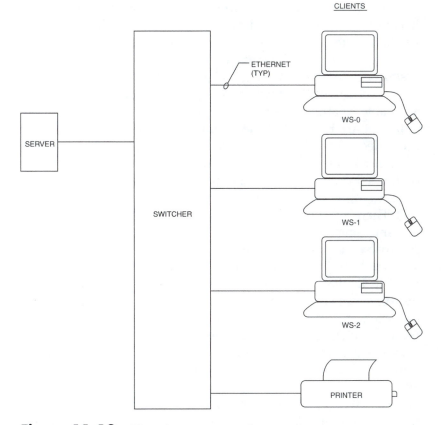

Figure 11-12   Client/server network.

servers in case of a disaster that disables the primary servers. This allows for remote access to the data up to the second of the disaster in order to analyze the event and to provide a business continuity record of all network data.

CREATING NETWORK EFFICIENCIES

One of the major advantages of enterprise security systems is the opportunity for remote monitoring of distant buildings. This often requires blending the security system network with the organization's business network.

The most common requirement is to monitor remote sites. It is not necessary to send all of the data from the monitored site to the site doing the monitoring. The monitoring center only needs to see the data it wants to look at. When you are watching a sports broadcast on TV on channel 11, you do not usually care much about the opera playing on channel 4. Likewise, it is advisable to attach the remote monitoring center only to those data that are relevant at the moment. You do not need to send the video of all the cameras all the time. Using this method, great efficiencies can be gained. Overall network bandwidth can be limited only to the cameras being monitored. I use cameras as an example here because they consume the most bandwidth.

There are two very efficient ways to remotely monitor over a business network: browser and virtual private network (VPN). A browser connection is quick, easy, and does not consume any bandwidth when it is not sending data. It consumes only what it displays. One can configure simple monitoring centers with browser connections to the remotely monitored sites. When one wants to see the site, one makes the connection; otherwise, the connection is closed. However, browser connections consume data even when minimized, whether or not the data is sent to the screen. This will consume both network bandwidth and workstation processing power. So it is advisable to close browsers when not being viewed. Alarms can be sent on a separate data link to alarm monitoring software that is always open. These consume virtually no bandwidth, so they can stay open at all times. Browsers should be run under https rather than http (https is a higher security environment), and secure socket layer encryption is often advisable to ensure the security of the system being monitored. Even so, browsers are not as secure as VPNs. Browser connections can be hacked.

A VPN can open and close like a browser, but it has vast advantages in terms of network security. A VPN is a tunnel between the server being monitored and the server that is requesting its data. That tunnel is firewalled and encrypted. It is as good as gold for security. It takes extremely high skill levels to hack a VPN. The disadvantage of VPNs is that they utilize a fixed bandwidth. When a VPN connection is open, that amount of bandwidth is in use regardless of the number of cameras

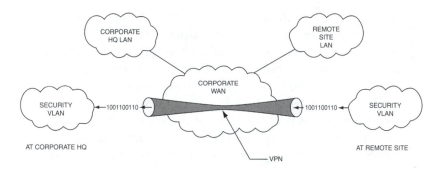

Figure 11-13 Virtual private network.

being monitored. That bandwidth is no longer available for the business network connection to that site (Fig. 11-13).

DIGITAL VIDEO

Cameras and Codecs

Digital video cameras are available in two types: digital cameras or analog cameras with digital codec converters. Digital cameras are an emerging trend. The predominance of cameras available are still analog, and to use them in a digital video system one must add a codec.

Digital cameras do not provide a baseband video output (PAL or NTSC). They are equipped with either a USB or Ethernet connection. They issue digital images directly.

A codec is a device that converts analog to digital. There are a variety of codec types, in the following categories:

- Number of channels: Single-channel codecs support only one camera. Multiple-channel codecs support multiple cameras. Single-channel codecs are the best choice when the wiring infrastructure is predominantly digital, and multiple-channel codecs are a good choice when most of the wiring is analog. Multiple-channel codecs facilitate wiring a number of cameras to a single point where perhaps an analog video switch used to be, its space now being occupied by codecs.

- Number of video data streams: Many codecs output only one data stream per camera. Some support two, which is better. Each data stream can typically be configured to adjust the frame rate and resolution. With two data streams, you can adjust one for live viewing and the second for archiving. You might adjust the live viewing data stream at, for example, 15 frames per second (fps) and at medium resolution and the second stream at 4 fps and high resolution. Generally, it is desirable for archiving retrievals to display higher resolution than for live viewing since you are looking for detail rather than just a transient image.
- Audio/no audio: Some codecs support an audio channel and some do not. The audio channel will be its own separate data stream, usually under the same TCP/IP address.
- Input and output contacts: Many codecs also provide one or more dry-contact inputs and outputs. These are useful to control nearby devices or to cause some activation in the system. For example, it could be used to unlock a door or to cause an alert if a door opens.
- Compression schemes: Different codecs use different compression schemes, which are discussed later.

A basic digital image such as a BMP (bitmap) is composed of a large number of picture elements called pixels, with each pixel having its own data attributes. These images take a lot of data space. It is common for a single BMP image to require several megabits of data. These large files are not useful for network transmission because they use too much network bandwidth. The images can be compressed (made into smaller packets) literally by throwing away useless data.

There are two major types of digital video compression schemes: JPEG and MPEG. JPEG (Joint Photographic Experts Group) is a scheme that results in a series of fixed images, strung together like a movie. MPEG (Moving Pictures Experts Group) is a similar group that from its inception created compression algorithms specifically meant for moving pictures.

- MPEG-1 was the earliest format and produced video CDs and MP3 audio.

- MPEG-2 is the standard on which digital television set-top boxes and DVDs are based. This is very high-quality video.
- MPEG-3 (MP3) is an audio codec.
- MPEG-4 is the standard for multimedia for the fixed and mobile web.
- There are also MPEG-7 and MPEG-21, which are for future projects.

Digital video security codecs and cameras are typically either MJPEG (a series of JPEG images strung together as a stream of data) or MPEG-4.

BMP images are resolution dependent. That is, there is one piece of data for each separate pixel.

JPEG compression basically replicates similar data rather than storing it. For example, if there were a picture of a flag, the red portion might only be stored in a single pixel, but there will be a note to replicate the red pixel everywhere it existed in its original BMP file. This can achieve very high compression compared to BMP files.

MPEG compression takes this process one step further. For a sequence of images, the first one is stored as a JPEG image, and each subsequent image stores only the differences between itself and the previous image. The first frame is called an "I-frame", and subsequent frames are called "P-frames." When too much updating is occurring, the process stores a new I-frame and starts the process all over again. The MPEG protocol results in very efficient file compression.

Advantages and Disadvantages

Each JPEG image is a new fresh image. This is very useful where the frame rate must be very low, such as on an offshore oil platform with a very low bandwidth satellite uplink, or where only a dial-up modem connection is available for network connectivity. I used JPEG on an offshore platform with only a 64 kb/s satellite connection available. MPEG is most useful where there is adequate data bandwidth available for a fast-moving image but where it is desirable to conserve network resources for future growth and for network stability.

DIGITAL RESOLUTION

Digital image resolution is the bugaboo of digital video. You can never have enough resolution. However, high resolution comes at a high price in network bandwidth usage and in hard disk storage space. There is always a trade-off between resolution and bandwidth/storage space. Thankfully, the cost of storage keeps dropping (I think we will soon see terabyte hard drives blister-packed for 99 cents), but I think that network bandwidth will always be a problem.

JPEG resolution is measured in pixels per inch (PPI). Proper resolution is required for good viewing. Ideally, you should be displaying one pixel of video image onto each pixel on the video monitor. If you display a JPEG image at a greater size on paper or screen than its native resolution, you will see a very fuzzy image (Fig. 11-14). Common file sizes are from 120×160 to 720×480. Larger sizes are available with even higher resolution.

MPEG resolution is measured in CIF (Common Intermediate Format). In NTSC, CIF provides 352×240 pixels. In PAL, it provides 352×288 pixels. The lowest resolution MPEG image is a quarter CIF (QCIF) at 176×120 pixels, followed by CIF, 2CIF (704×240, NTSC) and (704×288, PAL), and finally 4CIF

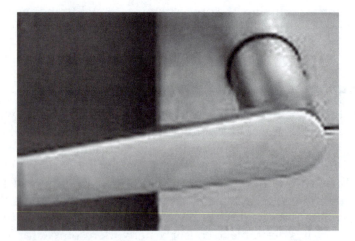

Figure 11-14 Fuzzy JPG image.

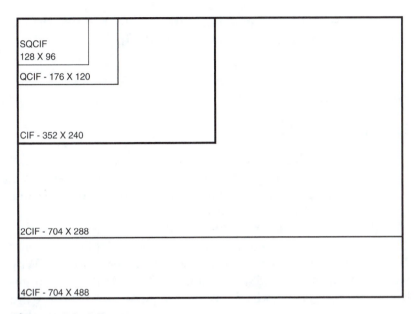

Figure 11-15 MPEG resolutions.

(704 × 480, NTSC) and (704 × 576, PAL). 16CIF will soon be available with very high resolution (1408 × 1152 for both formats), and there is also an amazingly low-resolution SQCIF (128 × 96, NTSC). Most digital codecs provide CIF, 2CIF, and sometimes 4CIF resolutions (Fig. 11-15).

FRAME RATES

In order to see moving images, they have to move. Frame rate is the rate at which one frame of video is replaced by another. The speed at which this occurs is measured in frames per second (fps). Some unique applications result in very slow frame rates of seconds per frame.

The human eye can visualize real-time motion as low as 12 or 13 fps. A minimum frame rate of 15 fps is recommended for real-time images. Many users prefer 30 fps because that is what is displayed on analog video. However, that frame rate is not required unless objects are moving rapidly.

Like resolution, frame rates affect both bandwidth and storage capacity, in direct proportion to the fps.

DISPLAY ISSUES

Display Parity

One of the problems that the security industry has not dealt with is that of display parity. Display parity is achieved when the number of pixels being sent to a screen is exactly the same as the number of pixels on the screen.

If one is displaying nine cameras in a window on a 20-in. LCD high-resolution screen, one might have only 160×120 pixels available on the screen for each image. Why would one want to send a 4CIF image (704×480) to that number of pixels? Why indeed? What happens to all those extra pixels? They are wasted, thrown away. The problem is that they are thrown away on the screen. They occupy tons (if that is a measure of screen processing) of central processing unit (CPU) and video card processing power before it gets thrown away on the LCD monitor.

No problem you say? Who cares? You do, if you are smart. Here is the problem. A 4CIF image generates 337,920 pixels. Each individual pixel requires a lot of CPU processing power and many more graphics processing units (GPUs). Both CPU and GPU are consumed for each pixel. The original supercomputer, the Cray-1 developed at Los Alamos National Laboratory in 1976, was capable of 80 megaflops of processing power. (Flops is a unit of CPU or video card processing effort; it is an abbreviation of floating point operations per second.) Although there is not a direct correlation between flops and pixel processing (there are approximately 40 variables involved in the calculation, making a calculation essentially meaningless), you can rely on the fact that it takes a lot of processing power to process video to the screen or to archive. At 30 fps, the computer is processing 10,137,600 pixels (10.1 megapixels) for each image at 30 fps. Remember, we were displaying 9 images. That calculates to 91.2 megapixels per second, and that is just for the video. You are also running the video application, and on larger systems you are also processing audio for the intercom, alarm/access control, and perhaps other data. One can easily exceed 100 megapixels being processed per screen on one's desktop. For 16 images, at 30 fps at 4CIF the number exceeds 160 megapixels being processed in real time, and that is just on one screen. That will crash virtually any workstation regardless of processing power. High-resolution times high frame rate times many images can easily equal a computer crash. Additionally, pixels thrown away on the screen present a rough look to the images. Without a doubt, display parity results in the best appearance.

The ideal process here is to have software in the server that disposes of unneeded pixels before they are sent to the workstation. This approach of prerendering the video image has many advantages in quality of display and network throughput. However, to date, no software vendor that we know of is even thinking about this problem.

So what is a designer to do? Well, there are only three variables available to manage this problem: image resolution, frame rate, and processing power.

First, there is little need to display images at 4CIF or greater unless one is displaying at full screen. It is better to send live images to the screen at 2CIF because the extra pixels will just be thrown away and no good will be served by the extra resolution that is consuming unneeded network bandwidth and processing power.

Second, archived images do not usually need to be displayed at 15 or 30 fps. Use a slower speed and higher resolution for archived video. When one calls up archived video, one is usually interested in seeing as much detail in the image as possible. Use higher resolution and lower frame rate. There are a few applications in which this is not appropriate, such as for casino environments, where fast-moving hands hold the secret to cheating.

Finally, I usually design systems with lots of processing power, typically dual Xeon™ computers as workstations. Dual-core processors better that. Expected advances will put teraflops of graphics processing power at hand.

Storage Issues

As with display, storage consumes lots of data and processing power. Unless there is a compelling reason otherwise, it is best to store data at a slower frame rate than for live viewing. This not only saves disk and tape space but also helps ensure growth capacity.

MANAGING DATA SYSTEMS THROUGHPUT

Network throughput management requires math, sometimes lots of math, but it is a good investment. I do not recommend running any network or network segment beyond 45% of its rated capacity. If there is a segment that has a capacity of 100 Mbps, keep traffic to 45 Mbps. If it is a gigabit backhaul segment, keep the traffic to 450 Mbps. If you have to exceed 450 Mbps, it is better to use multiple gigabit communications paths or a 10 gigabit path. Your client will not likely understand, but he or she will not sue you either.

There are two ways of managing network throughput: more capacity and network segmentation. The cost/benefit is usually in favor of network segmentation.

By segmenting the network into subnets or VLANs, one can manage the traffic to manageable levels. All traffic does not have to be everywhere. By recording video remotely rather than centrally, traffic is diminished. If a backup is needed, or if there is a concern about the loss of data in remote storage, centralized recording is possible at far greater cost in network traffic and infrastructure cost. An alternative is "neighborhood" archiving, where a few sites are gathered together for storage, limiting traffic on the enterprise network.

SYSTEM ARCHITECTURE

Servers

Servers provide the guidance and direction for the entire system and store its activities and history. A server can operate several applications simultaneously, and a server equipped with a dual-core CPU can also prioritize those services, ensuring that, for example, intercom calls always go through. Servers provide several basic services.

Directory Service

The directory service provides the routing information to locate cameras, intercoms, and archived video on demand. It also maintains the necessary information for all system devices to communicate effectively.

Directory services can be local or global. In an enterprise integrated security system, the directory service may be both, with a global directory service centrally controlled, and local servers may maintain their own subordinate automatic fail-over directory services in case of loss of communications with the global directory server.

Enterprise integrated security systems also typically use an automatic fail-over server that runs parallel to the main server but in another location, ready to take over its activities immediately upon a failure of the main server.

Archiving Data

The server will typically archive alarm/access control, video, and intercom activity, indexing it by date and time and often correlating video and voice data to alarm and security events so that the operator has immediate access to appropriate video and voice as he or she views alarm activity. Enterprise systems also typically use an automatic fail-over archive server.

Remote Access Services

Web Access

A VPN helps ensure data integrity for offsite Web service connections. Remote access from within the domain is often accommodated by use of a VLAN.

E-mail and Pager Notification Service

The server software may support e-mail and pager notification. These will require exchange server or similar software or a dial-up or Web connection for a pager.

Hardware Configurations

CPUs

Generally, it is appropriate to specify the fastest or nearly fastest CPU available for the server with significant cache memory and a very fast front side buss.

Memory

More is better. At least 2 GB of RAM should be considered in 2007 era terms. As this book ages, more memory should be considered. Fill the thing to capacity. You will not regret it, and memory is almost cheaper than candy bars.

Disk Storage

Operating Systems and Programs

All system servers should be equipped with multiple disks, including two mirrored automatic fail-over drives for operating systems and programs, complete with current configurations. These should be kept up to date so if one fails, the other takes over immediately. This is also less expensive than a full hot redundant off-site fail-over server and should be done even when a redundant server is used.

Additional disk slots should be dedicated to data archive up to the server's capacity. Disks are so inexpensive that it is almost always appropriate to specify the largest disks available. RAID-5 should be considered, configured to 500 GB segments for rapid searching of archived data.

Where additional disk capacity is necessary, external storage capacity should be considered. There are two methods of external storage.

Tape or Disk

External storage is available in both tape and disk. It is generally recommended to use both. Disks can store up to a given time depth. Beyond that, you can store endlessly on tape. For very large storage requirements, a tape carousel automatically handles the process of keeping fresh tapes loaded and used tapes stored, ready for use. The carousel can be expanded to store as much or as little as is appropriate based on network archive usage and the length of time storage is desired.

Network Attached Storage

Network attached storage is external storage that is attached directly to the server switch. This is the least expensive option, but it has a negative effect on network throughput. Accordingly, I do not recommend NAS.

Storage Area Network

A SAN is a separate network on the backside of the server that is dedicated only to moving storage data between servers and the external storage media. There is a perception that SANs are unnecessarily expensive, but this does not necessarily have to be so. A SAN can be created simply by placing an additional NIC in the server and porting archive data out the back to the external storage. Where multiple servers or multiple external storage units are required, a SAN switch handles the task. SANs make the best use of the primary data network over which live data are flowing. They place virtually no additional burden on the live data network, conserving its spare capacity for system growth. SANs are always recommended for external storage, even if there is only one server and one external storage unit.

Workstations

A workstation is a computer used by a person who operates the system. There are a variety of basic workstation types.

Security Monitoring (Command) Workstations

Security command workstations are used in security command centers, typically in enterprise security systems. A security command center typically includes two or more security command workstations and may include an array of large-screen video monitors to support the joint viewing of images by operators at several consoles. These workstations typically include alarm/access control/digital video and security intercoms as well as report writing programs.

Guard or Lobby Desk Workstations

A guard or lobby desk workstation is a single computer dedicated to supporting a guard's desk duties in a lobby. These may include alarm/access control, digital video, and intercom.

Administrative Workstations

An administrative work station supports management of an integrated security system, including system configuration, database management, and reports.

Photo ID Workstations

Photo ID workstations are used to create identification badges for use with the access control system. A photo ID workstation typically includes a camera, backdrop, light source, sitting chair, digital camera, and workstation and may include a posing monitor to help the subject pose to his or her satisfaction. On larger systems, there may be several photo ID workstations in a single area.

Access Verification Workstations

On high-security installations, an access verification workstation may be used in conjunction with a man-trap and card reader to ensure that the person passing into a secure area is indeed who he or she claims to be and that his or her credential is valid for the secure area. The access verification workstation displays a photo of the cardholder each time a card is presented. This allows a guard at the workstation to verify that the face is that of the valid cardholder.

Edge Devices

Edge devices include cameras, intercoms, card readers, alarm detection devices, electrified door locks, and request-to-exit detectors. These are the devices that interface with the user. On a typical integrated security system, the edge device connects with a data controller or codec, which converts its native signal (audio/video, dry contact, or data) to a uniform TCP/IP standard. Thus, controllers and codecs are also edge devices. The edge devices typically connect to the system through a data switch.

Infrastructure Devices

Between edge devices and servers/workstations is the digital infrastructure, which connects the system together and manages its communications rules.

Switches

Digital switches are the connection points for almost all system devices. A digital switch is a device that not only provides a connection point but also can manage how each device communicates with the system. A digital switch is like a mail carrier on a mail route, who ensures that each house gets the mail that is addressed to it for the neighborhood it serves.

Switches can segregate communications between devices and manage the priority and limit the bandwidth of the data of different devices. Switches generally have a number of RJ-45 eight-conductor modular jacks (typically 8–48) and can cascade communications in either a ring or tree architecture. The switch must be specified to support the amount of data that is expected to go into its edge ports and out of its infrastructure ports. It is wise not to exceed more than 45% of the rated capacity of any switch for all signals combined, under worst-case conditions. Switches are OSI layer 2 devices, but better switches can also perform OSI layer 3 management functions. These are commonly called "managed" switches. Switches should be able to support IGMP querying and IGMP snooping in order to support video multicast. Ample memory is recommended (at least 100 KB per port), and the switch should be able to support VLAN operation. If the switch may need to become part of a trunk within a VLAN, then it should also be able to support 802.1Q protocol. For outdoor operation, a robust environmental tolerance is needed. The switch should be able to operate from well below freezing (−10°F/−23°C) to high temperatures (160°F/70°C is ideal). These are commonly called "hardened" switches. Redundant power supplies are also recommended.

Routers

Routers manage data traffic at a more global level. Routers are OSI level 3 devices. An edge router is like a local post office that routes mail from one locale to another, where it will be handed off to the neighborhood postal worker (the switch). A router that manages traffic for an entire organization to the Internet is called a core router.

Routers are capable of segregating traffic into subnets and VLANs, creating logical separations of data and making communications within the network much more efficient and secure.

Firewalls

A network firewall is a computing device that is designed to prevent communications from and to some devices in support of an organization's network security policy.

Wireless Nodes

Wireless nodes are radio frequency transceivers that support network communications. Often, they also incorporate network switches, and sometimes they can incorporate routers and even firewalls. They also commonly encrypt data placed on the wireless link.

Network Communications Speeds

There are four common speeds of network communications:

- 10Base-T: 10 Mbps
- 100Base-T: 100 Mbps
- 1000Base-T: 1 Gbps
- 10,000Base-T: 10 Gbps

Cabling

Network cabling can be either wired or fiber optic. Fiber-optic cabling types include single mode and multimode.

Wired Cabling

Category 5e and 6 cables are used for network cabling. Both have a native distance limit of 300 ft. Cat5e and Cat6 cables can support 10Base-T, 100Base-T, and 1000Base-T connections, with distance decreasing as the speed increases.

Fiber Optic

Fiber-optic cabling can support faster speeds, longer distances, and simultaneous communications. Unlike wired cable, fiber only supports a single communication on a single frequency at one time.

Multimode

Multimode fiber uses inexpensive LEDs operating at either 850 or 1500 nm to transmit data. Multimode fiber is made of inexpensive plastic. In multimode fiber, the light propagates through the fiber core, bouncing off its edges (thus multimode). Multimode fiber can support only one communication at a time on each frequency. Typically, two fibers are used together, one to transmit and one to receive.

Single Mode

Single-mode fiber uses more expensive lasers and optical glass. Single-mode communication is right down the center of the glass fiber, never bouncing (thus single mode). Single-mode fiber can stand higher power and thus yields longer distances.

Scaling Designs

Systems can be scaled by creating subnets, which can segregate the system based on function or location. This approach allows the master system to have oversight and observation of the activities of all of its subsystems while not allowing the subsystems to see or affect each other.

INTERFACING TO OTHER ENTERPRISE INFORMATION TECHNOLOGY SYSTEMS

Enterprise LAN or Wide Area Network

The fundamental interface of the integrated security system is to the organization's enterprise LAN or wide area network (WAN). The recommended interface is to configure the enterprise security system as a VLAN on the enterprise LAN/WAN.

Remote monitoring from inside the enterprise LAN can be accomplished by placing the monitoring computer on the VLAN. If the monitoring computer must also be used on the business network, it should be equipped with two NICs to better segregate the VLAN from the LAN.

Remote monitoring over the Internet should be accomplished by use of a VPN.

Process Control Networks

Integrated security systems are classified as process control networks. A process control network differs from a business network in that it is a closed network, dedicated to a special purpose, and is segregated from the business network. The integrated security system may integrate with other types of process control networks, including building automation systems, elevators, telephony systems, fire alarm systems, parking management systems, and vending systems.

Building Automation Systems

Building automation systems (BASs) include controls for heating, ventilation and air conditioning, lighting, signage and irrigation control, and the control of other building systems. BASs may interface to the integrated security system via either RS-232 or TCP/IP. The common interface language is ASCII delimited files, although sometimes database integration is possible.

Elevators/Lifts

There is often good reason to integrate security systems with the elevator system of a building. This interface permits the control of who goes to what floor on which elevator at what time. Additionally, it is common to place video cameras and intercoms within elevators.

There are two basic types of elevators: traction and hydraulic. Traction elevators are used in high-rise buildings, and hydraulic elevators are commonly used in low-rise buildings and parking structures.

Access Control Interfaces

There are two common types of elevator access control interfaces: floor-by-floor control and hall call control. Hall call control simply enables or disables the hall call pushbuttons in the elevator lobby. Floor-by-floor control allows control over the selection of individual floors in each car for each cardholder. Floor-by-floor control components include a card reader in the elevator and an access control system controller that enables or disables each floor select button based on the authorizations for the individual card presented to the reader in the car.

More sophisticated floor-by-floor access control systems provide an indication of which floors the card can select by turning off the button lights to floor select buttons for which the cardholder is not valid and may also keep a record of which floor was actually selected. Today, those functions are handled in the programming of the elevator controller. For older elevators, as was done in the past, those functions can be accomplished with elegant relay logic programming.

Elevator control mechanisms affect the design of the elevator access control system. There are three common types: automated, relay, and on-the-car control. These are covered in detail elsewhere in this book.

Video cameras can be interfaced up the hoistway by using coax, ribbon cable, laser, or radio frequency methods.

Intercoms can be either the direct ring-down type or dedicated intercom type. They must ring to a location that will always be answered and must never be unmanned, even for a few minutes.

Private Automatic Branch Exchange Interfaces

Private automatic branch exchange (PABX) systems facilitate the connection of a number of analog or digital station sets to a central switch. The PABX switch will accommodate a number of central office telephone lines (from a couple to hundreds) and a number of telephone station sets (from six to thousands). The PABX switch routes incoming calls to the correct extension and routes outgoing calls to an available central office line.

Additional features of PABX switches may include direct inward dialing so that certain extensions can be dialed directly from the outside without going through the switch, an automated attendant, call waiting, voice mail, and many other unique features. Internal intercom functions are usually standard.

Station sets may be simple or complicated. Simple station sets may look like a home phone, whereas more complicated sets may display time/date, incoming caller ID, and the set may have many speed-dial buttons and may also show the line status of frequently called internal numbers. An operator's station set may display the status of every extension in the system either by a field of lamps and select buttons or in software.

PABX systems are normally controlled by a dedicated computer located in the main telephone closet. PABX systems are capable of sophisticated interfaces to other systems, including security systems.

The security designer can use the PABX system as a security intercom system by utilizing door stations in lieu of standard station sets (depending on the manufacturer and model of the PABX system).

For almost every installation, it is important for the security console to be equipped with a direct central office telephone that is not routed through the PABX switch. This serves as an emergency communication link in case of total power or equipment failure.

Voice over IP Systems

PABX switch systems are rapidly being replaced by Voice over IP (VoIP) systems. VoIP systems do not rely on central office telephone lines for their connection to the telephone company. Rather, they utilize the Internet for that connection.

The telephone station sets may be either conventional station sets with a VoIP converter or network devices.

VoIP phone systems are extremely flexible since all of their functions operate in software. However, they suffer from two major potential problems relating to the security of the organization they serve. VoIP systems are subject to Internet outages, which are much more common than central office line outages that operate on battery power from the central office. With central office lines, if electrical power fails, it is likely that the telephone lines will still work. This is not the case with VoIP phones. Additionally, VoIP phone systems are subject to intrusion by skilled hackers, making communications on a VoIP phone extremely unsecure.

VoIP phones are a natural for integration with other systems, although those interfaces have yet to be developed by the industry.

VoIP systems should easily accommodate integration with IP-based security intercoms and with pagers. Digital two-way radios are also a natural point of integration. I expect to see such integration before the first revision of this book.

Fire Alarm Systems

Fire alarm systems are among the oldest of process control networks used in commercial buildings. These typically have their own proprietary infrastructure that may be unique to the manufacturer. However, they often interface to other systems by means of either RS-232 serial data streams or TCP/IP Ethernet. Typically, the interface is an ASCII delimited data stream that identifies the change of state of a fire alarm zone. Occasionally, a designer may see access to a database that displays real-time status of all points in the system.

Public Address Systems

Public address systems can be configured with either an analog or a digital infrastructure. The interface to a public address system will always be a one-way audio signal from the security system to the public address system for paging purposes.

Typically, the interface between the systems includes both an audio signal and a zone selection, plus a push-to-talk momentary trigger. The interface may be either analog or digital. Typically, analog interfaces are used on smaller public address systems, and larger systems may receive either an analog or a digital interface for the audio stream.

Analog interfaces employ a microphone or line level input to the paging system and one or more dry-contact inputs to select one or more zones. Often, it is possible to select groups of zones or an "All Call" selection, in which all zones will be paged.

Digital interfaces employ a digitized audio feed and a data string that performs the zone selection. On larger systems, both analog and digital, multiple public address amplifiers may be used to support different areas of a building or different buildings on a campus. In such cases, the zone selections employ a hierarchical zone selection, in which one string may select the building, another selects the amplifier, and still another selects the zone on the amplifier.

We have also used the alarm/access control system to perform zone selections, controlling a single audio buss. This is an effective way to make a simple public address system operate like a very expensive one.

Parking Control Systems

Parking control systems perform a number of functions:

- Allow vehicles into a parking structure (car park) or parking lot
- Direct cars within a parking structure to one area or another
- Meter the number of cars in the structure
- Display up/down count signage of available spaces to drivers of cars entering
- Produce tickets for cash transactions
- Read the tickets and facilitate cash transactions for parking
- Use buried vehicle sensing loops to verify the presence of a car at a card reader or in the path of a barrier gate, or to notify the gate that it can close after a car has passed through
- Access control systems interface with parking systems to facilitate the entry of cars to the parking area
- Access control readers may simply provide a dry-contact closure to notify the gate to open

The parking system may also feed back a dry-contact signal that causes the card reader to refuse to read cars if the parking area is full. Access control card readers may be short range (6 in.) or long range (3 ft), or they may be overhead vehicle tag readers that do not require the driver to roll down the window.

The access control system may also be integrated with the parking monthly cash control system such that the card is enabled or disabled based on payment of a monthly fee. The card readers may also permit special privileged parking for handicapped, expectant mothers, high-rent tenants, high-level executives, etc.

Vending Access Management Systems

Vending access management systems are a variation of access control systems that are interfaced with a product vending system to provide product in kind for a prepayment or a charge account. In effect, the access control system is used like a credit or debit card.

Vending systems may include fuel management and vending machines, or the card may be used at a school bookstore, etc. This requires a database interface between the access control system and the vending system such that the vending system has daily status on the validity of the card and it keeps a running database of credits and debits.

More Protocol Factors

Wired and wireless digital security systems both use unicast and multicast protocols to communicate. Unicast protocols, commonly TCP/IP, are meant to communicate a signal from one device to another device. They ensure that the communication occurs by verifying the receipt of every packet of data. Unicast protocol is commonly used for pure data, such as alarm and access control data. Most networks are inherently based on TCP/IP protocol.

Multicast protocols such as UDP/IP and RTP/IP are used to broadcast data to any number of receiving devices. Unlike unicast TCP data, if a packet is not received, there is no mechanism or attempt to verify that and resend the packet. Multicast is widely used for video and audio data.

Do not confuse multicast protocol with multipath. Multipath is the phenomenon caused by radio frequency reflections, and multicast is the distribution of a single digital signal to more than one destination using a single signal to which each receiving device signs up on a subscription.

Multicast can both reduce and increase network traffic, depending on how the network is configured. Multicast can reduce network traffic because there is no attempt to resend data. It is sent only once. Especially for radio frequency and satellite systems, where latency (circuit delays) can be a factor, the receiving computer can make many requests for unreceived packets. This has the effect of increasing data traffic for no good purpose because the video frame or audio signal cannot be received in time to be useful, having already been displayed or heard.

However, because multicast transmits to any device that will listen, it is important to configure the network to adapt to multicast protocol so that devices that do not need to process the data will not hear it. Otherwise, many devices are kept busy trying to process data that is of no use to them. On security systems, some devices have a capability of only 10Base-T (10 Mbps). Their input can be swamped by the signals of only a few video cameras, rendering them incapable of communicating. The effect is similar to a denial-of-service attack on a Web site, where it is flooded with unwanted traffic, bringing it down.

It is important to understand that multicast was designed for an entirely different application than to support distributed video cameras. Multicast was designed to support a single source transmitting data to many destination devices. In video systems, there are many sources (cameras and intercoms) transmitting to a few destination devices (servers and workstations). This difference can have unintended consequences for the uninitiated. For example, in conventional multicast environments, the "edge" switches (those at the outermost devices) do not have to be managed switches. However, in distributed digital video systems, the outermost switches should be managed because when multicast touches a device that cannot handle multicast protocol, that device broadcasts a return message for each packet it sees, often bringing down the entire network. When managed edge switches are used, however, each individual port can be set up with IGMP snooping to prevent multicast signals from getting to unicast devices (e.g., alarm/access control system panels).

Multicast Anomalies

Additionally, be advised that multicast traffic can have unanticipated side effects even on systems that are properly configured for it. For example, adding a set of mirrored backup archive servers to a security system requires the system to operate in multicast mode since both the primary and the backup servers are receiving the data of all digital cameras at all times. On a typically configured digital video system, this can result in directing 200 Mbps of data traffic across the backhaul network to the backup servers. It is a little known fact that multicast data traffic can have an adverse effect on intercom codecs. I was once confronted with an enterprise security system that exhibited audio distortion in its intercoms when the backup servers were turned on. The additional data traffic was enough to cause the intercom talk codecs to distort the audio only when the archive servers were turned on (changing the system from unicast to multicast for all video signals). By reducing the volume setting of the talk intercoms, the "clipping" of audio signals was eliminated. This condition is especially obvious where audio converters are used to convert two-wire intercoms to four-wire for use with conventional audio codecs because the two-/four-wire converter also inserts an additional volume control in series in the circuit.

Multicast is a very "user surly" environment. Multicast is especially not friendly to radio traffic and should not be used on such by the unsophisticated designer. Many configuration settings are required to operate multicast on a wireless mesh network (discussed in Chapter 12) to ensure that the radios do not retransmit the multicast traffic endlessly, thus flooding the mesh with unnecessary traffic.

It is ideal to configure the digital video network into two distinct VLANs, where VLAN1 is the camera-to-server network and VLAN2 is the server-to-workstation network. Run VLAN1 (the cameras) in unicast and VLAN2 (clients) in multicast. Configure IGMP querying on a primary and backup core switch, and configure all switches to support IGMP snooping to ensure that no unicast devices retransmit multicast signals. IGMP querying asks which switch ports want to sign up for multicast signals, and IGMP snooping sends those signals only to those ports. Utilize managed switches to ensure IGMP conformance.

SUMMARY

Understanding information technology infrastructure is the basis for a successful integrated security system design. The reader should carefully read and understand this chapter in order to succeed as a designer.

The TCP/IP suite of protocols is the basis for information technology networked systems. This chapter provides a detailed description of how TCP/IP works. The designer will not achieve success without a comprehensive understanding of TCP/IP.

TCP/IP operates on levels 3 and 4 of the OSI networking model. Data is encapsulated from the application program through the seven layers down to the network wire, sent across the network, and then decapsulated back up the seven layers to the application on the other end.

TCP protocol is able to fix bad communications. Other protocols in the TCP/IP family include UDP and RTP, which do not fix bad communications but which are better suited for streaming data, such as video and audio.

TCP/IP is also an addressing scheme. Each network connected device is assigned a TCP/IP address that identifies its location on the network. Addresses can be assigned either automatically or manually.

Common wiring schemes include Ethernet and fiber-optic cables. Ethernet is available on Cat 5, Cat 5E, and Cat 6 cable at speeds of 10, 100, and 1000 Mbps or 10Base-T, 100Base-T, or 1000Base-T (gigabit Ethernet). Fiber-optic runs can be on either single-mode or multimode fiber. Single-mode fiber can carry more data farther. Multimode cable and transducers are less expensive. Gigabit switches are often available with fiber connectors to link switches together over long distances, and RJ-45 connectors are used for short runs of Ethernet cables to local devices.

Edge devices include IP video cameras, IP intercoms, and codecs. Network infrastructure and wiring is connected using hubs, switches, routers, and firewalls. Hubs are rarely used today because they simply connect wires together and do nothing to handle network contention. Switches handle the connection of local devices. Routers control where network communications can go. Firewalls exclude unauthorized devices from gaining access to the network. Intrusion detection systems monitor the network firewall to detect any attempt to intrude into the network.

Integrated security system network computers include servers and workstations. Servers can include directory service servers (Windows directory service), Internet information services, domain name service, and other network management services. Other services may include archiving, application program service, ftp, http, e-mail, and broadcast services. Workstations provide the interface between users and the network. Printers and mass storage systems round out the network attached devices. Mass storage systems include network attached storage and storage area networks.

Network architecture includes simple networks, local area networks, and wide area networks. Advanced network architecture includes backhaul networks, subnets, and virtual LANs. Network connection types include peer-to-peer and client/server configurations. Systems can be monitored remotely and safely using browser (http) or virtual private networks. Digital cameras can link directly to the network, whereas analog video cameras require a codec interface.

Typical video compression schemes include MJPEG, MPEG-2, and MPEG-4. MJPEG is a stream of individual images strung together to show movement, whereas MPEG schemes display a single image and then update subsequent frames only with the changes in the image.

Workstation types include security monitoring centers, guard or lobby desk workstations, administrative workstations, photo ID workstations, and access verification workstations.

Integrated security systems can interface to many other types of systems, including process control networks, building automation systems, elevators, PABXs, VoIP systems, fire alarm systems, public address systems, parking control systems, and vending systems.

Multicast protocol is sometimes used in digital video systems, but it is fraught with many nuances requiring special skills and knowledge. I recommend a thorough understanding before implementing multicast protocol.

CHAPTER NOTES

1. www.lewistech.com/rlewis/Resources/JamesBondOSI2.aspx.
2. *TCP/IP Foundations* is no longer available, but references to it still exist on a number of Internet web pages, most notably on www.wikipedia.com under the search string "OSI model".
3. The Institute of Electrical and Electronics Engineers (IEEE) is the world's leading professional association for the advancement of technology.

4. *1000Base-T Gigabit Ethernet Tutorial*, Hewlett-Packard, September 15, 2000. Available at http://docs.hp.com/en/784/copper_final.pdf.
5. A waveguide is a structure that guides very high-frequency radio waves (radar, microwave, etc.) down a tube from a transmitter to an antenna or from a receiving antenna to a receiver. Above normal radio frequencies, conventional wires are useless for carrying the signal because of the "skin effect." The skin effect is an effect of physics that results in radio waves traveling increasingly closer to the outside of a conductor as the frequency rises, eventually losing connection with the conductor altogether. Above that frequency, a waveguide must be used to contain the transmission because normal wiring is unusable. The low-frequency cut-off of a waveguide is half of the wavelength of the frequency being passed. Generally, waveguides are useful above 1 GHz.
6. American Fibertek 47-LX series 1000Base-LX Ethernet Fiber Optic Media Converter uses a single multimode fiber and transmits and receives on two frequencies (1310 and 1550 nm). This company also makes a 100Base-LX converter "45-LX series." Both units use a laser to transmit and receive on a single multimode fiber. This company also makes LED two-fiber single-mode and multimode solutions, as do many other firms.
7. Cisco Gigabit Interface Converter 1000Base-ZX GBIC media converter using premium single-mode fiber or dispersion shifted single-mode fiber.
8. *Telecommunication Essentials: The Complete Global Source for Communications Fundamentals, Data Networking and the Internet, and Next Generation Networks*, by Lillian Goleniewski. Addison-Wesley, December 2001.
9. For example, FibroLAN TX/FX H.COM 10/100 provides 100Base-T speeds up to 93 miles (150 km) over single mode or multimode. Their GSM1000 and GSM1010 provide gigabit speeds up to 75 miles (120 km) over single mode or multimode. Prices vary from a few hundred to a few thousand dollars, depending on the range required and the required data speed.

12

Radio Frequency Systems

BASIC RADIO FREQUENCY THEORY

Radio frequency (RF) systems are never as reliable as wired systems, but they are nonetheless useful when wired alternatives are too costly and total quality of service is not required.

FREQUENCIES AND TRANSMISSION SCHEMES

Frequencies

Analog AM and FM Frequencies

There have been a variety of different types of RF methods used for security systems throughout the years. Common analog communications have included both AM and FM communications at a variety of frequencies from low kilohertz to gigahertz.

Digital Frequencies

Common frequencies include 900 MHz, 2.4 GHz, 4.9 GHz (public safety), and 5 GHz.

Range

Transmitters and receivers are available at 5.0, 5.8, and 5.2 GHz.

Other Frequencies

Other less used devices operate at 8 GHz, 20 GHz, and as low as 108 MHz.

Transmission Schemes

Analog

Analog video and audio can be transmitted across many frequencies, from AM and FM to more than 20 GHz.

Digital

Spread Spectrum Systems

The idea for spread spectrum was conceived by actress Hedy Lamar in 1940. Married to a defense mogul, she thought of a way to eliminate surface ships from jamming the radio transmissions of submarines while playing four-handed piano. She envisioned a transmitter that could send its signal on numerous frequencies and that would hop around the frequencies like her and her partner's hands on the piano and be received by a group of receivers that could demultiplex the signal. The idea was patented by her and an engineer in the early 1950s and was immediately put into use by the U.S. Navy.

Today, spread spectrum is a means of transmitting noiselike radio signals that are very difficult to disrupt or interpret or interrupt, providing a reliable means of digital communications for data systems. The most common version of spread spectrum radio is the 802.11a/g/i transceiver.

Wireless Security

Wireless systems have many uses in security, including retail loss prevention, proximity access cards, vehicle tag readers, wireless alarm transmitters/receivers, and digital infrastructure for entire security systems. Understanding the capabilities and limitations of these systems is the key to success or failure as a RF system designer.

Wireless alarm systems operate on a variety of frequencies, including but not limited to 315, 505, 418, 433.92, and 868 MHz. They commonly emit several short data bursts at variable intervals over a period of several seconds. The signals can be encoded so as not to duplicate or interfere with other transmitters in the vicinity. Wireless alarm systems are useful for environments that do not have extensive steel or concrete with rebar. Interference is not always obvious until later.

Proximity access control cards and readers operate at 125 kHz and at 902–928 and 868–870 MHz. The newest class of contactless read/write smart cards operate at 13.56 MHz.

Old style proximity cards respond to a RF signal being emitted by the card reader and transmit an answer signal as a short data burst including the card's identity number. Contactless read/write proximity cards operate in the same fashion but can store from 64 bits to 256 kilobits of data. Card readers can be configured to load the data onto the card or read it as appropriate. This could also allow the card to keep track of its own activities.

COMPONENTS

All RF systems have several basic elements, including a signal source, power injector, transmitter, receiver or transceiver, transmission line, and antenna. A basic RF system mixes a signal source with a RF carrier frequency. This process is called modulation. The carrier frequency has three main attributes: frequency, amplitude, and phase (Fig. 12-1).

Analog RF systems modulate the amplitude of the carrier frequency (AM radio); they can also modulate the frequency

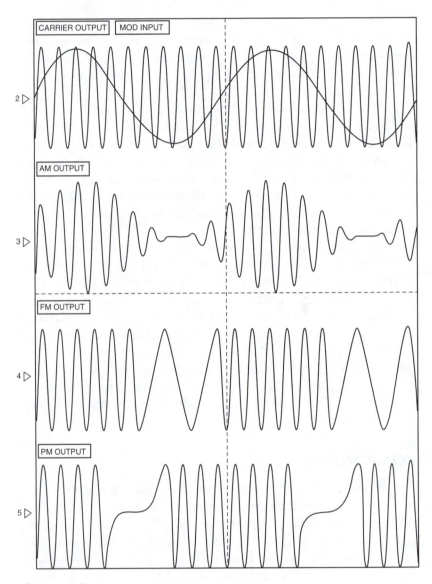

Figure 12-1   RF modulation schemes.

(FM radio) or the phase (phase modulation). Other modulation techniques include single sideband modulation, vestigial sideband modulation, and sigma-delta modulation.

Digital RF systems use a number of distinct signals to represent the data. The signal can use PSK (phase-shift keying), FSK (frequency-shift keying) or ASK (amplitude-shift keying). Amplitude-shift keying is similar to pulse code modulation (PCM), which is a digital representation of an analog signal. PCM is widely used in digital telephony and digital audio, including MP3 and other standards.

Antennas

An antenna is an arrangement of one or more electrical conductors that are designed to radiate an electromagnetic field in response to the application of an electromotive force from a fluctuating electrical current.

Antennas are to radios like tires are to cars. It is where the rubber meets the road. If the antenna is well matched to the RF signal and the environment, a good signal is emitted or received. If the match is poor, poor results are to be expected. Most RF problems are antenna problems.

Antennas are designed to operate (resonate) at a given optimum frequency, depending on the electrical length of the antenna. This is typically the length of the wire multiplied by the ratio of the speed of wave propagation in the wire. Other attributes of the antenna can be varied by its design. These include radiation pattern and impedance (dynamic resistance to the electrical current). Antennas can be configured to propagate their signals either horizontally or vertically. The signal is best received from a similar antenna operating in the same plane.

Patterns

Omni Antennas

A basic antenna radiates in a circular pattern around the conductor (the antenna). This is called an omnidirectional (or omni) antenna pattern. This antenna transmits equally in all directions, either horizontally or vertically, based on the physical orientation of the antenna (Fig. 12-2).

The omni antenna can be made to focus its transmission or receiving pattern more in one direction than in others by changing its physical configuration. This is accomplished at the expense of its transmission or reception ability in other directions. Typically, a directional antenna will have a longer front lobe and weaker rear and side lobes in its pattern (Fig. 12-3).

Antenna Gain

Antenna gain is the ability of the antenna to radiate more or less in any direction compared to a theoretical antenna. If an antenna could be made as a perfect sphere, it would radiate equally in all directions. Such an antenna is theoretically called an isotropic antenna and does not in fact exist. However, its mathematical model is used as a standard of comparison for the gain of a real antenna.

Omni antennas typically radiate with a gain of 2.1 dB over an isotropic antenna. For a vertically oriented omni antenna, this gain in transmission horizontal distance from the antenna is at the expense of transmission above and below it. Its pattern looks similar to a donut.

Directional antennas can be configured with gains up to more than 20 dB. These carve a significant part out of the omni-directional pattern of an omni antenna and can significantly extend its projection distance. A disadvantage of extreme gain antennas is that they can be very sensitive to improper position displacement due to wind conditions. There are a variety of configurations that can result in good directional RF signal transmission, including Yagi antennas, dish antennas, Luneberg lenses, and phased arrays.

Bandwidth

Each antenna is cut to resonate at a particular frequency. The bandwidth of an antenna is the measurement of its ability to operate above and below its resonant frequency.

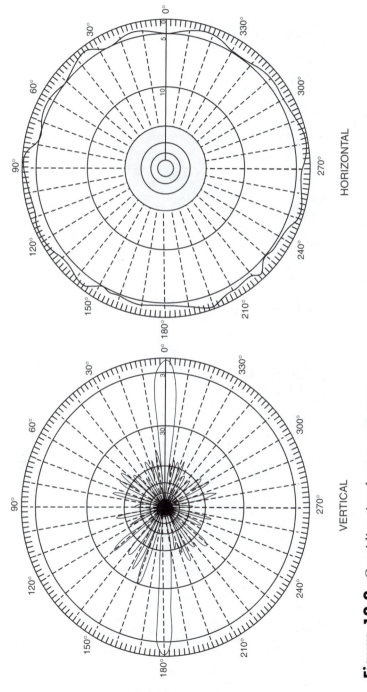

Figure 12-2 Omnidirectional antenna pattern.

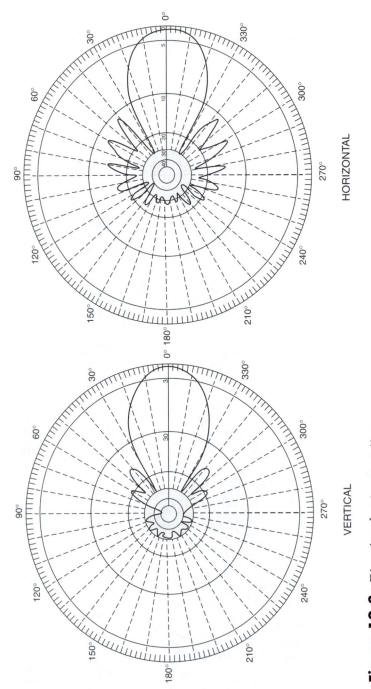

HORIZONTAL

VERTICAL

Figure 12-3 Directional antenna pattern.

Impedance and Coupling

Each antenna is designed to match the electromotive force of the current being applied to it. Every antenna will reflect some of that power back into the transmitter, forming a standing wave in the feed line. That power is effectively lost to RF energy and goes back into the transmitter, where it generates unwanted heat.

The amount of power reflection is measured by its standing wave ratio (SWR), which is a ratio of maximum power to minimum power in the transmission line. Too much SWR and the transmitter can burn up. As SWR increases, power out of the antenna decreases.

A SWR of 1:1 is ideal. A SWR of 1.5:1 is very good, especially for low-power applications in which the SWR consumes available transmitter power. Generally, the lower the SWR, the better.

SWR can be reduced by matching the total impedance of both the antenna and the transmission line to the output impedance of the transmitter. Every physical component in the line has an effect on impedance, including the connectors, the transmission line, and the antenna. The age of connectors and the quality of connection can cause impedance to change over time and in different environments, such as in icing conditions. The components should be closely matched to minimize antenna SWR.

Interference

Many things can interfere with good RF transmission, including automotive ignition noise, other transmitters operating in the same range, fluorescent lamps, microwave ovens and microwave intrusion alarm detectors, reflections from or blockages by large structures, and weather.

Multipath

Antennas are made to transmit across clear air and with no reflections. This is called a line-of-sight (LOS) signal. When a RF signal reflects off a large structure or body of water, that signal may also arrive at the receiving antenna. When it does, it will arrive later than the LOS signal and often out of phase from the original signal. These two signals will both be "read" by the receiver, which will try to make some sense of what it is seeing. Often, the reflected signal will interfere with the LOS signal, sometimes even to the extent that the receiver can no longer effectively act as a receiver.

Dr. Jack Nilson designed and patented a unique multi-polarized omnidirectional antenna that is especially designed to reduce the effect of interferences and multipath signals in the 802.11 ranges. With its radome removed, the antenna looks like a large spider, on its back writhing in agony. These antenna "legs" are angled precisely to gather the signals that are late and out of phase, and the antenna recombines them at its base into a single in-phase and real-time signal. The result effectively is gain produced from interference.

To optimize RF transmissions, it is advisable to encourage a good RF performance and interference study in the real-world environment.

How RF Systems Differ from Cabled Systems

Circuiting

Although designers do not often think of RF systems as having "circuits," it is easier to imagine how they work.

- Point to point: The most basic type of transmission, a point-to-point RF circuit, involves a single transmitter/receiver pair transmitting only to each other.
- Point to multipoint: In a point-to-multipoint circuit, a number of transmitters or transceivers point to a single antenna.
- Wireless mesh: A wireless mesh system is one in which the radios can communicate with any number of nearby radios. Wireless mesh systems are usually more reliable, robust, and redundant than point-to-multipoint systems.
- Cascading design: Wireless mesh systems can also be configured to retransmit the signal of a single camera down a line

of other wireless mesh nodes like a daisy chain or string of pearls, sending the first signal a long distance and combining it with the signals of other cameras along the way. This is a specialized application that requires very high expertise to design properly.

Weather Factors

Weather has an important effect on the effectiveness of wireless communications. The effects of weather should be taken into consideration in any RF design.

TRANSMISSION PHYSICS

RF systems are fraught with problems for the uninitiated. Virtually all of them are solvable. One just has to know how to solve them. The major obstacle is not knowing what you do not know. The following sections discuss RF problems and how to prevent them. Where they cannot be prevented, I will talk about how to solve them.

Transmitter Power

RF security systems are typically transmitting digital data and may transmit a mix of video, alarm/access control data, and voice. The first issue is one of transmitter power. As for most RF problems, the system works best in a "Goldilocks and the Three Bears" comfort zone. That is, not too much power, not too little power, but enough to be "just right." Just right differs from one system to the next, so check the system specifications.

There are two factors at play to achieve this goal: distance and transmitter gain. For distance, the inverse square law applies. That is, for each doubling of distance from transmitter to receiver, you will see one-fourth of the power. So the energy twice as far from the source is spread over 4 times the area (therefore, at any point at that distance there is one-fourth the power). At three times the distance it is spread over 9 times the area (one-ninth the power), at four times the distance it is spread over 16 times the area (1/16th the power), etc.

There is a maximum distance beyond which a given transmitter and antenna will not have enough power to be received by their corresponding receiver and antenna. Likewise, there is a distance below which there is simply too much power for the system to work.

Therefore, it is important to know the acceptable minimum and maximum power at a receiver and then adjust the transmitter power and antenna gain to accommodate that figure. In most cases with better RF data equipment, it is possible to adjust the transmitter gain to accommodate the required receiver signal strength of the closest and farthest wireless nodes to which each transmitter is intending to send data. Transmitter power is usually adjustable in 3-db (half-power) increments, and antenna gain is also rated in decibels.

Antenna Loss/Gain

Transmitter power is rated based on a 0-db antenna load—that is, the resistance and output of the antenna are assumed to be exactly the same as those of the transmitter feeding it. A dipole antenna (simple rubber duck-type antenna) is often configured as a 0-db antenna.

Antennas are also available with either gain or loss. Antennas with gain perform better than a 0-db antenna, and antennas with loss perform less well (not always a bad thing).

Antenna gain and loss are factors of physics. A 0-db antenna inherently transmits an omnidirectional pattern (perfect circle horizontally). To visualize the pattern, imagine a donut. The hole in the center is where the antenna is placed vertically oriented. The donut pattern would be the pattern of transmission from the antenna. To achieve gain, one must understand the principle of balloons. When inflated, balloons have a finite volume and a finite surface area. If a balloon is round, like the donut, one can make one side larger by pushing in on the other side. More here equals less there. Antenna patterns are similar. To get gain in one part of the antenna pattern, one must create losses in another. Directional antennas achieve gain by their directionality. That is, they have farther reach in one direction (gain) by sacrificing reach in other directions.

Antenna Patterns

The following are common antenna patterns:

- Omnidirectional—circular
- Cardiod—heart shaped
- Yagi array—long node on one side and little radiation elsewhere

Transmission Losses

Transmission losses result in lower signals than the math would indicate. These typically result from any of the following conditions:

- An obstruction in the path of the transmitter–receiver field
- A reflecting surface (see Multipath)
- Poor connections to the transmitter, transmission line, or antenna
- Poor ground for the transmitter or antenna
- Adverse environmental conditions (fog, rain, humidity, etc.)
- Transmitting cable losses (which can be significant)

Of all the conditions that can cause problems, environmental effects are the most difficult to calculate (some say virtually impossible). This is one of the most important reasons to design the system with adequate headroom in the circuit to accommodate unpredicted losses. I recommend that any data system should not be taxed above 45% of its rated headroom. That is, if the system is designed to accommodate 100 Mbps, do not send more than 45 Mbps across it. For 54 Mbps, send no more than 24 Mbps.

Line of Sight

LOS transmissions are the basic form of RF transmission. In a LOS transmission, there is a transmitter, receiver, and free air in between with no obstructions or reflecting objects such as buildings. LOS transmissions are the ideal. This rarely occurs.

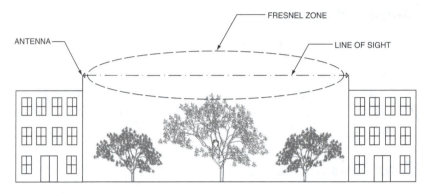

Figure 12-4   Fresnel zone.

Fresnel Zone

If a transmitter and receiver are located on two buildings some distance apart, their communication path is not defined by a single thin line of RF energy between the points. Rather, its pattern looks something like a cartoon cigar (thin on the ends and thick in the middle). The Fresnel (pronounced fra-nel) zone is the area around that thin line between the transmitting and receiving antennae (Fig. 12-4).

Certain RF signals (especially 2.4-GHz waves) are absorbed by water, such as the water in trees. Thus, if trees lie within the imaginary cigar around the line of sight, then the received power may be less during wet periods than during dry periods and will certainly be less than if the trees were not there at all.

Additionally, any buildings, oil tanks, ships, bodies of water, etc. that lie within the Fresnel zone can also create multipath reflections, including the potential for gains, losses, and secondary data images.

Multipath

What is multipath? Multipath is the effect on RF signals of reflected signals. Whenever a RF signal is transmitted, there exists the opportunity for secondary (undesired) reflections of the signal reaching the receiving antenna, not just the intended (LOS) signal (Fig. 12-5).

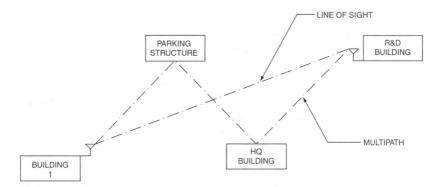

Figure 12-5 Multipath.

Multipath can most easily be understood by considering a television signal received off the air. If you tune through the channels, you will likely find a channel on which you can see a good image, but you may also see a ghost image just to the right, perhaps 1 in. to the right of the sharp image. That secondary image is multipath. It is caused due to the television signal being reflected off a large building or other distant object. The primary signal is the sharp image you see, and the multipath signal is the softer one, displaced to the right of the primary image.

Delay Losses

The multipath signal is shifted to the right because the reflected image takes longer to travel to the receiving antenna than the primary signal. That greater distance causes the secondary (multipath) signal to be delayed by a factor of the greater distance and the wavelength of the frequency of the channel on which it is operating. Accordingly, because it arrives at the receiving antenna later, it gets processed later. On an analog television signal, it will be displayed to the right of the primary signal by the amount of time between the arrival of the primary and secondary signals.

The results of multipath delays on digital signals display as dropped packets. This is because for every primary packet, there is a duplicate secondary packet that is being received by the receiver. So for each reflection, there is a doubling of the number of packets being sent. More reflections, more packets by a multiple of the number being reflected. On strong multipath environments, this can swamp the front end of the receiver, causing it to fail because it cannot process all these extra packets. The result is dropped packets.

For video images, the result can be seen as splotchy images because the receiver cannot keep up with the primary signal stream, and it ends up mixing secondary packets in with the primary packets as it attempts to reassemble the packet sequence of the image.

For audio, it results in lost packets, which sound like dropped syllables or just extraneous noise. You can hear these commonly on hand phones in bad areas.

For data systems, the result is lost connections or no loss at all. Data systems use the TCP/IP protocol, which goes back to get a replacement for any lost packets and does not present the information until the entire data group is reassembled. When it cannot, it simply drops the connection.

Cancellation Losses

Because multipath signals arrive not only later but also often out of phase (not oriented the same as the transmitting antenna—pure vertical or pure horizontal), some signal cancellations can occur. Additionally, the simple fact of the delay can cause signals to arrive out of phase. Out of phase signals can effectively reduce the quality when they combine with a good signal at the receiving antenna. This has the effect of creating artificial distance for the good signal, reducing its effectiveness and sometimes making the multipath signal the only one seen by the receiving antenna. Multipath is a major problem and should be eliminated where possible by careful positioning of the antennae.

When it is not possible to eliminate multipath, a special antenna exists that seems to effectively minimize multipath signals. Underneath its radome, this antenna looks like a spider that has died in agony, lying on its back. The spider legs are twisted into many different angles, forming curves, all carefully calculated to either accept or recombine multipath signals or to cancel them out. The antenna effectively gets gain from multipath while nearly eliminating its bad effects.

Cascade Losses

As wireless digital signals are propagated through a sequence of nodes, cascade losses occur. These are discussed in the section on full-duplex wireless mesh networks. Antenna patterns must also be observed.

Power Stability and Reliability

Stable system operation depends on stable alternating current power. In most of the developed world, stable power is taken for granted. However, that is not always the case. Increasingly, even in the developed world, power instability is becoming a problem as increasing demands create brownouts and rolling blackouts. Stable power must be ensured, especially for mission critical systems, such as for nuclear power plants, central banks, museums, hospitals, and research and development facilities.

In order to ensure stable power, the designer should check the history of power stability in the area. If power is suspect, arrangements should be made for emergency power. This might include an emergency generator and a uninterruptible power supply. Both should be sized to accommodate the expected load plus 50%, with a lower limit of 25%.

Grounding and Powering

After reliable power, grounding is the second most important aspect regarding system power. The two chief issues regarding grounding are ground stability and ground loops.

System grounds can cause reliability problems for any data system. In an analog audio system, a poor ground can easily be heard as a persistent 50- or 60-cycle hum (depending on whether a facility is in a 50- or 60-Hz power grid). Although one cannot

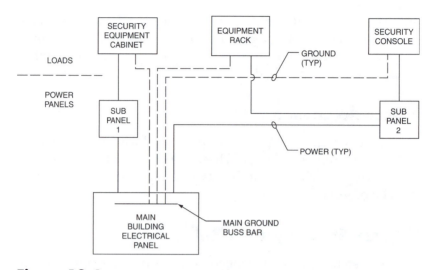

Figure 12-6   Hospital ground scheme.

hear the persistent hum of a poor ground in a data system, its effects are equally as evident in poor system performance.

I recommend a so-called hospital ground (IEEE 602-1996 and NFPA 99-1996) as a cure-all for system grounds. A hospital ground depends on a single ground point tied to the copper ground bar of the main electrical feed of the building. All system grounds to all assemblies should emanate from this one location (Fig. 12-6). Power receptacles, power strips in assemblies, racks, consoles, etc. all should ground to this one point. This alone ensures a reliable ground.

Ground loops can also create many system reliability problems. A ground loop is created when two devices are powered and grounded from separate locations and there is a voltage difference between the ground points. Since the system is attempting to reference ground from two different voltage potentials, it may not be able to pass data between the signal connections of two different parts of the system because they no longer have a single point of reference (Fig. 12-7). To eliminate this problem, system components in different buildings, or those fed from different main electrical panels, should be electrically isolated by fiber optics or RF connections. There should

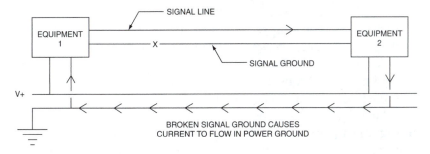

Figure 12-7 Ground loop.

be no exceptions to this rule because ground faults can be fatal, especially between buildings.

The security designer should intimately know the source of electrical power for his or her systems. Never assume that the power is acceptable or that all is well. As former U.S. President Ronald Reagan once said: "Trust but verify."

System Resets and Restores

The security designer should also ask, What happens if power to any component of the system is interrupted? Will the system reset itself or will manual intervention be required? The answer to that of course is that manual intervention should never be required. The system should be designed such that in the event of a cold reset of any part of the system, it will restore quickly to its appropriate operating configuration, fully automatically. Surprisingly, a number of major systems fail this test. It pays to know.

Special Power Problems

The secret to successful design is to always understand the environment in which one is operating. This is especially true of extreme environments. Extremes of cold, heat, and power can often be encountered.

One example is that of unmanned offshore oil platforms or oil pipeline lift stations. In both cases, there is no utility company power available; power is typically available only from an uninterruptible power supply that is refreshed by solar panels. For such environments, power usage calculations are essential, as is a design philosophy tilting toward using little or no power. Sometimes these conditions require one to totally rethink one's approach to systems design. One method is to eliminate as much standard equipment as possible. Instead of wiring conventional or digital cameras to a digital video recorder, one can use digital cameras that have a built-in processor and memory in lieu of a recorder. Also, instead of using a conventional digital switch, the SCADA PLC or similar equipment already on the platform or lift station can often be used as a digital switch. Finally, there is no need to power the cameras except when actually viewing one. Cameras can be turned on automatically in response to alarms, and alarms can be managed by the SCADA system, instead of a conventional alarm panel. All this eliminates unnecessary power consumption.

Each unique environment may present its own challenges. Thinking outside the box, one can often find unique and workable solutions.

SUMMARY

RF systems can be either analog or digital. Wireless systems operate on many frequencies. Antenna patterns include omnidirectional and directional. Directionality is achieved in one direction at the expense of all other directions. Reducing an antenna's reach in one direction achieves gain in another. Antennas transmit along a LOS to each other. The designer should observe the Fresnel zone around the LOS transmission, within which interference can occur. Interference includes RF (ignition noise or other radios), multipath, and obstructions (trees, etc.) as well as weather. RF architecture includes point to point, point to multipoint, and wireless mesh. Protocols include unicast and multicast, TCP, UDP, and RTP. The design must be adjusted to accommodate multipath and delay losses.

Stable power is the basis for a high-quality security system. Grounding is the source for many system problems. A hospital ground is the most reliable grounding method. Special power problems can be solved by thoroughly understanding the environment.

13

Interfacing to Legacy Systems and Emerging Technologies

THE CHALLENGE OF LEGACY SYSTEMS

Virtually no organizations move from nothing to a complete integrated enterprise security system in one single step. Rather, these systems tend to be built upon a fabric of older, legacy systems that must be updated to newer, more capable technology.

Commonly, organizations find themselves owning a number of incompatible security systems in different areas of the world and in different business units. How then to integrate these all into one single system that can manage alarms, access control, video, and security voice communications all from one or two security command centers? How then to weave this fabric of different, incompatible systems into one that can permit management to begin a comprehensive program of uniform application of corporate security policies?

This is the challenge of legacy systems. There are actually three challenges: A technical challenge, a budget challenge, and a political challenge. You can try to influence the political issues, but there are usually forces at work to which the security designer will not be privy. However, once a decision has been made to go forward with integrating legacy security systems, the budget and technical approaches usually present themselves. If budget is an issue, and usually it is, then decisions must be made as to how to prioritize the integration implementation program.

LEGACY ACCESS CONTROL SYSTEMS

Access Card Legacies

One of the most expensive challenges awaiting organizations wishing to integrate their various alarm/access control systems is that there may be numerous different card types, with varying card bit formats. Some sites may use magnetic stripe cards, others may use Wiegand swipe cards, still others may use one brand or another of 125-kHz proximity cards, and some may use smart cards. Of course, where the card formats are the same, it is possible that the bit formats may still differ.

Therefore, one challenge is for the client to make a decision regarding what card technology to use. At the time of the writing of this book, the National Transportation Workers Identification Card (TWIC) had not yet been implemented. TWIC cards provide a single uniform credential that are more difficult to counterfeit and to misuse than many past cards. Several different card technologies are all present on a single TWIC card, including a biometric credential reference standard for the cardholder that is embedded in the smart card. TWIC cards are a good choice to use to merge older card populations into a single new standard.

Interfacing Multiple Access Control Systems from Differing Manufacturers into a Single Comprehensive System

One of the normal challenges faced is that alarm/access control systems software and hardware are almost always completely incompatible from one manufacturer to the next. Integrating different brands and models of video and intercom systems is not nearly as complicated as integrating different brands of alarm/access control systems. Thus, if your client is one of the many whose many security systems involve numerous alarm/access control systems at various sites, one of the key decisions is to determine whether or not to immediately implement full and total integration of the alarm/access control system.

The obvious advantage to having a single alarm/access control platform is that it makes both alarm monitoring and access control management very easy. The disadvantage is that it may require substantial replacement of various alarm/access control systems with a single brand. There are other options, however.

One option is to leave the access control management integration for later and integrate the alarm management portion first to achieve centralized monitoring. That is relatively easy.

Several options exist for achieving centralized monitoring.

The Old-Fashioned (But Still Very Reliable) Way

Each individual site's existing alarm/access control system can be configured with output control boards that are then connected to a central office-type alarm panel. The central office alarm panel reports by dialer to a central office alarm receiver at the remotely located security command center. The central office alarm receiver connects via RS-232 to the digital video server's alarm database input. This results in a reliable cascading transmission of any alarms at the remote site via telephone line to the security command center, where they will be displayed on the alarm mapping software of the digital video system. They will also be logged into its alarm database.

Newer (Still Reliable) Way

For each type of alarm/access control system in the various sites, install a new alarm/access control system controller at the security command center (one or each type of system). Link each type of controller to its equivalent at the remote site, and enable remote global alarm reporting. In this model, the alarm/access control system assumes that you are going to have a printer at some remote site that will print all system alarms. From the RS-232 alarm printer output of the alarm/access control system controller, feed this to a corresponding RS-232 input on the digital video system server, from which the printer outputs will be displayed on the alarm mapping software of the digital video system. They will also be logged into its alarm database.

As the phasing of the enterprise integration project moves forward, it is likely that older sites will be gradually converted to a single alarm/access control system standard. When that is done, it is recommended to use the alarm/access control system rather than the digital video system as the alarm history database because of its inherently better reporting capabilities.

Interfacing Old Wiring Schemes

Older alarm/access control systems may use a variety of field wiring schemes, including RS-485, Protocol A, Protocol B, Class A, 20 ma current loop, RS-232, Lantronics, fiber, and Ethernet. As the alarm/access control systems are replaced with a single brand, it may be necessary to replace some wiring infrastructures. The standard will usually be Ethernet and/or TCP/IP on fiber since that has become the uniform standard of the security industry. For difficult or extremely expensive retrofits within buildings or across campuses, it may be less expensive to utilize 802.11 or another wireless data protocol in lieu of replacing the wiring infrastructure.

LEGACY VIDEO SYSTEMS

Like alarm/access control systems, legacy video systems present unique challenges. Analog video systems have evolved into a complicated array of devices, each of which performs a unique task, whereas digital video systems can perform all these tasks with minimal hardware. They also have the flexibility to perform all of these tasks at once, or they can be programmed as needed to perform one task or another. For example, video multiplexers allow for the display and recording of multiple cameras on a single monitor and video recorder. These tasks are inherent in every digital video system, regardless of type.

The challenge with conversion to a new integrated video system is not to repeat the mistakes of the past. Any new system should be virtually universal in its architecture so that the client is not locked into any brand of cameras, codecs, digital recorders, computers, or software. Although digital video systems are being developed today that replicate the old paradigm of locking clients into a single manufacturer, arguably that should be avoided if possible. (The manufacturers might argue for it, but clients rarely will.)

There are three major types of digital video systems:

- Digital video recorders
- Proprietary hardware-based server-type configurations
- Nonproprietary software-based server-type configurations

Digital video recorder-based systems are inexpensive to begin using and make an easy migration path from analog to digital infrastructures. However, some designers (myself included) believe that they are a transitional technology. Server-type systems are generally regarded as more powerful than digital video recorder-based systems. They are inherently friendly to digital infrastructures and digital video cameras. This makes the entire system, not just the recording portion, much more scalable. Server-type systems are available in both hardware and software types. There are valid arguments for and against each approach.

Digital Video Recorder-Based Systems

The arguments for:

- Digital video recorder systems can be built from small systems to fairly large systems over time with minor incremental cost for each step.

- The client has only to buy as many digital video recorders as he or she needs to add at the time.
- Digital video recorders can be networked together (some better than others) into fairly large systems.

The arguments against:

- Digital video recorders often become obsolete in a very short time, having been replaced by a newer recorder with more recording capacity and better features in less than 2 years.
- Digital video recorders lock the client into a single brand of equipment because their operating formats are generally not compatible from brand to brand.
- Many digital video recorders only work with analog video cameras and cannot work with signals transmitted to a switch across a digital infrastructure.
- Digital video recorders may become obsolete due to their inability to keep up with new recording capacity demands. What seemed like a lot of storage 2 years ago may seem totally inadequate today. The cost of updating the storage capacity for a digital video recorder may outweigh the benefits.
- Some digital video recorder manufacturers have produced a nonlinear progression of recorders such that the client may have to abandon all previous recorders in order to expand the system beyond a certain capacity. This obviates the benefit of the scaled approach to building a digital video system.
- Digital video recorders have a finite life, and the entire unit may have to be replaced more often than the client would like.

Proprietary Hardware-Based Server-Type Configurations

The arguments for:

- Proprietary hardware-based server-type systems have most of the advantages of software-based systems but do not have some of their disadvantages.

- Specifically, hardware-based systems are very easy to install and configure. Because they are hardware based instead of software based, most system configurations are built into the hardware. Once it is connected, it boots up and works as planned.
- System installation and reliability over time are likely to be very high.
- The system may require far less expertise to install correctly.
- It is less likely that a computer-savvy guard would try to reconfigure the system to his or her own taste, possibly rendering the system inoperable in some capacity.

The arguments against:

- Hardware-based systems lock the client entirely into that manufacturer's products. This may not be bad, if the products are available for installation from a variety of contractors, can be maintained by a variety of agencies, and have enough installation and maintenance options to make the product competitive over time. If not, what may look like a very good deal in the first installation may become quite costly as the client realizes that he or she has limited options for availability of the product. Many many clients wish they had never made proprietary decisions.
- Hardware-based system functions are built into the hardware. They do what they do because of what they are physically. If a need develops for a function that was not realized when the system was purchased, it may not be possible to add it.

Software-Based Server-Type Configurations

The arguments for:

- Software-based server systems are the purest form of digital video technology: Almost all are composed of off-the-shelf network hardware with the functions operating entirely in software.

- Because they are based on standard computer switches, routers, servers, and workstations, software-based systems provide the ultimate in system configuration flexibility.
- The systems operate on conventional servers and workstations, so the client can have his or her choice and use the product that fits his or her own corporate culture, making the system easy for the information technology department to service.
- Many software-based systems are completely nonproprietary. That is, the client can use any digital video camera, and the software can be replaced without loss of stored data.
- Some software-based systems are far more flexible in their functions than their comparable hardware equivalents.
- Some software-based systems make integration to legacy analog and digital video systems much easier than their hardware counterparts.

The arguments against:

- Software-based systems are based on standard servers and computers, so they suffer from all of the flaws, vulnerabilities, and foibles that go with nondedicated systems, including some dangerous operating system vulnerabilities.
- Because they are based on conventional operating systems, the configuration of the operating system and data infrastructure require higher skills in order to ensure a stable, secure system. A skilled (or even improperly inquisitive) guard can easily corrupt the configuration of an improperly configured operating system that serves as a platform for the digital video software system. To be fair, this can also be a factor in conventional alarm/access control systems and even hardware-based digital video systems, if the workstation operating system is not configured correctly.
- Software-based systems require higher skill levels to commission properly.

Analog Switch Interfacing

Interfacing a digital video system to an existing analog matrix video switch can be either straightforward or an extreme challenge, depending on the digital video system to which it is to be connected. Some software-based systems are very well thought out with regard to this issue, whereas digital video recorders and some hardware systems are, at best, a mixed bag.

The objective of legacy matrix video switch integration is to make the matrix switches of various manufacturers at various locations all operate as though they belong to the family of the digital video software. This is actually not a difficult task since most analog matrix video switches provide a data interface format for their switches. By engineering a communications protocol based on the data interface format, the digital video software vendor can create a toolkit of interfaces for each brand. At least one software manufacturer has done this; more will follow.

Thus, it is important to ensure that the digital video product you specify can interface to a legacy analog video matrix switch if such exists within the enterprise for which you will be designing. Communications with older matrix switches should be through a method that facilitates Ethernet connections so that the interface can be made across wide geographic expanses.

Multiplexer Interfacing

Multiplexer interfacing is not as easy as it is for analog switches. It is possible for digital video manufacturers to write interfaces to control multiplexers, although this is not commonly done. The other way is to take the output from the multiplexer's monitor output into a digital video switch codec input. This will allow the digital video system to display the output of the multiplexer as though it were itself a video camera. When this is done, it will also be necessary to control the multiplexer, which can be done through the multiplexer's data control input. Most multiplexer manufacturers make accessory products that can allow the networking of their multiplexers under a single remote keyboard command. In this case, the digital video software will provide the commands to control the multiplexers.

LEGACY INTERCOM SYSTEMS

Two-Wire Intercom Systems

One of the most common security intercom products is a two-wire intercom made by Aiphone™. This versatile intercom has been used extensively in very small to relatively large applications for many years, so it is likely to be encountered repeatedly throughout a security designer's career.

The two-wire intercom incorporates talk, listen, call, and remote door release functions onto a two-wire infrastructure. Although this is economical on cable, it presents challenges to convert to a digital infrastructure.

The two-wire intercom manufacturer makes an Ethernet converter for its intercom stations, as does at least one digital video software manufacturer. The product converts the intercom directly to an Ethernet signal, whereas other products convert the Aiphone signal to a standard four-wire intercom interface, suitable for use across a variety of other codecs. Either of these two approaches provides a reasonable migration path for this popular two-wire intercom.

Four-Wire Intercom Systems

There are a variety of so-called four-wire intercom systems. Some of them actually use more than four wires, although designers still lump them into the four-wire group. A four-wire intercom uses two wires for talk, two for listen, and may use separate cables for intercom call and remote door release, or it may include these functions on the original four wires. Several digital video and intercom manufacturers make four-wire-to-Ethernet converters, and most digital video codecs will accommodate a four-wire intercom directly.

DIRECT RING-DOWN INTERCOM SYSTEMS

Direct ring-down intercoms are essentially telephones that ring to a specific telephone number and no other. This type of intercom connects to a standard telephone line. Often, there are several ring-down intercoms all connected on a single phone line.

This is not a problem because they are so rarely used that there is little likelihood of a conflict between the phones. It is not likely that they will compete for a line at the same time.

Another type of direct-ring down phone also supplies its own ring voltage so that it does not need to connect to a standard telephone line. This type of ring-down intercom can connect over relatively long distances (up to 1 mile and sometimes farther) and is useful for environments in which the ring-down intercoms may be a long distance from a security command center, such as with emergency phones on a college campus.

Currently, there are no options to interface ring-down phones to VoIP systems. However, I expect that such an interface will be available in the near future. In the meantime, another method is to replace the existing ring-down stations with analog two-wire intercom stations, using the existing infrastructure and placing a codec on the intercom to convert it to an IP infrastructure.

SWITCHED INTERCOM BUSS SYSTEMS

A switched buss intercom system is an innovative system that uses a single audio buss (one talk and one listen) throughout a facility, and switching is accomplished by means of a dry contact from the nearest alarm/access control system controller panel (Fig. 13-1). Audio is provided by a single-channel intercom system.

This is a very economical and extremely expandable system since additional field intercoms can be added anywhere at any time just by linking to the closest point on the audio buss and controlling the new intercom station from the nearest alarm/access control system output control panel.

These systems are very easily converted by linking the individual field intercom stations into the nearest digital video camera or codec.

Intercom Matrix Switches

Another type of intercom system designed to accommodate larger installations is the intercom matrix switch. This operates

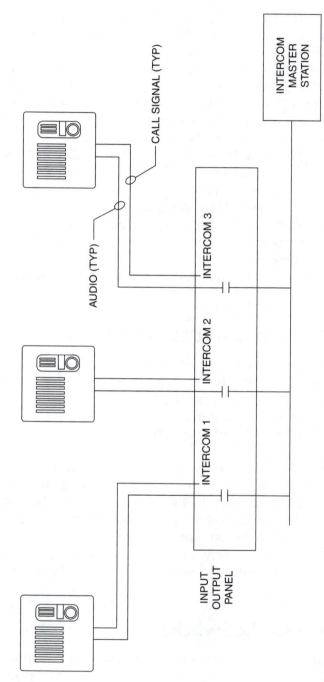

Figure 13-1 Switched intercom buss.

much like a PABX, but it is dedicated to intercom use only. Matrix switches are offered by a number of manufacturers, but their use is likely to decline with the advent of digital intercom switches. Like a PABX, there is a matrix switch, one or more intercom master stations, and a number of intercom field stations. On larger systems, there may be a number of intercom matrix switches all networked together via audio and control lines.

Some of these are very difficult to convert to digital systems, particularly older matrix switches. Newer switches often have a data interface protocol that will allow an outside unit (in this case, a codec) to act as the talk path, and the matrix switch can accept RS-232 commands and provide call requests via RS-232. In a few cases, a software API or XML interface may be possible.

Check with the manufacturer of the specific matrix switch to determine how they can adapt to a digital intercom system. Many of these companies offer digital intercom systems of their own, making this transition easier.

EMERGING TECHNOLOGIES

New Alarm/Access Control System Technologies

Expect to see a new architecture for alarm/access control systems begin to emerge in the near future. Unlike existing alarm/access control system architectures that wire a number of field devices from doors and alarms back to a closet where there is an alarm/access control panel, expect to see a new architecture in which each door may be served by its own individual controller, locally at the door. The system will likely be powered over Ethernet and will have connections for up to four Ethernet devices, including an up/down link connection with minimal latency and fast Ethernet throughput (or gigabit throughput). This will allow for the connection of one or two card readers, door position switch, request-to-exit device, low-power door lock, one or two digital cameras, and a digital intercom (on Ethernet connections) all on the microcontroller. The microcontroller should also be able to cascade down a corridor from

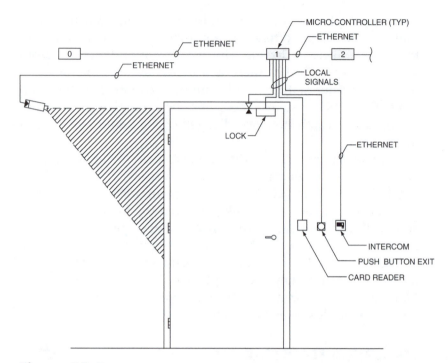

Figure 13-2 Microcontroller.

door to door, perhaps up to 10 hops before arriving at a digital switch, where they will go onto the larger security system digital infrastructure (Fig. 13-2).

New Digital Video Technologies

Light Field Camera

A team of Stanford researchers has developed a light field camera that can create photographs whose subjects universally appear in sharp focus, regardless of their depth. The light field camera overcomes the challenges of high-speed and low-light conditions. The light field camera adds a microlens array to conventional cameras that contains almost 90,000 miniature lenses to sift through converged light rays. Processing software then produces a synthetic image drawn from a consideration of the many different depths where the various rays would have landed. The light field camera disentangles the relationship between the depth of field and the aperture size, which traditionally entailed a trade-off between scope and clarity. The microlens array yields the benefits of larger apertures without compromising the clarity or depth of the image. Surveillance cameras could be improved significantly by this technology because they frequently produce grainy images with poorly defined shapes. At night, when a security camera is attempting to focus on a moving object, it is difficult for the camera to follow it, particularly if there are two people moving around. The typical camera will close down its aperture to try to capture a sharp image of both people, but the small aperture will produce video that is dark and grainy. The light field camera does not exhibit these problems.

Digital Signal Processing Cameras

As video systems migrate from analog to digital, it is expected that full digital video cameras will become the norm and codecs will disappear. One expectation is that in order to conserve digital infrastructure throughput, digital cameras may begin using "push" technology. This will allow the camera to send a low-resolution, low frame rate signal if there is nothing of interest (e.g., within an empty corridor) and switch immediately to a higher frame rate and higher resolution if a video motion alarm occurs.

Extreme Low Light Color Video Cameras

Extreme low light cameras have been around for some time; however, none have been color. One manufacturer has developed an extreme low light color video camera. The camera achieves full color with as little as 0.00025 lux.

SUMMARY

Digital integrated security systems often integrate to legacy analog systems. Legacy access card technologies present a simple challenge. TWIC cards are a good way to migrate from older cards to newer ones.

Interfacing multiple access control systems requires an alarm management system that can receive signals from multiple other systems. This allows the monitoring of alarms across the various systems and the control of remote doors and gates. Centralized monitoring can be achieved by using a central station alarm receiver. The printer output of some alarm/access control systems can be interfaced to some digital video systems to graph alarms. With all access control systems, the alarms can be programmed to trigger dry-contact outputs that can be read by an input of a codec on a digital video system and interpreted to an alarm map.

Legacy video systems can be interfaced using a variety of methods. There is no consistent method that works with all types and brands. Proprietary digital systems have a limited ability to interface to other systems, making them more difficult to develop into a true enterprise system. Nonproprietary software-based systems are often easier to interface with a wider variety of legacy systems from many manufacturers.

Analog switches can be controlled from the data interface of the switch. Multiplexers do not interface so easily and may require immediate conversion to a digital technology. Legacy intercom systems can be adapted to digital by using a codec and/or intercom interface module. Direct ring-down intercom systems do not have an interface. Switched intercom buss systems can be interfaced similarly to four-wire systems. Older intercom matrix switches can be very difficult to convert. Some newer systems have a data interface.

Emerging technologies include local access control system controllers at each door, digital light field cameras, advancements in digital signal processing cameras, and extreme low light color video cameras.

14

Interfacing to Related Systems

BUILDING SYSTEM INTERFACES

By interfacing the security system to other building systems, it is possible to control lights, doors, ventilation systems, announcement systems, irrigation systems, elevators, and other building systems to the overall benefit of the security of an organization's assets and safety of its users. Building system interfaces are of two types: information inputs and control outputs.

Information Inputs

Other systems can provide information to the security guard force. For example, when an office building occupant places a 911 call to emergency services (police, fire, or ambulance), that call can be logged on the alarm/access control system, the location of the desk from which the call originates can be displayed on an alarm map, and the call can be recorded on the audio track of the digital video system and announced at the security console.

This prepares the security force to be the first responder to the desk where the emergency is occurring, rendering appropriate assistance, and it also enables the force to greet members of the responding public agency and guide them quickly to the appropriate location. All this places facility ownership in the enviable position of being informed and truly helpful in a timely fashion, with all the facts in hand from the phone call.

Control Outputs

The ability to control the environment to the benefit of the users' safety and security has profound effects on the welfare of the client, and it is a service of real value to the client's constituents.

A good example is that of irrigation systems. Upon triggering a perimeter alarm, if an intruder is proceeding across a grassy area, the intent of the intruder can be determined quickly by the remote triggering of the irrigation system. Only the most determined intruder will proceed across a large grassy area toward a target while in the embrace of a sprinkler system when a shorter path to escape is available.

Imagination

The use of building interfaces is limited only by the designer's imagination. Wherever it can be imagined that a process could be facilitated by hand, it is probably possible to place that process under remote control from the console.

MORE ON BUILDING SYSTEM INTERFACES

Fire Alarm Systems

In most cases, the security system is not rated as a fire alarm system and should not be used as such. However, for large buildings and facilities, it is useful to use the security system as a secondary annunciator for the fire alarm system. This does not replace the fire alarm system as a primary annunciator.

Usually, the fire alarm annunciation panel will be located in a fire control room that is convenient to the fire department when it accesses the building. The fire control room may not be convenient to the security control room.

A useful interface between the two systems involves placing a summary or secondary lamp annunciator within the security command center (this fulfills the requirement that the primary annunciator is the fire alarm system) and also interfacing the fire alarm system to the security system such that any alarm from the fire alarm system will be displayed on the security graphic maps.

By interfacing the fire alarm system to the security system in this manner, it is assured that the code requirements are fulfilled while at the same time allowing for the display of fire alarms on a single graphical user interface map that displays all other types of alarms.

Fire/Life Safety Interfaces

When a fire alarm occurs within a high-rise building, it is recommended practice to pressurize the fire stairwells so that smoke cannot infiltrate the stairs while the occupants are using them to exit. A problem is that very often when this protective system is needed the most, it is found that someone has propped a stairwell door open, rendering the safety system inoperable.

By combining the fire/life safety system with the security system, and creating a Boolean algebra logic system, the security console officer can instantly determine if a door has been propped or is not reclosing after it was opened. This is done by coupling the fire alarm system input with the inputs of door position switches in the fire stairwell and displaying these on a map that specifically shows all the fire stairwell doors in a riser. When the stairwell is in use for a fire and someone props a door open, the security staff can quickly dispatch to that location, preventing a buildup of potentially fatal smoke within the stairwell.

This process can also be automated by placing magnetic holders on the fire stairwell doors so that if anyone does prop them open, they can be easily closed after the door prop alarm engages. This is an optimal implementation allowing instant release of the door remotely from the console, preserving the life-saving value of the system.

ELEVATORS AND ESCALATORS
Access Control

Access control in elevators is a valuable function in any multifloor building. There are four basic types of elevator access control systems.

Hall Call Control

Hall call readers allow access to the hall call push buttons in the elevator lobby. This is very useful for parking structure elevator lobbies and elevators that are intended to serve a specific group, such as staff elevators in a hospital or educational institution. Hall call readers are also useful to prevent vandalism to elevators in areas where pedestrian access to the elevators cannot be prevented, such as in a parking structure.

Floor-by-Floor Control

Floor-by-floor control combines a card reader within the elevator car with control over the individual floor select buttons to ensure that the cardholder is allowed to go only to the floors to which he or she has access privileges.

Scheduled Operation

Because any access control system can be placed on a schedule of operation, the elevator can be placed on free access during normal building hours and on access control during off-hours.

Remote Operation from the Console

The ultimate implementation of elevator access control is direct control over the floor select buttons by the security console officer. This method ensures that visitors to the building after-hours do indeed get off on the floor they stated as their intent. This is particularly useful in residential high-rise buildings, where unauthorized visitors can create significant liability for the building owner.

Emergency Operation

Elevators

During emergencies, all elevators can be programmed for fire recall, bringing all elevators down to the lobby level. This can be especially useful in areas where demonstrations or swarming attacks in the lobby could occur because it ensures that the elevators cannot be used to infiltrate the building.

Escalators

Similarly, escalators can be placed into a down-only mode after a short pause to allow those on board to exit. This creates a barrier to rising through the building and helps large numbers to exit down.

BUILDING AUTOMATION SYSTEMS

Building automation system integration to the security system can have numerous benefits.

HVAC

Very popular in certain locales, the integration of access control and HVAC systems provides users of tenant spaces with a convenient way to activate air-conditioning service during hours when it would normally be off.

The basic implementation of the system includes a card reader for each floor and a zone select button for each of several HVAC zones for that floor. The card reader enables the appropriate zone, much like the floor select buttons of the elevator access control system. Each pressing of the HVAC buttons provides for a fixed time period of HVAC service, typically 2 hours. Often, these services are coupled with after-hours HVAC usage accounting, facilitating a monthly charge for the services that would otherwise not be available.

More elegant versions of this system incorporate telephone access to activate the HVAC services. This is especially useful because the office can be cooled down prior to arrival when a call is made from a car on the way to the office. Access control identification in these cases is based on a user password or pass-number entered into the phone. This system can also light corridors at night that would otherwise be darkened, making working late at night much more pleasant.

Lighting

It can be disturbing to go to one's office late at night when the area is unoccupied and dark. However, by coupling together the parking lot/structure access control system with the building automation system, it is possible to light the parking structure upon entry of the car and then light a path from the parking area to the user's office area. Presentation of the user's card to a reader in the elevator lobby can also light the return path to the parking structure.

Lighting can also be automated in response to alarms, particularly perimeter alarms to ward off intrusions. Finally, in reactive electronic automated protection systems (REAPS), lighting can be extinguished, leaving the intruder in total darkness while the security officer can see the intruder through infrared illuminated video cameras.

Signage

There is little more frustrating than to enter a parking structure only to drive every level and never find a parking space.

The security system that controls access to a parking lot or structure can also be used to count up and down to manage the capacity of the structure.

By linking an up/down counter to the access control system, lighted signage can inform potential users that the parking structure is full, saving them time. The building automation system makes a useful up/down counter for access control systems that are not so enabled.

IRRIGATION

A REAPS technology, irrigation systems are often controlled by the building automation system. As stated previously, irrigation systems are a useful tool in augmenting perimeter security.

DELUGE FIRE SPRINKLER CONTROL (ANOTHER REAPS TECHNOLOGY)

For any environment such as an outdoor shopping mall, where competing gangs of criminal youths could engage in gunfire, nothing can disperse a crowd immediately quite like 10,000 gallons of water in 60 seconds. Afterward, although people are most likely to be upset and drenched, the gunfire will probably have stopped and the perpetrators will likely have fled, thus dissipating the danger and protecting the innocent public.

Coupled with gunshot recognition software, pan/tilt cameras can instantly zoom in on the offender, providing visual verification of the condition requiring action.

Deluge activation systems should only be installed after careful consideration and advice from legal counsel, but they may be appropriate for any venue where there is a potential or history of gunfire in public spaces.

PABX INTERFACES

PABX systems facilitate the connection of a number of analog or digital station sets to a central switch. The PABX switch will accommodate a number of central office telephone lines (from a couple to hundreds) and a number of telephone station sets (from six to thousands). The PABX switch routes incoming calls to the correct extension and routes outgoing calls to an available central office line.

Additional features of PABX switches may include direct inward dialing so that certain extensions can be dialed directly from the outside without going through the switch, an automated attendant, call waiting, voice mail, and many other unique features. Internal intercom functions are usually standard.

Station sets may be simple or complicated. Simple station sets may look like a home phone, whereas more complicated sets may display time/date and incoming caller ID, have many speed-dial buttons, and show the line status of frequently called internal numbers. An operator's station set may display the status of every extension in the system either by a field of lamps and select buttons or in software.

PABX systems are normally controlled by a dedicated computer located in the main telephone closet. PABX systems are capable of sophisticated interfaces to other systems, including security systems.

The security designer can use the PABX system as a security intercom system by utilizing door stations in lieu of standard station sets (depending on the manufacturer and model of the PABX system).

For almost every installation, it is important for the security console to be equipped with a direct central office telephone that is not routed through the PABX switch; this acts as an emergency communication link in case of total power or equipment failure.

VOICE OVER IP SYSTEMS

PABX switch systems are rapidly being replaced by voice over IP (VoIP) systems. VoIP systems do not rely on central office telephone lines for their connection to the telephone company. Rather, they utilize the Internet for the connection.

The telephone station sets may be either conventional sets with a VoIP converter or network devices.

VoIP phone systems are extremely flexible since all of their functions operate in software. However, they suffer from two major potential problems relating to the security of the organization they serve. VoIP systems are subject to Internet outages, which are much more common than central office line outages, in which case the telephone lines operate on battery power from the central office. With central office lines, if electrical power fails, it is likely that the telephone lines will still work. This is not the case with VoIP phones. Additionally, VoIP phone systems are subject to intrusion by skilled hackers, making communications on a VoIP phone extremely unsecure.

VoIP phones are a natural for integration with other systems, although those interfaces have yet to be developed by the industry. VoIP systems should easily accommodate integration with IP-based security intercoms and with pagers. Digital two-way radios are also a natural point of integration. I expect to see such integration in the near future.

PUBLIC ADDRESS SYSTEMS

It is often useful to interface the C3 console to a public address system in order to make announcements. By using the microphone of the C3 console, it is one less system to keep track of at the security command center.

For single-channel (all-call) paging systems, this interface is straightforward. Simply provide an audio output from a codec into the line-level input of the paging amplifier. The output control of the codec will control the push-to-talk input of the paging amplifier.

Multichannel paging amplifiers will have a series of push buttons according to the zone to be paged. One dry contact for each zone will be needed. These can be provided by the alarm/access control system or an output relay interface panel from the digital video system, if it is so capable.

Some paging systems are actually a subset of an intercom or telephone system. These require an interface appropriate to the type of system. There is no single interface that will work with all such systems.

PARKING CONTROL SYSTEMS

Parking control systems are a common point of integration. In the simplest form, the integration may involve controlling gates in response to a card reader. In more complex cases, the integration may include counting cars, lighted automated signage, fee systems, and vehicle tag access control systems. Each element should be taken on its own, always considering the complete system picture, not just the small elements.

FUEL MANAGEMENT SYSTEMS

Fuel management systems are a subset of access control that will permit access to a fuel pump in response to presentation of a valid access card at the pump. In more elegant systems, the database may also be linked to fuel usage. In some advanced alarm/access control systems, this feature is available.

SUMMARY

Integrated security systems really begin to perform miraculous functions when they are interfaced to other building systems. Interfaces are of two types: information inputs and control outputs. Common integration tactics include

- Fire alarm interfaces

  Remote secondary annunciation (observe local codes)
  Fire/life safety interfaces

- Elevators and escalators

  Hall call control
  Floor-by-floor control
  Scheduled operation
  Remote operation from the console
  Emergency operation

- Building automation systems

  HVAC for convenience

HVAC for fire/life safety support
Lighting control
Signage
Parking control up/down counters

- Irrigation systems
- Deluge fire sprinkler control systems
- PABX interfaces and VoIP systems
- Public address systems
- Parking control systems
- Fuel management systems

15

Delaying Technologies and Response Technologies

REACTIVE AUTOMATED PROTECTION SYSTEMS

Reactive automated protection systems (REAPS) technologies are agile, automated systems that provide the security console officer with the ability to react to security events. REAPS technologies can interfere with the advance of an attacker. They range from the subtle (lights and intercom) to the extreme. REAPS technologies include intercoms, deployable barriers, and takedown technologies. The organization should consult its council before implementing any countermeasure that could cause bodily harm, as some takedown technologies can do. Takedown technologies are normally only appropriate where the risk of injury of the subject is offset by the potential risk of harm to others if the asset is destroyed or misused, such as might be the case with a suspension bridge or nuclear power plant.

INTERCOMS

Intercoms give the console officer the ability to intervene immediately on discovery of a security event. When the attacker's determination is manageable, intercom intervention can often stop an attack and send the attacker away.

DEPLOYABLE BARRIERS

For the purposes of brevity, we review a number of REAPS systems together under the heading of deployable barriers. Deployable barriers are used to slow the progress of an attacker once an attack is detected. There are three main types of barriers: vehicle barriers, marine vessel barriers, and pedestrian barriers. This list is by no means exhaustive.

Vehicle Barriers[1]

Vehicle barriers are typically manufactured either to deter or to prevent an entry and will be rated using the U.S. Department of State Crash Test Certification method. Unrated barriers should be viewed as being appropriate for deterrence only and not to stop a vehicle. Barriers are rated for their ability to stop a 15,000-lb (6800-kg) vehicle (including its load) at a given speed and with a given amount of penetration (the bed of the truck must not penetrate the barrier by more than a given distance– "L" rating). There are three "K" ratings and three "L" ratings:

- K4 barriers are rated to stop a 15,000-lb vehicle going 30 miles per hour (mph) [48 kilometers per hour (kph)].
- K8 barriers can stop the attack vehicle at 40 mph (65 kph).
- K12 barriers can stop the attack vehicle at 50 mph (80 kph).
- L1 barriers will allow the attack vehicle to penetrate not less than 20 and not more than 50 ft.
- L2 barriers will allow the attack vehicle to penetrate not less than 3 and not more than 20 ft.

Figure 15-1 K12 barrier in action. Image used with permission of Delta Scientific Corp.

- L3 barriers will not allow the attack vehicle to penetrate more than 3 ft.

Thus, a K4/L1 barrier can stop a 15,000-lb vehicle at 30 mph within 20–50 ft, and a K12/L3 barrier will stop the same vehicle at a speed of 50 mph with no more than 3 ft of penetration of the bed of the truck (Fig. 15-1).

Rising Bollards

Many manufacturers make bollards that rise out of the pavement to deter or prevent vehicular entry to an area. Bollards are useful in areas where it is desirable to permit pedestrian entry while limiting the entry of vehicles. Rising bollards are available in a vast array of cosmetic and mechanical design. Typically, rising bollards are either electric motor driven or hydraulic, although pneumatic bollards still exist. Rise time is typically 2 seconds to full height and 2 seconds down again. Rising bollards are usually capable of lifting a vehicle, so careful design and use is indicated to avoid such occurrences. When it does occur, it will usually be an ambassador's limousine that will be captured. Murphy's law indicates that the ambassador will be in the back seat with

Figure 15-2 Rising bollards. Image used with permission of Delta Scientific Corp.

his wife and children or with another ambassador or a head of state (Fig. 15-2).

Rising Wedges

Rising wedges (also known as phalanx barriers) are the mainstay of serious vehicle stopping systems. Like rising bollards, they deploy in approximately 2 seconds and can take out a vehicle on top. Many phalanx barriers are K12/L3 rated. Phalanx barriers have wonderful psychological value. They send the message. If the message does not get through, they are one of the few barriers that can withstand a multiple vehicle attack in which one vehicle is used to clear the barrier and a second and sometimes third vehicle carry the bomb payload (Fig. 15-3).

Semaphore Parking Gates

Semaphore parking gates are commonly found at the entrance to car parks and car lots. They are a psychological barrier. They will not stop any serious attack. They will not even stop drunk or confused patrons. However, they can cause a fair amount of damage to a car's paint (Fig. 15-4).

Figure 15-3 Rising wedge barrier. Image used with permission of Delta Scientific Corp.

Cable Beams

Cable beam barriers are the killer bunny of semaphore arms. They look warm and fuzzy but they sure have a painful bite. Although they are not K/L rated, a good one can stop a 10,000-lb attack vehicle at 27 mph or a 6000-lb vehicle at 40 mph. These are useful in tight spots where a large, fast attack vehicle could not likely maneuver well, such as a parking lot. At slower speeds, they do a good job. Cable beams can either swing up or to the side of the road (Fig. 15-5).

Box Beam Barriers

Box beam barriers are similar to cable beam barriers but they are able to stop larger attack vehicles traveling at higher speeds. These are typically custom fabricated and counterbalanced. They are very heavy (several tons) and are often manually operated because motors for them are very expensive. These are normally used in areas where local fabrication costs are low enough to make them viable. I use them extensively in Third World

Figure 15-4 Parking barrier gate. Image used with permission of Traffic and Safety Control Systems, Inc., of Wixom, MI.

Figure 15-5 Cable beam barrier. Image used with permission of Delta Scientific Corp.

Figure 15-6 Grab barrier. Image used with permission of USR, Inc.

environments. Although I have never submitted one for K/L rating, the math supports a K12/L3 rating on better designs.

Net Systems (Grab Barriers)

USR Inc. manufacturers a barrier that deploys fast and is effective against all types of vehicles (motorcycles to tandem trailers) as well as pedestrians. It presents as a web fabric made of high-strength aircraft cable and, unlike other barriers, is effective as both a vehicle and a pedestrian barrier. Also unlike other barriers, it is designed to achieve its stopping results without fatal injuries in most cases. (All bets are off if the offender has a weapon and your people do too.) The grab barrier is available in K4, K8, and K12 ratings. The barrier can be configured for either industrial or cosmetic installations (Fig. 15-6).

Swing Gates

Swing gates are used in low-security environments in which a psychological barrier is appropriate for vehicle traffic, and they make a useful pedestrian barrier.

Rolling Doors and Gates

Some installations require sliding gates. These are available in a variety of types, with the least expensive being chain-link or estate-type fence fabric on a rolling frame. Box frame gates can be fabricated that present as a more formidable barrier, although most of these are not K/L rated.

Serious stopping power is available in the form of true K/L-rated steel fabricated sliding gates. These take major gate operators because the mass to move is significant and it requires much power to get them moving and stopped when fully open or closed. Typically, the robust K/L-rated sliding gate operators are included with the gate (Fig. 15-7).

Air Bags

Esoteric developers are reportedly working on an air bag system to stop vehicles. These would be deployed virtually instantaneously at a full-height vehicle portal and would trigger upon detection of a fast-approaching vehicle or manually.

Figure 15-7 K12 sliding gate. Image used with permission of Delta Scientific Corp.

Inventive Systems

It is possible to create a variety of other vehicle defense systems using common materials applied in unusual ways. For example, a roadway trench can become a barrier with the use of a grille (cattle guard) fabricated with explosive bolts to cause the grille to collapse into the trench upon approach of a known threat.

Marine Vessel Barriers

Antiboat Barriers

Deployable antiboat barriers are floating obstacles that can be reeled into place across a berthing basin or waterway on demand. They are capable of stopping small craft and act as a visual deterrent. They are typically deployed by boat but can be deployed by reeled cable that sits on the bed of the basin (Fig. 15-8).

Figure 15-8 WhisprWave antiboat barrier. Image used with permission of Wave Dispersion Technologies, Inc.

Water Monitors

Water monitors are an adaptation of fire-fighting equipment that serve as an effective deterrent or to fend off attackers in a small craft. The volume of water that can be deployed against a small craft is capable of turning it away or sinking it. Water monitors can be controlled remotely and aimed by video camera on the monitor or by a synchronized pan/tilt/zoom camera.

Pedestrian Barriers

Pedestrian barriers range from the totally inoffensive (intercoms to challenge a subject verbally) to the extreme (ballistic weaponry).

Intercoms

Intercoms are the most basic and inoffensive barrier. When an intrusion is detected, the first step is to assess the seriousness of the offense. The combination of video and intercom is a very good way to do this. A console officer can quickly determine the capabilities and motivation of an intruder using a brief and standardized interview procedure.

Lighting

When it is determined that an intruder's motivation is to ignore directions over an intercom, the console officer can remotely turn off all available lighting in an unoccupied building. This is very useful indoors in buildings in which there are no windows, such as in the anchorage building of a suspension bridge. Unless the attacker is carrying a flashlight, he or she is quite literally "in the dark." The console officer, of course, will be equipped with a quantity of low-cost infrared-illuminated indoor video cameras. The intruder cannot see, but the officer can see the intruder. The console officer can then return to the intercom, and will likely find that the attention of the offender has been captured.

Alternatively, outdoors, turning on all available lighting sends the message that it will be difficult for the intruder to

Figure 15-9 Operable wall. Image used with permission of Modernfold.

acquire cover from a patrolling officer. The point of lighting manipulation is to make the subject feel exposed.

Rolling Grilles and Operable Walls

Deployable grilles and operable walls are available in a variety of styles, from steel grilles to folding operable walls and moveable walls. When motorized, these can be deployed rapidly to present a wall where the intruder was pretty sure a passage used to be. This a good place for another intercom and camera. Most intruders get the message by this point (Fig. 15-9).

Deployable Doors

Automating critical passage doors or simply placing those doors on magnetic holders can cause the doors to release and close in a locked condition. The addition of magnetic locks with an intrusion override can prevent travel in either direction, making an effective barrier. Intrusion overrides require a fire authority variance and a safety switch at the console (Fig. 15-10).

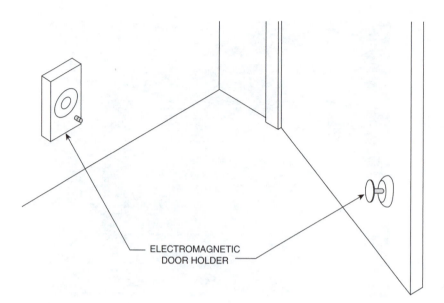

ELECTROMAGNETIC
DOOR HOLDER

Figure 15-10   Magnetic door holder.

Revolving Doors

Revolving doors can be used for positive access control and serve as an effective deterrent against illicit entry. They can also be locked to prevent the progress of an intruder.

Irrigation Systems

Irrigation systems make a surprising barrier to outdoor intruders. Only the most determined intruders will proceed across a field of sprinklers. If the intruder does proceed, at least you know he or she is motivated (Fig. 15-11).

Fog Barriers

Smokecloak™ is a glycol-based visual barrier that can fill an area with an impenetrable fog within seconds, rendering anyone in it fully incapable of seeing anything. The barrier dissipates over a period of approximately 15 minutes and is effective when lights-out is not enough. An intruder cannot see his hand in front of his face, let alone anything else. It effectively blinds the intruder,

Figure 15-11   Irrigation system.

even in daylight, making his progress painfully slow, and that is usually toward wherever he imagines the exit to be (Fig. 15-12).

Prejudiced Barriers

Quick Setup Foam Barriers

Specialized applications call for a foam barrier. Rigid foam is deployed by combining two separate chemicals into a single nozzle, which sets up into a self-hardening block in the shape of the containment area. This can block and trap (and even encapsulate) the aggressor. Sticky foam has been developed at Sandia National Laboratories but is not yet commercially available; it is a single-component chemical that is dispensed from a pressure vessel to block the adversary's path. The more the adversary fights with the sticky foam, the more sticky and tenacious the foam acts against him or her. See the section on dispensable barriers in Garcia's *Design and Evaluation of Physical Protection Systems*[2] for a more detailed discussion of sticky foam.

Drop Chains

For small, confined spaces such as the cable-splay room of a suspension bridge, it is possible to position a large quantity of heavy chain links (about ceiling to knee length) from the ceiling in an

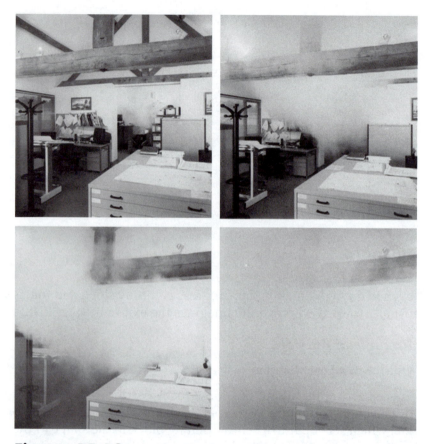

Figure 15-12 Smokecloak™. Image used with permission of Smokecloak – Martin Security Smoke A/S. www. smokecloak.com

array on approximately 6-in. centers. These are held in place by two trays that are themselves held in place by explosive bolts. If the intruder makes it to the asset, the console officer blows the bolts and the chains drop in a manner that defies anyone in the room to stand up, let alone wield any kind of harmful weapon.

Acoustic Weaponry

The human body is sensitive to infrasonic sounds. Tigers are reported to be able to emit a stunningly loud 18-Hz roar immediately before attacking, stunning their prey. Sperm whales reportedly emit high-volume infrasonic pulses, disabling squid from making a quick getaway.

According to a report prepared for the United Nations in 1978, the frequency of 7 or 8 Hz is thought to be most dangerous to humans. This is the resonant frequency of flesh and theoretically can disrupt or destroy internal organs. At lower volumes, it is certainly able to cause intense discomfort, even making the subject evacuate at both ends.

High-amplitude infrasonic weapons can be created simply by combining two high-volume ultrasonic frequencies at a difference of 8 Hz and aiming them at the desired subject. Because the source transducers are ultrasonic, they can be placed some distance apart and "vectored" onto a single subject in a crowd of people. This creates a compelling wish to be somewhere else. Patents were issued for some acoustic weapons in 1999 and 2000. Experiments on infrasonic weapons in the 1970s by French robotics researcher Dr. Gaverau, without the benefit of the ultrasonic-to-infrasonic conversion, resulted in the test building being shaken to the point of nearly being destroyed, and the researchers were subjected to what they referred to as an "envelope of death." Gaverau and his team were critically ill for days, with their internal organs experiencing painful spasms as a result of their body cavities having resonated at the deadly frequency. The jury is still out on this one. As this book was being written, the first commercial acoustic weapon was introduced, called the Long Range Acoustic Device (LRAD)™. The LRAD combines two ultrasonic frequencies together, creating a third "Beat" frequency. Since ultrasonic frequencies are highly directional, and the beat frequency can be any frequency, even ultra low frequencies of 7 to 8 Hz, it is possible to create very high amplitude, very directional very low frequencies. This is a feat never possible before. In November 2005, pirates off the coast of Somalia who were attempting to fire on a passenger cruise ship were effectively repelled by an LRAD.[3] (Fig. 15-13)

Useable Acoustic Security Devices

I have successfully addressed gang activity near convenience stores by implementing outdoor speakers playing peaceful

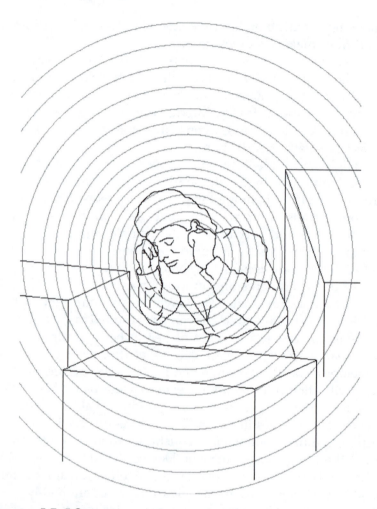

Figure 15-13 Sonic weapon.

symphonic pop elevator music on satellite radio. This drives gangbangers totally nuts. The designer is advised to use bull-horn speakers enclosed in a vandal-deterrent cage. Bullhorns are recommended because they sound very bad. The music is not offensive to legitimate customers, but it creates an environment that does not support the business model of drug dealers. This has also been used in Australia to good effect to rid public buildings of unwanted gang behavior.[4]

A Welsh firm makes a near ultrasonic tone generator, amplifier, and piezo speaker that creates a sound like fingernails on a chalkboard. This also drives young people crazy. Older people cannot hear it due to natural age-related high-frequency hearing loss.[5]

High-Voltage Weaponry

Essentially a Tesla coil on steroids, high-voltage weapons are a Taser™ for protecting buildings. Useful to disperse crowds, they emit an attention-getting amount of high voltage at very low amplitude all around the vicinity of the spike transducers.

Another version of this weapon is the spark-gap transmitter. Similar to its portable cousin the stun gun, the spark-gap transducer can be mounted on top of a protective perimeter fence at distances of approximately 10 ft. When an intruder suspected of carrying satchel charges or improvised explosive devices is detected attempting to make entry through the fence, after a video assessment of the situation and a polite verbal warning through a camera-mounted 30-W bullhorn, if this intruder still is not getting the message, the console officer and his or her supervisor throw a pair of safety switches after selecting the appropriate fence zone, and all the spark gaps along that fence section ignite in a bright array of high-voltage arcs. If the intruder is carrying explosives and electrically activated detonators, this display of high-voltage can also be accompanied by an explosion in the vicinity of the intruder, followed afterward by a repair of the fence. This approach is most appropriate in serious threat environments and in countries in which such methods are approved by the government. This approach is much less expensive than a helicopter gunship and requires less maintenance than automated guns.

Remotely Operated Weaponry

Most of the defeat technologies discussed previously are non-lethal, but when the asset value is exceptional or the risk of a successful attack to the public is high, and nothing else will get the job done, one can always rely on guns. At least

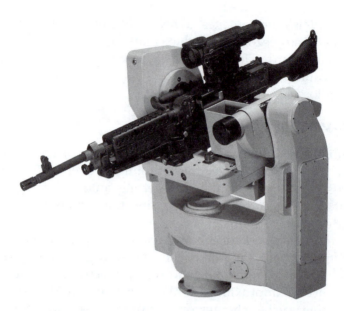

Figure 15-14 MacKenzie River Partners Orion 300 weapons system. Image used with permission of Mac Kenzie River Partners, Inc. www.mackenzieriverpartners.com

two manufacturers make remotely operated weaponry. From 7.62-mm to twin 50-caliber guns and a range in between, remotely operated weapons are the final answer to intruders that just will not take no for an answer. These are products that couple a pan/tilt/zoom video camera with an appropriate weapon. These are available in either temporary or permanent installation versions. I have also seen them fabricated on site where budget is a factor and low-cost maintenance personnel are available (Third World countries). These are also deployed in the United States at critical installations (Fig. 15-14).

Deluge Systems

For any environment such as an outdoor shopping mall, where competing gangs of criminal youths could engage in gunfire, nothing can disperse a crowd immediately quite like 10,000 gallons of water in 60 seconds. Afterward, although people are most likely to be upset and drenched, the gunfire will probably have stopped and the perpetrators will likely have fled, thus dissipating the danger and protecting the innocent public.

Coupled with gunshot recognition software, pan/tilt cameras can instantly zoom in on the offender, providing visual verification of the condition requiring action.

Deluge system activation should only be installed after careful consideration and advice from legal counsel, but they may be appropriate for any venue where there is a potential or history of gunfire in public spaces.

INTEGRATING THE ELEMENTS

It is one thing to find REAPS equipment (that alone can be a difficult task), but it is quite another to appropriately apply them. The reader can contact the author for help in finding them. There are three factors in applying them.

Appropriateness

It is wholly inappropriate to apply lethal or even less than lethal countermeasures in anything but a serious threat environment in which the asset under protection could cause harm (munitions, nuclear reactors, etc.) and in which adequate public safeguards are not possible. The use of any of these systems in an environment in which an innocent could be harmed is completely inappropriate. I have refused to employ them where the government requesting the countermeasure was of questionable moral ethics. They should be used in close consultation with the manufacturer.

Operationally

The operation of such barriers and weapons should be limited to circumstances in which multiple layers of security are in place and the intruder has demonstrated firm determination to proceed toward a goal of harming or destroying a critical asset. Adequate evidence can be achieved by either the amount of force used or the determination with which the intruder continues undeterred by instructions toward the asset. If the attacker uses lethal force, it is arguably appropriate to defend with lethal force. If the intruder continues through other deployed barriers and refuses verbal instructions, it is reasonable to assume he or she will be undeterred by mild measures.

In any case, the system should be configured with adequate operational safeguards to absolutely prevent accidental deployment. This typically requires a deployment action by both an operator and a supervisor or some action by the intruder that is unmistakably hostile and will result in the death of innocents, such as driving a large truck full of explosives toward a Marine barracks compound at 5:00 AM at high speed past a guard post.

Safety Systems

For any REAPS technology that could cause bodily harm, it is imperative to build in deployment safety systems. These can be effected electronically, mechanically, and procedurally.

Electronic Safety Systems

Design REAPS systems to include at least two separate electronic circuits to trigger the system activation. For potentially lethal systems, it is advisable to use at least three triggering systems. These should be activated by totally separate electronic circuits such that no single point of failure could cause any more than one electronic triggering system to activate unintentionally. By separate systems, I do not mean separate dry-contact points on the same circuit board. I mean separate circuit boards on separate power systems with their own battery or uninterruptible power supply backup and with separate communication lines to each individual board. It is advisable to locate the boards in different areas on separate circuit breakers, on separate electrical phases, and, ideally, on separate electrical transformers. The dry contacts should be triggered in series, not in parallel. It is also advisable to protect the conduit within which the triggering circuit runs with a conduit intrusion alarm system. Use only metallic electrical conduit, preferentially rigid, not flexible, and waterproof where appropriate. For fast vehicle capture systems, at least two sets of loops should be used, coupled with optical sensors, if possible, to prevent accidental triggering by an unusual positioning of slow-moving vehicles.

Mechanical Safety Systems

Mechanical safety systems are a backup to electrical safety systems. For example, on drop chain systems, the explosive bolts should be on separate electrical circuits and the bolts should be wired such that all of them must break in order for the chains to drop. By using four separate circuits to drop the exploding bolts, the chains will only drop if all four circuits blow, thus assuring that a single point of failure type of accident does not cause injury.

Procedural Safety Systems

Any lethal or less than lethal REAPS system should also have procedural safety systems. These can include the requirement for both a console officer and a supervisor to trigger lethal systems after verifying intent and capabilities to cause great harm to the protected asset or the organization's people or the public.

For nonlethal systems, such as deployable doors, gates, and grilles, these measures are not necessary since the deployment of a door is not an unusual or life-threatening event.

SUMMARY

REAPS technologies provide the designer with the ability to react to security events. REAPS technologies include intercoms, deployable barriers, and takedown technologies. Intercoms can often stop an attack and send the attacker on away.

Deployable barriers may include vehicle barriers, marine vessel barriers, and pedestrian barriers. Vehicle barriers are rated by their stopping power. They are assigned K and L ratings based on the weight of a vehicle they can stop and how far the vehicle may penetrate past the barrier. Vehicle barriers include rising bollards, rising wedges, semaphore parking gates, cable beams, box beam barriers, and net systems. Vehicle gates include swing gates and rolling doors and gates. Marine vessel barriers include antiboat barriers and water monitors. Pedestrian barriers include intercoms, lighting, rolling grilles and operable walls, deployable doors, revolving doors, irrigation systems, and fog barriers.

Prejudiced barriers include quick setup and sticky foam barriers, drop chains, acoustic weaponry, high-voltage defense systems, remotely operated weaponry, and deluge systems.

REAPS technologies should be carefully vetted for operational, legal, and safety standards.

CHAPTER NOTES

1. A wonderful guide for vehicle barrier design is available from the U.S. Department of Defense, MIL-HDBK-1013/14—Selection and Application of Vehicle Barriers. The document is referenced at www.wbdg.org/ccb/NAVFAC/DMMHNAV/1013_14.pdf.
2. Garcia, M. L. (2001). *The Design and Evaluation of Physical Protection Systems*, pp. 216–219. Butterworth-Heinemann, Oxford.
3. BBC News - Saturday, 5 November 2005.
4. Reuters (2006, June 5). Bothered by Loud Cars? Try "Copacabana": "Sick and tired of souped-up cars with loud engines and pulsing music? Barry Manilow may be the answer.

   Officials in one Sydney district have decided to pipe the American crooner's music over loudspeakers in an attempt to rid streets and car parks of "car hoons" whose antisocial cars and loud music annoy residents and drive customers from businesses.

   Following a successful experiment in which Bing Crosby music was used to drive teenage loiterers out of an Australian shopping center several years ago, Rockdale officials believe Manilow is so uncool it might just work.
5. The Mosquito product by Howard Stapleton, Compound Security Devices of Merthyr Tydfil in Wales, uses the medical phenomenon known as presbycusis or age-related hearing loss, which, according to the *Merck Manual of Diagnosis and Therapy*, begins after age 20. Available at www.snarkhunting.com/2005/11/a-name-with-buzz.

16

Alarm Detection and Emerging Video Technologies

ALARM DETECTION TECHNOLOGIES

Alarms are the mainstay of security. The oldest security systems involved a public responsibility of citizens to stay awake all night and patrol in shifts, calling out for help if any threat was discovered.

There are three basic types of detection systems:

- Point detectors (door position switches, glass-break sensors, duress switches, etc.)
- Volumetric detectors (including infrared, microwave, ultra-sonic, and video)
- Line detectors (seismic, pressure, capacitance, etc.)

Alarm detectors may be used indoors or outdoors. Indoor applications can be of any type. Outdoor detectors are most commonly used on the perimeter, although there is some use of volumetric detectors.

Point Detectors

Magnetic Switches

Simple Magnetic Switches

Simple magnetic switches are used to detect the opening of doors and windows. A basic magnetic switch comprises two parts— the magnet and a magnetically sensitive switch (usually a reed switch enclosed within a glass envelope). Switches may be either normally open (close on alarm) or normally closed (open on alarm). Some are available in a Form-C contact (your choice of normally open or normally closed, both in one switch).

There is a wide variety of magnetic switch form factors for every need. Switches are available both for surface mount and for concealment within the door and its frame.

Economical switches are usually surface mounted and enclosed in a plastic case, whereas better switches may be concealed. Switches are made for unique applications, such as concealment within a wood door or a hollow metal door. These cannot be used in place of each other.

Switches rated for industrial or outdoor use may be fitted with heavy aluminum enclosures, some even with integral conduit fittings.

Balanced Bias Magnetic Switches

One problem with simple magnetic switches is that it may be possible for an intruder to place a magnet next to the switch while opening the door, fooling the system into missing the fact that the door or window has opened.

Balanced bias magnetic switches are designed for high-security applications. By floating the magnetic switch in its case between two magnets oppositely polarized (one horizontal and the other vertical), any disruption in the magnetic field, such as opening of a door or window, will cause a change in state of the magnetic switch. The very act of placing a magnet next to the switch to fool the switch will be seen by the switch as an alarm.

Duress Switches

Duress switches are a class of switches that are intentionally triggered as a call for help by a person who believes that he or she is under threat. Usually, these are in the form of a switch placed under a counter or in the knee-well of a desk that the victim can activate while in his or her normal working position. Duress switches are common in banks, emergency rooms, convenience stores, public counters, and other places where a person might express angry or violent behavior.

There are three factors of concern in the design and use of duress switches:

- The switch must be convenient and quiet so as not to alert the subject of the duress alert.
- The switch must exhibit a positive feedback so that the victim knows that a call for help has gone out.
- The switch must not activate accidentally.

A number of designs have been created to deal with these concerns:

Two-Finger Switches

Two-finger switches are a type of switch that requires two separate push button switches to be pressed simultaneously in order for an alarm to occur. The two switches are best arranged as a finger and thumb squeeze configuration to ensure that they cannot both be triggered accidentally by a knee or object. These switches are very effective but must be custom made.

Pull and Plunger Switches

Pull switches require the victim to pull out a plunger with the thumb and forefinger. This is a positive action and cannot be accidentally triggered. Plunger switches require that a plunger be pushed deep into a ring around the switch that otherwise protects the plunger from accidental triggering.[1]

Footswitches

Footswitches are common in areas where the victim may be asked to keep his or her hands above a counter, such as in a bank. Footswitches are activated by placing one's foot under a lever and lifting it with the toe, thus activating the switch.

Bill Traps

For banks and cash counters, a type of duress switch called a bill trap causes an alarm if the last bill in the drawer is removed. The bill is placed in the bill trap and left there constantly, thus separating two contacts of a switch. When the bill is removed, the switch makes contact, sending a silent alarm. Thus the famous movie line, "I think I hear the silent alarm!"

Resets

All duress alarms should be configured to latch until reset. This is important so that if one of several duress alarms is tripped along a line of cash drawers or service counters, it is possible to determine which one was tripped.

Elegant Duress Switch Implementations

Although simple duress alarms are very helpful, it is not good to send security officers (or even police) into a situation with guns drawn where innocent people could be harmed. These implementations help ensure that the console security officer knows exactly what is going on at the location of the duress switch:

- Audio and video activation: Wherever a duress alarm is used, a video and audio verification is appropriate. It is difficult to explain to a courtroom why such verifications were found to be important at a back door but not where an angry, confrontational, possibly gun-toting person was anticipated. A microphone at the counter (you do not want two-way communications here) and video camera with a commanding view of the room are very useful in assessing the situation.

- Ring-back: A ring-back system has been used to assure the victim that his or her duress call was acknowledged and that help is on the way. A simple wrong number to the victim's phone will keep the subject blissfully unaware that he or she is under observation.
- Visual indicator: Some clients want some kind of visual indicator that the alarm has been acknowledged. This can be in the form of a normal-appearing activity. I have used everything from a momentary and unconcerning telephone ringing across the room (a nonstandard ring tone for the users) to a ceiling fan that switched on in response to a duress alarm. In both cases, those actions were inconsistent with normal operations to the authorized users but would not create an alert to the attacker.

Volumetric Detectors

Volumetric detectors are designed to detect movement within a defined space. All volumetric detectors sense a change in some condition within the space, typically a change in heat signature or motion.

Passive Infrared Field Detectors

Passive infrared (PIR) field detectors sense a change in heat across an infrared phototransistor. The phototransistor does not sense motion, but by fabricating a lens in front of the phototransistor, it is possible to create a series of invisible "fingers" across which a subject might walk or crawl. As the subject moves across the fingers of detection, the phototransistor senses a change in heat signature from the heat generated by the subject versus the ambient heat in the space. As the change is sensed, the transistor current crosses a predetermined detection threshold, activating a dry-contact relay in the detector.

PIR detectors are most useful in areas where the ambient temperature is below 95.6°F (35°C) because above that temperature the sensor cannot distinguish the difference between the heat generated by a human body and the ambient heat.

PIR detectors are also most useful when configured so that a subject must walk across the fingers of detection. They are least sensitive as a subject walks toward or away from the detector. This is because the detector lens is configured to create temperature differentials between the fingers of detection that the phototransistor can easily detect. When walking across the fingers, the detection is natural; when walking toward the detector, a subject must transverse an area comprising at least two or three fingers of detection before detection occurs.

PIR detectors are used both for alarm detection and to sense the presence of a person about to exit through an access controlled door. In the latter case, the detector is often configured to unlock the electric lock and to bypass the door alarm to allow the legal exit without an alarm. The former type of detector is configured with detection patterns of from a few degrees to 150 degrees of arc. The latter type of detector is configured to position directly above a door and creates a "curtain" pattern looking down on the door handle. They can often be positioned to look back a few feet to sense a person approaching the door.

Active Infrared Detectors

Reflection Detector

The simplest type of active IR detector is one that has an infrared photodiode coupled with an infrared phototransistor in the same enclosure. The photodiode generates infrared light, and the phototransistor senses the infrared light. These are both visible through lenses on the side of the enclosure. The enclosure is positioned opposite a prism reflector, usually across a door, gate, or other portal. The detector is used to sense an interruption in the beam, typically a person, vehicle, or object moving through the beam.

Reflective detectors are useful for short distances and best used indoors, where ambient light is less likely to overwhelm the phototransistor. These are commonly used as door alarms to alert a shopkeeper that a customer has entered the shop. They are popular because they are easy to install, having only one active element so wiring is simplified.

Beam Detectors

Infrared beam detectors overcome the inherent problem of reflective IR detectors—that is, the problem of ambient light interfering with the detection. They do this by separating the photodiode and phototransistor into separate enclosures. For long-distance detection, the photodiode may be replaced by an IR laser. This configuration allows the phototransistor to more precisely sense the IR light.

IR beam detectors are commonly used to detect entry through a perimeter and may be used to surround a property or asset. These are typically high-value assets, including high-end homes, industrial sites, and corporate headquarters. Because of the value of the assets, exploits for early IR beam detectors were developed. These mainly involved replacing the true IR light source with a handheld source in the possession of the intruder. To counter this, manufacturers developed pulsed IR beams. Any attempt to replace the true IR light source with a false source automatically causes alarm detection.

IR beams are most useful on ground that is flat or on a continuous smooth grade without intervening hills and valleys because these create opportunities for the intruder to crawl under the beams. IR beams are available to span distances from 10 to 600 ft.

IR beams are useful wherever a long straight line over level grade must be protected. Exploits for IR beams include the use of ladders, trucks, and even pole vaults—anything that can be used by the subject to go over the top of the beams.

Microwave Detectors

Microwave detectors are made in a variety of types for use indoors and outdoors. Microwave detectors have either an elliptical-shaped detection pattern or a balloon-shaped pattern. Microwave detectors are either monostatic or bistatic. Monostatic detectors have a microwave transmitter and receiver both in one package. Bistatic microwave detectors separate the transmitter and receiver into two units.

Monostatic Detectors

Monostatic detectors are commonly used indoors and in small, contained areas. They are most sensitive to subjects moving toward or away from the detector. Monostatic microwave detectors are essentially small radar units that detect the "echo" of the transmitted signal.

Monostatic detectors operate at such a high frequency[2] that they are able to detect the movement of gasses within the space, including gasses within fluorescent fixtures. Many designers have been surprised to discover that their systems false alarm when fluorescent fixtures start flickering. Designers are also sometimes startled to discover that frequent false alarms are in fact caused by the detection of people moving on the other side of a wall. Microwave detectors operate at a frequency high enough to detect movement through walls, particularly gypsum board walls.

Exploits for monostatic detectors include very slow movement (less than 1 ft every 5 minutes) and creating a string of continuous false alarms over a long enough time so that the monitoring center may ignore the alarm when it is real.

Bistatic

Bistatic detectors operate completely differently from monostatic detectors in that they are not detecting an echo signal but more closely resemble the operation of active IR beams. By separating the microwave transmitter and detector, greater definition of the detection zone is possible, as well as greater distances. Bistatic microwave detectors can "reach" distances of up to 1500 ft.

Bistatic microwave detectors operate at a very small wavelength (0.75–3 cm), making detection of any object larger than 3 cm a virtual certainty within their detection field. Bistatic microwave detectors should be overlapped when used to protect a perimeter so that there are no areas where an intruder can step over or between the patterns of any individual detector. Detection patterns can be adjusted from very narrow to up to 40 ft.

Microwave detectors are prone to false alarms when positioned across any body of water (even a small mud puddle) and during weather patterns such as snow, high wind, rain, or fog. Wind is problematic due to the number of small blowing objects, including leaves and debris.

Bistatic microwave detector exploits include transiting during periods of heavy wind and rain, when the detectors are likely to be yielding many nuisance alarms.

Ultrasonic

Ultrasonic detectors use a high-frequency transducer just above the range of human hearing (typically 40–60 kHz). Ultrasonic detectors predate the introduction of monostatic microwave detectors for indoor use and have largely fallen into disuse.

Ultrasonic detectors broadcast a high-frequency audio signal and listen for the same signal. They detect the Doppler shifted wave reflected by a moving object within the field of detection. Ultrasonic detectors are prone to nuisance alarms caused by keys jingling, vacuum cleaners, and numerous other problems.

Acoustic (Glass-Break) Detectors

Acoustic glass-break detectors comprise a microphone and discriminating circuit designed to listen for the specific sound signature of glass breaking. Acoustic glass-break detectors are placed within close acoustic proximity of the glass to be monitored (typically within 15 ft). They must have a clear line of sight to the glass and may not detect reliably if they are obstructed.

Early acoustic glass-break detectors were prone to all of the same problems as ultrasonic volumetric detectors, but these have largely been resolved by use of discriminating audio circuits.

Do not confuse ultrasonic detectors with glass-break detectors that sense in the ultrasonic range. The difference is that glass-break detectors do not transmit an ultrasonic frequency but instead use a microphone to listen for the specific sound of glass breaking within the ultrasonic frequency range.

Dual Technologies

Serious designers always try to design detection systems that complement the weaknesses of each other in order to ensure detection in any circumstances. Recognizing that infrared and monostatic microwave detectors have complementary nuisance detection factors, manufacturers have packaged both together into a single unit, thus ensuring reliable detection in most circumstances. Many can be configured to alarm if either ("or" logic) or both ("and" logic) detectors sense the presence of an aggressor. The infrared and microwave each have different sensing patterns and responses to objects moving in their path. Infrared detectors sense most readily when an aggressor is moving across their pattern,[3] and microwave detectors sense most readily when an aggressor is moving toward or away from the detector.[4]

These detectors can detect objects moving any direction within their field (when set to "or" logic) and are considered more reliable than either infrared or microwave detectors alone.

EMERGING VIDEO TECHNOLOGIES

Volumetric Detectors

Video detection systems are somewhat unique in that they combine both detection and assessment into a single process. As the video algorithm detects possible inappropriate behavior, the system makes the video available for further human assessment.

Video Motion Detectors

The simplest form of video volumetric detection is motion detection. Such algorithms are available on even the least expensive of multiplexers, digital video recorders, and other video processing units. In their simplest form, they define an area on the screen using large block pixels. Settings include sensitivity (how many shades of gray each pixel must change in order to cause a detection) and duration.

Intelligent Video Detectors

Anyone looking at a specific video image can easily distinguish motion and certain troubling behaviors. Using advanced digital signal processing image evaluation algorithms, it is possible to detect a number of inappropriate behaviors on many cameras simultaneously without the need to have console officers viewing all those images at all times.

The term the industry uses for this is *intelligent video.* Although intelligent video still has a long way to go in terms of both accuracy and cost, it shows great promise. Video detection algorithms can be programmed as to the area of detection, the type of detection (motion, absence of motion, loitering, left objects, etc.), and the schedule of detection.

This approach allows for much better utilization of human resources, freeing guards for patrol and response. These solutions are also highly scalable. Where increased video detection tasks quickly overwhelm human resources, computers can efficiently process dozens to hundreds of video images simultaneously. Intelligent video detectors are also much better than their human counterparts at enforcement of security and surveillance policies since they do not rely on the integrity or attention span of the monitoring guard.

Typically, a computer is used to render the images to the detection algorithm. Each computer can typically handle 3–16 cameras.

The systems are also capable of organizing detections into classifications, times, and dates in order to develop trend-tracking reports. They also generally archive the detection video, including a period of pre- and post-alarm activity. Intelligent video detectors typically work one or more algorithms for each camera.

One type of intelligent video detection shows great promise. One company has developed a set of detection algorithms that index their findings so that searches can be made very rapidly (in milliseconds). The system is also capable of rendering alerts, like a normal intelligent video system, and it requires many times less processing power than other systems. This system is especially useful for security analytics and is the first system to make deep video analytics practical for the typical user.[5]

Some intelligent video systems are better suited for indoor scenes and some are better suited for outdoor scenes, based on the type of algorithm. For example, outdoor systems are often designed to look for human-sized objects moving in a large field and may also be able to identify boats, planes, cars, trucks, and busses and even animals. One current system is able to identify the location of the object in three-dimensional space and whether or not that object is moving toward, away from, or across or into a zone that has been identified for intrusion detection.[6] Such capabilities as plane and bus identification obviously have little use indoors.

Other intelligent video detection systems are especially adept at indoor scene detection. These often include such capabilities as identifying people loitering in a crowd or a crowd developing or dispersing, and they may be able to identify the facial features of a subject for later or real-time identification. Based on facial identification features, the level of certainty can be calculated. Some systems are pretty good at determining if an object has been left or taken. Some systems are capable of ignoring certain types of ongoing activity, such as trees blowing in the wind and mild wave action.[7]

Triangulation Detectors

Another type of video detector that is undergoing testing is quite unique in that it uses three video cameras to triangulate on an area in three-dimensional space to determine if an object is moved, placed, or affected in any way. Each of three cameras is set up to detect the same object from different angles. The combination of the cameras allows for much more accurate detection to determine if an object is targeted in the presence of high traffic. This system has had considerable success in early tests, such as in museum environments.

Perimeter Detection Systems

Line Detectors

Leaky Coax Detectors

Ported coax or "leaky coax" detectors comprise a direct-burial coaxial cable on which the center conductor is continuous and the shield is woven in such a fashion as to allow the signal from the center conductor to leak through the shield by virtue of the fact that the shield has openings in the weave, unlike a normal shielded coaxial cable. A radio frequency signal is sent down the coax, and some of its energy leaks into the atmosphere. The cable is buried so as not to make possible intruders aware of its presence. When the intruder steps into the field of the coax, he or she interrupts the field, causing detection. Advanced systems can pinpoint within a few feet exactly where the detection occurred.

Leaky coax systems are useful wherever there is a long expanse of perimeter to cover and the detection method should be unseen (Fig. 16-1).

Leaky coax systems must be well integrated to their environment. The systems can fail to alarm or to false alarm by virtue of their environment. For example, leaky coax systems will not detect under ponding water and may yield nuisance alarms from

Figure 16-1 Leaky coax detector.

larger animal activity. Thus, they should be installed along crest lines if possible and in areas not prone to animal activity.

Leaky coax exploits are few where they are properly installed. Leaky coax systems can fail to detect if movement is less than approximately 1 ft every 10 minutes. Few intruders have such patience.

Capacitance Detectors

Leaky coax systems are a form of capacitance detector. Other types can be mounted on or above a fence. Capacitance detectors work best if configured so that the intruder must come into close contact with the sensor, such as when used in lieu of barbed wire at the top of a fence, set off of the fence fabric by a few inches.

Seismic Detectors

Seismic detectors are basically microphones that are placed into the ground which detect acoustic disturbances. A typical seismic detector is configured as a spike that is driven into the ground. These are arrayed in a line along a perimeter. Usually, the cables

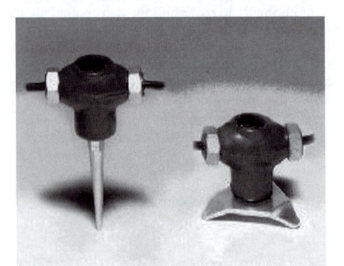

Figure 16-2 Seismic detector. Image used with permission of Safeguards Technology, LLC.

can be covered to obscure their presence (Fig. 16-2). Seismic detectors work well in remote areas and areas where there is little adjacent vehicular traffic.

A common seismic detector exploit is to use a large vehicle to mask the sound of foot traffic.

Fiber-Optic Detectors

Fiber-optic cable can be configured to detect either breaking or deflection in the cable. It can also be configured to act as a microphone along a fence line.

A fiber-optic detector injects a pulsed signal down the fiber and monitors it for differences at the receiver, where it is compared to the signal that was sent. Any sudden change in the signal triggers an alarm. Fiber-optic detectors are immune from most environmental effects and operate reliably over a wide range of environmental conditions.

A common fiber-optic exploit is to "accidentally" cut or damage the cable, necessitating a repair. An intrusion may occur during the repair interval (Fig. 16-3).

Common-Mode Wire Detectors

Common-mode wire detectors are similar in physical installation to fiber-optic detectors. Common-mode detectors comprise a pair of wires strung within a single insulation jacket. A balanced signal is sent down the cables, and they detect any

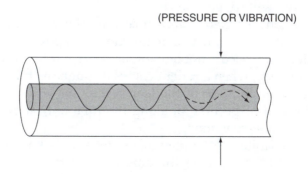

Figure 16-3 Fiber-optic detector.

difference in the signal resulting from a disruption in the cables. Common-mode detectors are typically strung onto a chain-link fence. The detector acts as a microphone, "listening" for the sound of the chain-link mesh being cut or climbed.

Common-mode detectors are subject to their environment, particularly fence condition. Fences that are loose, have large signs loosely attached to the fabric, or are connected to gate posts that might "clang" when a gate closes can all cause false alarms.

Common-mode detectors are best used on expanses of fence that are free from vegetation and animal activity and also on fences that are well maintained.

Exploits for common-mode detectors are the same as for fiber-optic detectors, in addition to the placement of an object that can cause false alarm activity.

Pneumatic Weight Detectors

Pneumatic weight detectors are a variation on the old gas station driveway alert, which was common years ago. They comprise a tube filled with air, plugged at one end, and at the other end there is an atmospheric pressure sensor.

The pneumatic tube is buried just underneath the surface and when an intruder steps onto the ground above the tube, detection occurs. Unlike fiber-optic and capacitance detectors, the area of the detection is imprecise; only the zone is detected, not the location on the zone.

Unlike capacitance and fiber-optic detectors, pneumatic detectors are immune to water, brush, small animals, etc. Only a heavy step will trigger the zone.

Pneumatic detectors are subject to the diets of certain rodents, so the tubes must be maintained with positive pressure so that detection occurs not only on pressure but on the absence of pressure (e.g., when a rodent chews through the tube). When this occurs, the location of the tear is impossible to determine without visual inspection all along the tube until it is located. This can be time-consuming.

If the location of the pneumatic detector is known, it can be exploited by going over the tube with a structure such as a ladder.

Monostatic and Bistatic Perimeter Microwave Detectors

These were described under Volumetric Detectors.

Perimeter Video Detectors

Video can be used as an alarm detector with the addition of either simple video motion detection or complex intelligent video algorithms.

Miscellaneous Detectors

Most designers believe that the alarm inputs on security systems are binary inputs, sensing open and closed positions. In fact, most alarm inputs are measuring current flow across a constant voltage. Typically, the acceptable range is 4–20 ma. Anything less than 4 ma or greater than 20 ma is an indicator that the alarm loop is in a trouble condition, or that it has been subject to tampering. By using end-of-line resistors, in series with and across the alarm dry-contact switch, an open or closed condition of the switch can be accurately measured because it results in precise 4- or 20-ma conditions on the loop.

A few systems can also use their alarm inputs to measure a current gradient, allowing analog measurements such as temperature and water level.

Other common miscellaneous detectors include water level detectors, humidity detectors, and temperature detectors.

SUMMARY

Alarm detection technologies include point detectors, volumetric detectors, and line detectors. Point detectors include magnetic door switches and duress switches. Volumetric detectors include passive and active infrared, microwave, ultrasonic, and acoustic detectors. Dual-technology detectors reduce nuisance alarms.

Video systems can also serve as volumetric detectors and as either a security alarm system or a forensic analytic system.

Perimeter detection systems include leaky coax detectors, capacitance detectors, seismic detectors, fiber-optic detectors, common-mode detectors, and pneumatic weight detectors. Miscellaneous detectors include 4- to 20-ma current loop detectors and temperature, humidity, and water level detectors.

CHAPTER NOTES

1. United Security Products HUB-2B latching panic switch.
2. The frequency range will be between 0.3 and 300 GHz; Fennelly, L. J. *Effective Physical Security*, 2nd ed. 1997, Butterworth-Heinemann, Oxford. ISBN 0-7506-9873-X.
3. Security Industry Association. *Passive Infrared (PIR) Motion Detector: Testing Standards for Interior PIR Detectors Intended for High Security Use.* Security Industry Association, Alexandria, VA.2006.
4. Ron Nelson, Security Distributing & Marketing magazine, November 1, 2004.
5. 3VR Security, www.3VR.com.
6. VistaScape, www.vistascape.com.
7. Object Video, www.objectvideo.com.

17

Design Standards Development

Design standards help ensure a consistent look for all drawing packages published by a designer or design firm. Design standards also improve quality and consistency of design projects, reduce the possibility for errors, and improve the quality of the installation in the field.

ENVIRONMENTAL ISSUES

Temperature

All specified devices should be rated for the temperature in which they are operating. For outdoor applications in the north and south, these may include temperature extremes. Be sure to specify equipment that can operate at all anticipated temperature extremes, or specify placement of the equipment in a suitable enclosure or environment to keep the equipment within its specified range.

National Electrical Manufacturers Association and Ingress Protection Environments

National Electrical Manufacturers Association (NEMA) devices and cabinets are rated according to their environmental capabilities. NEMA enclosures are rated as follows:

- NEMA-1 enclosures are intended for indoor use and provide only a degree of protection against contact with the equipment in areas where normal service conditions prevail.
- NEMA-2 enclosures are intended to protect indoor equipment from falling dust and water.
- NEMA-3 enclosures are intended primarily for outdoor use and provide some protection against windblown dust, rain, sleet, and external ice formation.
- NEMA-4 enclosures are intended to protect against typical rain, sleet, and dust conditions that occur outdoors.

Ingress protection (IP)-rated equipment and enclosures are rated as follows:

- IP-0: No protection
- IP-1-4: Protected against solid objects such as hands and tools
- IP-5: Limited protection against dust and water ingress
- IP-6: Totally protected against dust and generally protected against high-pressure water jets from any direction
- IP-7: Protected against immersion to 1 m
- IP-8: Protected against long periods of immersion under pressure

Explosive and Flammable Environments

Explosive and flammable hazard environments are rated by class and division by the Canadian Electrical Code (CEC) Section 18 and the National Electrical Code (NEC) as those areas in which the potential for fire or explosion could occur in the presence of flammable gasses or vapors, combustible dust, and easily ignited fibers or flyings. Both agencies adopted the same zone area classification system of the International Electrotechnical Commission as part of their own codes; NEC did so in 1996 and CEC in 1998.

Classes

- Class I is flammable gasses and vapors.
- Class II is combustible or electrically conductive dusts.
- Class III is easily ignited fibers or flyings.

Divisions

- Division 1 indicates that a facility, which is operating within its design parameters, has explosive gas or dust mixtures present; that is, this is the normal condition of the environment.
- Division 2 indicates that the explosive or flammable material, while it is still present, is normally confined in enclosed systems or containers and will only be in the atmosphere if the system is operated incorrectly or containers are accidentally ruptured. This is an abnormal condition for the substance. Division 2 areas are almost always adjacent to Division 1 areas.

Zones

A zone is the combination of a class and a division—for example, Class I, Division 2.

Equipment Classifications

Equipment is classified according to its ability to operate within a zone. Ratings are commonly listed according to the zone; however, there is still some equipment that is rated under the following overlapping definitions:

- Explosion-proof apparatus: "Apparatus enclosed in a case that is capable of withstanding an explosion of a specified gas or vapor that may occur within it and of preventing the ignition of a specified gas or vapor surrounding the enclosure by sparks, flashes, or explosion of the gas or vapor within and that operates at such an external temperature that a surrounding flammable atmosphere will not be ignited thereby" (see NFPA 70).

- Intrinsically safe apparatus: "Apparatus in which all the circuits are intrinsically safe" (see UL 913).
- Intrinsically safe circuit: "A circuit in which any spark or thermal effect is incapable of causing ignition of a mixture of flammable or combustible material in air under prescribed test conditions" (see UL 913).
- Purging: "The process of supplying an enclosure with a protective gas at a sufficient flow and positive pressure to reduce the concentration of any flammable gas or vapor initially present to an acceptable level" (see NFPA 496).
- Pressurization: "The process of supplying an enclosure with a protective gas with or without continuous flow at sufficient pressure to prevent the entrance of a flammable gas or vapor, a combustible dust, or an ignitable fiber" (see NFPA 496).

Security equipment should always be rated for its zone of installation or placed within an enclosure that is appropriately rated. Class I, Division 1 devices are very costly, so this is important to observe in the design phase so that there are no surprises at installation acceptance time when the safety personnel ask about its rating. Often, a designer can avoid zone ratings by placing the equipment outside the zone. The health, safety, and environmental manager of a facility will be able to advise the designer about the zone areas.

POWER ISSUES

Grounding and Powering

Stable system performance begins with stable electrical power. I have seen many security systems that had chronic, seemingly unsolvable problems that turned out to be power related.

Power Phasing

Any system components that are connected together using copper wiring should be on the same electrical phase. It is common to find a single pan/tilt video camera on a different phase that can cause image problems across the entire system.

Hospital Ground

Use hospital grounding practices. This calls for a single common ground bar at the main electrical panel for the building to which all system electrical sources are grounded directly. This involves running a continuous ground wire from every power point in the system back to the same ground bar. Do not use any intervening ground bars or splices in ground cables.

Ground Isolation

Isolate grounds between buildings. Avoid the use of any copper wiring from building to building. Isolate all campus building systems with fiber optics to avoid interbuilding ground loops.

Panels and Breakers

Each electronic device should be marked as to the electrical panel and circuit breaker that is powering it.

Uninterruptible Power Supplies

Security equipment should typically be powered from an uninterruptible power supply (UPS) and backed up by some form of emergency power, which could be a generator or battery rated to last the duration of the anticipated power outage, brownout, or overvoltage condition. At a minimum, the UPS should be rated for the anticipated time to switch over from mains power to the generator or backup power multiplied by a factor of five. This is typically rated in seconds to minutes. Most emergency generators turn on automatically within 20 seconds to 5 minutes (depending on the programming of the emergency generator unit). This delay is normally programmed depending on the common frequency and type of power outages. For example, if it is common for power to "burp" on and off, as is the case in some Third World countries, the generator may not be programmed to turn on for 1–5 minutes in order to ensure that the generator and main power are not in contention. In developed countries where power is much more reliable, the generator may turn on immediately (20 seconds is common). The UPS also provides conditioned power, which avoids typical voltage spikes, voltage fluctuations, and other "dirty" power conditions. The UPS should also be rated for its operating environment, including temperature extremes and explosives/flammable area zone rating.

WIRING PRACTICES

Classes of Wiring

The NEC has developed classes for wiring based on its fire and shock hazard potential. These are commonly equivalent to voltage and current.

- Class 1: Both fire and shock hazards exist; in other words, the wiring can deliver enough current for a fire hazard and enough voltage for a shock hazard. Normal 120/240 VAC equipment is Class 1 equipment. This requires prevention of all touching and barriers against fire.
- Class 2: Neither fire nor shock hazard exists; in other words, the wiring cannot deliver enough current (by internal current limiting or fuses) for a fire hazard and not enough voltage for a shock hazard. Normal audio, fire alarm, and low-voltage security equipment is wired with Class 2 wiring. Any equipment that operates below 70.7 V is usually Class 2 equipment.
- Class 3: There is not a fire hazard, but there is a shock hazard; in other words, the wiring cannot deliver enough current for a fire hazard but can deliver enough voltage for a shock hazard. This requires touchproof terminals. This may include 100 V audio circuits, for example.

Integrated security systems work with two classes of wiring, Class 1 and Class 2. Class 1 wiring is from 108 to 305 V with higher power ratings, Class 2 circuits typically cover up to 70.7 V, and Class 3 circuits commonly cover the range of 70.7 to 108 V, depending on the installation application.

Wiring classes cannot be mixed within a single conduit unless the lower class wiring is insulated to the higher class rating. It is an uncommon but legal practice in the United States, for example, to place Class 2 wiring in 600-V insulated cable in the same conduit with Class 1 wiring. A designer must also observe the higher power of Class 1 cables and their effect on the Class 2 circuit. Inductive forces can cause "hum" in low-voltage circuits. Although hum used to be audible or visible in analog circuits, it can be maddening to find in data circuits, but is nonetheless bothersome to the quality of data transmission.

WIRE DRESSING

All wires should be dressed so as to be neat, free from loose copper ends, and not installed in a tangled fashion. The liberal use of wire ties is recommended so that wires will path in right angles alongside connectors and box walls. All wires should be labeled with the wire number corresponding to the same number on the device at the other end of the wire and corresponding to its documentation in the as-built drawings.

MOUNTING DEVICES
Mechanical Strength

Any device mounted to a wall or ceiling must be done so in a mechanically safe fashion. The installer must assume that the worst will happen. I recommend mounting all devices with a load factor of at least five (the mount should be capable of supporting at least five times the weight of the object it is holding and not less than 200 lbs). Anyone who thinks this is extreme has not seen an 8-year-old boy hanging from the support of a hospital television set. The State of California has adopted Office of Statewide Health Planning and Development (OSHPD) standards for mounting of all devices from ceilings and walls and for attachment of certain equipment to the floor in order to deal with the earthquake-prone environment there.

Aesthetics

For any finished area, visual aesthetics are important. Care should be taken in the design of device mounts to ensure that they are consistent with the surroundings. The use of small, unobtrusive devices when the choice allows is often preferred.

Earthquake Considerations

For any area with a history of major earthquakes, no matter how long ago, it is advised to observe earthquake mounting practices. This involves the use of a secondary support mechanism, such as a cable, within the mount, tied separately to the wall or ceiling in case the primary support should fail. Although this may not ultimately keep the object from falling in an extreme earthquake, it will at least give occupants in the area enough warning that it is about to fall so that they can stay clear from harm. Equipment racks should be tied to walls and floors at the top and bottom. There is very good material about this in California's OSHPD standards.

Physical Details

Physical details should illustrate all of the information necessary for an installer to properly mount the device and interface it to the building and the conduit system, including the following:

- Mounting height
- Type of mounting and attachment to the wall, floor, or ceiling
- Illustrate how power and signal get to the device in enough detail that the installer can achieve the desired structural and aesthetic objectives

Physical details should be included whenever there is any question as to how a device should be installed. I recommend the use of standard physical details for every mounting configuration in the project.

DRAWING STANDARDS

The designer should develop a standard set of symbols, notes, abbreviations, device nomenclatures, and schedule lists (devices, circuits, etc.). It is also advisable to design everything in a fashion so that the detail may be reused on a future project. In this way, the designer can build a library of standard details from which to draw on. Standard practices improves the quality of design packages and reduces their production cost over time.

Typical standards may include the following:

- The order of drawings can help the reader absorb the data more quickly. It is common to have schedules (circuit lists, etc.) in the front of the package, followed by outdoor site plans, indoor floor plans, elevations, reflected ceiling plans, physical details, and, finally, risers, single-line diagrams, and interfacing details.
- Text font and size for title blocks, detail titles and call-outs, notes, etc.
- Note and call-out leader angles, direction, and landing locations (e.g., always on the top line with the text justified below the leader ending point, and leaders that are always angled between 30 and 60 degrees with a specific arrow point).
- Locations and numbering schemes of physical details on a drawing page (I always number detail 1 in the lower right corner to detail 6 in the upper left corner so that a drawing reader does not have to open the entire set to find a single detail on a sheet).
- Standard line types and line weights in order to define boxes, text, outline dashed lines, etc. differently in visual terms.

All these and many other visual details will define your drawing set as uniquely yours and will assist readers in absorbing the material quickly.

SUMMARY

Design standards help ensure a consistent look for all drawing packages published by a designer or design firm. Design standards also improve quality and consistency of design projects and reduce the possibility of errors.

Design standards should include grounding and powering, wiring practices, wire dressing, mounting of devices, physical details, and drawing standards.

18

Finalizing the Installation

FINALIZATION AND COMMISSIONING CHECKLIST

The following steps should be taken in commissioning the system and its software. Each of these items is explained in detail following this list:

- Connect each field device to power and its digital switch as its installation is completed in the field.
- Load and commission the server and workstation operating systems.
- Set up the security system network infrastructure (primary switches, wireless nodes, servers, and workstations), get all devices communicating (backup servers will be set up later), and secure the security system information technology network.

- Load alarm/access control system primary server and workstation software and set up the access control system databases.
- Configure connections to all of the alarm/access control system field controller panels, reader interface boards, alarm input boards, and output controller boards.
- Load digital video system primary server and workstation software (including the archive server software) and set up the digital video system archive databases.
- Configure connections to all of the digital video system cameras and intercoms.
- Commission the alarm/access control system field devices.
- Commission the digital video system cameras and intercoms.
- Set up higher system functions (video guard tours, video pursuit, etc.).
- Set up alarm/access control system and digital video system integration.
- Implement Homeland Security threat level system policies and rules.
- Implement the organization's system policies and rules.
- Implement backup servers.
- Configure the system for remote monitoring.
- Present the system for acceptance testing.

After the devices are hung and powered, the server(s) is installed, the workstations are in place, and all the wiring is run in conduit and the racks are built, the system must be commissioned (put into operation). Included in this basic preparation is system server/workstation configuration, which may include ensuring that there is one master clock for the entire system and that all other servers and workstations take their time stamp from that one server. Ideally, that clock will be synchronized with an atomic clock.

Connect Each Field Device to Power and Its Digital Switch as Its Installation Is Completed in the Field

As the field devices (cameras, card readers, intercoms, etc.) are installed, connect each to their power source and the digital edge switch through which they will communicate. Also connect the network infrastructure elements together in the field (edge switches to field switches, etc.) and document each completion step.

Load and Commission the Server and Workstation Operating Systems

Load the server and main workstation operating systems, including any required support programs (antivirus, antispyware, and registry maintenance program), and delete any automatically installed programs that could be harmful to the system, including preinstalled web links.

Set Up the Security System Network Infrastructure

After the primary server and workstations are operating, get the primary server and all workstations communicating together on the core network. Next, connect the edge switches and any wireless nodes so that the entire network infrastructure is operating. Configure the infrastructure to support the communications rules sets that will be required on the network. This may include establishing IGMP querying on the main core switch to support multicasting (often also on a backup core switch) and IGMP snooping on it and all the other the switches.

If the system is being blended with the organization's information technology (IT) local area network (LAN) or wide area network (WAN), the system may require a virtual local area network (VLAN) or subnet configuration and the establishment of VLAN or subnet rules in order to segregate the two logical networks on the same physical infrastructure.

Finally, establish group policies on the server and switches to enforce basic network user-level security. A complete discussion on securing networks at all seven layers of the Open Systems Interconnection (OSI) network model is provided later. I recommend that all network-based security systems should be secured at all seven layers of the OSI network model.

Load Alarm/Access Control System Primary Server and Workstation Software

I am not sure if it matters whether the alarm/access control or digital video software is loaded first, but it seems to be an industry convention, perhaps because the network configuration is simpler. Once the alarm/access control system server and workstation software is loaded, it is time to set up the access control system database. There are a number of types of system databases, but two are most common: MS Access (for smaller systems) and structured query language (SQL) for larger systems. SQL databases are powerful and robust, and they can easily operate an enterprise access control system comprising thousands of sites and hundreds of thousands of authorized users. Access databases are adequate for small systems only. (A more complete description of SQL databases is provided later.)

Configure Alarm/Access System Field Connections

After the alarm/access control system software and database are established, connect the field hardware devices to the network by coding their TCP/IP addresses into the network and configure each device, including the system controllers, reader interface panels, alarm input panels, and output relay panels. At this point, we are only concerned with connectivity, not programming of the individual devices.

Load Digital Video System Primary Server and Workstation Software

In the same manner in which the alarm/access control system server/workstation software was loaded and its database configured, so now the digital video system server/workstation software is loaded and its databases are configured.

Configure Connections to All of the Digital Video System Cameras and Intercoms

Following the loading of the digital video server/workstation software, use the software to find and connect to all available digital video cameras and intercoms. You should be able to see images on every camera. You will also need to configure the system for multicast operation if more than one workstation or server will be in the system. For simplicity and reliability, I suggest that you configure the cameras and intercoms to communicate by unicast protocol to the primary server and then configure the server to communicate by multicast to its workstations and backup server.

For networks that are especially sensitive to multicast, such as blended corporate/security networks, it is recommended to separate the field components network from the workstation/ backup server network by means of a subnet or VLAN. This can be done by installing two network interface cards (NICs) in the primary server, one for the cameras and intercoms and one for the workstations and backup server. This approach creates multiple logical networks in the same physical network architecture, as though they were in fact separate physical networks. Typically, the security system will already be configured on its own VLAN in a blended network. This approach can help ensure that multicast signals never interfere with normal system operation.

Commission the Alarm/Access Control System Field Devices

After configuring the software of both main security systems, begin commissioning of the alarm/access control system field devices.

Groups

This involves first setting up the devices into groups and then setting alarm/access control system schedules of operation to the groups. For example, in a multitenant building, you might set floor access to each tenant (in this case, each tenant forms a group). For a corporate environment, this will normally involve setting groups to correlate with buildings, departments, divisions, etc.

Schedules and Time Zones

Once groups are established, you can set up the system schedules. These will include time zones (24/7, working hours, etc.) and holidays.

Then correlate the device groups to their normal operating schedules. For example, you may want the front lobby doors to be on alarm bypass and unlocked automatically during working hours but locked on access control at other times and on holidays.

Next, begin entering the system's user database. For a new system in a new facility, this is fairly straightforward. Simply input the data and take photos in the photo ID segment of the software. For existing systems, you will need to transport the existing user database to the new system. This can be a relatively simple process if the system is simply an upgrade of an earlier version of the same manufacturer's software, or it can be quite complicated if an entirely new system is being imported. The manufacturer will have explicit instructions on how to make this conversion, which should be followed exactly to achieve a successful database conversion.

Set Up Higher System Functions (Video Guard Tours, Video Pursuit, etc.)

Video Guard Tour Implementations

A video guard tour is a compilation of individual video guard tour stops. A video guard tour stop is a group of individual camera scenes that are brought up on screen together which convey an overall view of a contiguous area, such as at an airport security checkpoint. A video guard tour is a consecutive sequence of individual guard tour stops that allows the console operator to tour the entire facility in a coordinated fashion using groups of video cameras to get a good look at each stop on the tour. Video guard tours are a basic element of successful integrated security system functions and should be included in every system.

The ultimate expression of video guard tours is the video pursuit function. In video pursuit, each camera tile on the screen is an alarm button. By pressing on the tile of a video camera, that camera becomes the focus camera of a new video guard tour stop. The console operator can follow a subject simply by pressing on the video tiles into which the subject walks. This function is especially useful in large public venues, such as airports, casinos, convention centers, malls, and parking structures.

Situational Analysis Software Implementation

Situational Analysis Software (SAS) is an especially elegant form of Graphical User Interface (GUI) that includes information that places the alarm information in the context of a map or aerial or satellite photo of a facility. Situational Awareness Software also may update the movements of subjects based upon emerging sensor data, such as radar data. Situational Awareness Software is one of the most effective means of managing a security system from a console operator's point of view. The SAS provides a "top level" view of the system and how it relates to its overall physical environment. The SAS should have as a minimum the following basic elements:

- Alarm icons
- Camera icons
- Intercom icons
- Nested maps (to "drill down" into maps with greater detail)
- Linked maps (to move from area to area—east/west/north/south)

In addition, all alarm points should display a GUI screen.

In an ideal SAS implementation, each camera should also be a "pseudo-alarm" point that links to a SAS screen (as well as to nearby cameras), so that when an operator double clicks on a camera it becomes the new focus camera and related cameras around it also display (video guard tour); in addition, a SAS map shows the area of the selected camera. This facilitates the video pursuit function.

Set Up Alarm/Access Control System and Digital Video System Integration

After setting up both the alarm/access control and the digital video system, the real work begins. Set a camera link for each individual alarm in the system. Typically, the link should call up a guard tour stop from which the console officer can then follow the subject in question using video pursuit.

Similarly, link every intercom in the system to the nearest video camera so that the console officer can see the image of the person on the intercom during the conversation. Also, the GUI screen showing that intercom (and its related access controlled door or gate) should be displayed on the screen.

At access controlled doors, this can also be tied to the photo ID lookup function so that the console officer can look up the access control record of the person at the intercom and then let the system approve access for that person by dragging his or her photo over the door icon on the GUI screen.

In reverse, anytime a focus camera is selected, the intercom associated with that camera should be queued automatically, as should the GUI map on which that camera is shown.

Implement Homeland Security Threat Level System Policies and Rules

After all this, you can implement Homeland Security threat level policies and rules. Homeland Security threat levels[1] are as follows:

- Red—Severe: A terrorist attack has occurred, or credible and corroborated intelligence indicates one is imminent. Normally, this threat condition is declared for a specific location or critical facility.
- Orange—High: Credible intelligence indicates that there is a high risk of a local terrorist attack but a specific target has not been identified.
- Yellow—Elevated: Elevated risk of terrorist attack but a specific region or target has not been identified.
- Blue—Guarded: General risk with no credible threat to any specific targets.

- Green—Low: Low risk of terrorism. Routine security is implemented to preclude routine criminal threats.

You may set up the system to operate differently at each threat level. For example, when the threat level is changed from elevated to high, you might put two consoles online and dedicate one entirely to continuous video guard tours. At the same time, a high threat level policy would be implemented; for example, no one would be allowed to loiter near a suspension bridge anchorage building. This would be enforced by implementing intelligent video motion detection, looking for loiterers on the camera viewing the area surrounding the anchorage building, and then notifying the loiterers by bullhorn intercom to leave the area.

Implement the Organization's System Policies and Rules

The previous example illustrates one type of security policy implementation. The entire system can be designed to facilitate the organization's security policies. For example, if company laptops are issued to certain employees, you can install asset tracking tags on the laptops and then track them as they leave through building exits against the employee access credential. By using Boolean algebra logic cells (discussed in detail later), you can compare the laptop asset tag to the authorized employee list. If the computer is in the hands of an authorized employee, no action will be taken by the system. If, however, it is in the hands of an unauthorized employee or a noncredentialed person, an alarm will sound, allowing a nearby security officer to quiz the person when the laptop is sensed passing through an exit.

A thorough review of the entire organization's security policies should be implemented in order to fully exploit the power of the security system.

Implement Backup Servers

After implementing the primary servers, workstations, and the security application programs, backup servers may be implemented. The backup server(s) will provide two main services: archiving system activities in real time and providing a fail-over function to manage the system in the event of failure of the primary server.

Configure the System for Remote Monitoring

Following implementation of the backup server, remote monitoring can be implemented. There are two common ways to achieve remote monitoring: through an independent connection to the Internet or through the organization's WAN. Generally, for independent Internet connections, this is best handled only via a virtual private network (VPN) connection to ensure the security of the connection and vital security data. Remember that remote monitoring could theoretically expose the organization to a "takeover" attack in which an outsider can open doors and gates for accomplices using the alarm/access control system and may know the activities of the security force via use of the digital video system. Thus, the security of the connection is at all times vital.

For connections through the organization's WAN, permission must be obtained from the organization's IT department. Understand that the security system and its architecture, configuration, and management rules must necessarily then comply with the IT department's standards.

The main issues of concern are bandwidth usage and network security. Bandwidth to a remote monitoring location can easily exceed the maximum network capacity from a remote site. A typical site may be served by one or more T-1 connections.[2] A security system can easily require 3 Mbps to monitor unless it is well managed. Management is accomplished by controlling the amount of video to be sent, its image resolution, and its frame rate. For slow connections, it is advisable to use 2CIF or lower resolution and slow frame rates, perhaps one frame per second. I have designed around connections that would not support more than one frame every 20 seconds.

Network security can be ensured with proper system hardware and network configurations. Basic methods include the use of a stateful firewall.[3] Many large organizations use managed firewalls.[4] Managed firewalls are very expensive but provide the best possible protection.

Secure the Security System

The security system must itself be secure. The best way to do that is to secure the system at all seven layers of the OSI network model. A basic discussion of that is provided at the end of this chapter. Other important security methods covered include basic data encryption, IPSec, and wireless security.

Integrate the System to the Information Technology System

Where it is required to share the IT infrastructure for logistical or architectural reasons, there are three main concerns:

- Bandwidth preservation
- Network security (for both the organization's LAN/WAN and the security system)
- Multicast compatibility

Bandwidth preservation involves a simple number. No network infrastructure should ever be utilized to more than 45% of its rated capacity. If the connection is a 100Base-T connection, no more than 45 Mbps should be used. For gigabit links, no more than 450 Mbps should be used. These are absolute worst-case figures. Less utilization is better. Utilization over that amount will result in dropped UDP packets and lost camera image pixels. The worst-case utilization of both networks should be calculated in order to ensure that the infrastructure can accommodate the demands of both systems.

The best way to accommodate this requirement and to accommodate network security is to segregate the security system on its own VLAN. Each network operates in its own VLAN, even if none are implemented. The native VLAN is VLAN 0. You will implement a separate VLAN for the security system, which will both ensure bandwidth segregation and isolate the two networks so that the security system is not accessible from the organization's LAN users.

Additionally, it is important to implement IGMP querying and snooping on the data switches in order to isolate multicast traffic. Multicast traffic is also isolated automatically by the VLAN.

Integrate the System to Other Building Systems

Integrated security systems are often integrated to other building systems, including elevators, building automation systems, parking control systems, irrigation systems, lighting control systems, public address systems, and telephone systems. There are two basic types of interfaces to other systems: dry-contact relay interfaces and data interfaces between system computers.

Dry-contact interfaces are basic but powerful. They also have the advantage that changes in system software versions of either system will not likely affect the interface as long as the logic elements remain in effect. Their downside is space and capital cost. I am very fond of dry-contact interfaces because of their dependability and durability.

The best argument in favor of data interfaces is that the physical interface is very simple. Often, the physical interface is effected just by plugging both systems into switches (sometimes on opposite ends of the building). However, for the interface to work, both manufacturers must

- agree to the interface and its attributes and functions;
- coordinate an application programming interface or other method; and
- coordinate the databases of both systems so that information can be exchanged.

Many manufacturers have cooperated to create useful functions. However, if the function you need has not been previously agreed upon by the two manufacturers that you are considering using, it is best either to consider other manufacturers that have cooperated or create the function in relay logic.

Relays can be combined to perform almost any function. They can count, set timers, create "and" or "or" functions, and even create "exclusive or" functions. Although this may seem hardware intensive, the results can be excellent. I and other consultants have been asking the security system manufacturers for many years for products that can perform Boolean algebra logic cells. Finally, they are being developed. New alarm/access control and digital video systems are being developed that have counters, timers, and addressable memory and can perform all manner of logic functions. Many higher functions can be performed with these tools, as described next.

One of the best arguments in favor of relays and against data connections is that relays are fixed and are not subject to disconnection when a new software update is installed in one system that does not contain the necessary programming elements to communicate with the other software in the system, as did the original software version. Such unplanned obsolescence can occur if both manufacturers are not fully committed to maintaining interoperability through software version changes.

SPECIAL IMPLEMENTATIONS

Boolean Algebra Logic Cell Implementation

Boolean algebra logic cells are the key to amazing integrated security system functions as well as to truly cost-effective installations. You can achieve virtually any function you can imagine with a combination of counters, timers, input and output points, memory, and Boolean algebra logic cells. This section presents only four examples developed by me for various projects. Your imagination will undoubtedly develop an endless array of others.

"And" Gate Alarms

A petrochemical terminal had a perimeter alarm system that comprised 52 microwave zones just inside its outer fence line. These microwave alarms occasionally caused nuisance alarms, which the firm wished to reduce. I designed a system of 35 fixed video cameras on existing camera towers to view the microwave alarm zones. The fixed cameras were configured with video motion detection to detect movement within the areas of the microwave alarms. The triggering of a motion alarm by either the microwave detectors or the video motion detectors would cause an alert, whereas the triggering of motion detection by both systems simultaneously within the same zone would cause an alarm.

With an alarm/access control system with Boolean algebra logic cells, this can be accomplished by only 52 hardware-based alarm inputs for the microwave detectors. The video motion alarms are in the video software, and they are transmitted to the alarm/access control system via software. The alarm/access control system compares the inputs and causes either an alert or an alarm, based on the Boolean algebra logic cell formula.

In a conventional alarm/access control system without Boolean algebra logic cells, this same result requires (now this will not be easy to follow, so stay with me) 52 hardware alarm outputs for the video motion alarms from the video system to the alarm/access control system from the 35 video cameras, 104 hardware alarm inputs (52 for the microwave detectors and 52 for the video motion alarm inputs from the 35 cameras), and an additional 104 outputs to reflect the condition of the alarm inputs are then hardwired together to create the 52 And gates, which are then wired back into an additional 52 alarm inputs in the alarm/access control system as And gate alarm inputs. The total hardware count is 156 outputs and 156 inputs. Understand why Boolean algebra logic cells are so popular with designers who understand them and with the clients who would otherwise have to pay thousands of dollars for all those extra inputs and outputs? It is easy to understand why.

Local Alarms

Suppose we have a door that gets a lot of traffic during the day and that some people occasionally prop open (e.g., a stairwell door). We do not want it propped because this would violate fire code. In a system with Boolean algebra logic cells, we simply use the single door alarm input and a single output control near the door, two timers, and a logic cell. During the day, if the door is propped open, a timer is engaged when the door opens and it counts to perhaps 45 seconds. If the door is still open at 45 seconds, we engage the output control, which is connected to a local alarm at the door. This tells people in the vicinity of the door to close the door. If they do not close it within perhaps an additional 30 seconds, we send an alarm to the security console stating that the door is propped open so that the console operator can dispatch a patrol officer to close the door. At night, the door does not act as a propped door alarm but, rather, activates an alarm immediately upon opening, based on a software schedule. In a conventional system without Boolean algebra logic cells, this same function can be achieved by means of a hardware-based prop-door alarm, which has a key that a patrol officer turns on and off.

Lighted Paths

As a convenience to late-working employees, a client asked me to design a system that would turn on lights and air-conditioning for any employee who arrived late at night to work (these were IT workers, who often had to come in to work in the wee hours of the morning when something did not work correctly in the system). I established a database of workers and where they worked, and I designed a lighted-path algorithm to turn on the lights in the parking structure and all the way to their offices or cubicles, specific to each employee, as well as to the snack room and the bathrooms. The lights stayed on until the employees logged out of their computers.

Lights/HVAC After-Hours System Billing

In response to a client request, I designed a system that provided lights, heating/air-conditioning, and plug power for employees who worked late or on weekends. Each elevator lobby had a card reader on a panel with three buttons (lights, heat–A/C, and reset). Upon entering the workspace to work late, an employee would present his or her access card to the reader and press one or both service request buttons. This would energize lights, heat–A/C, and plug power for 2 hours. Ten minutes before the end of the 2-hour period, the lights would flash once so that the employee could request more time if needed. If the employee left during the 2-hour period, he or she could present his or her card once again and press the reset button, ending the timing cycle. At the end of each month, a report (custom written for this purpose) presented a bill to each tenant for their usage, with a full audit trail of who made the requests, the date and time of the requests, and the time outs or resets. The system was popular with the tenants. Although commercial products exist for this purpose, they cost tens of thousands of dollars. This system was installed in a small four-story building for only the cost of the readers and push buttons, plus a small cost for the creation of the Boolean algebra logic cells and the monthly report. The alarm/access control system had an additional user-defined field for each cardholder that defined what lighting zone the employee sat in so that it knew what lights and A/C to turn on.

You can probably imagine dozens of other applications for Boolean algebra logic cells.

CUSTOM SYSTEM REPORTS IMPLEMENTATION

In addition to the dozens of useful reports each access control system has available today, it is also possible to write custom reports that are very useful. One example was mentioned previously with regard to the after-hours lighting report. This section discusses a few more examples.

Exclusion Reports

It is important to know which employees entered and left the site each month. However, it is perhaps more important to know which cardholders did not use their cards within the past month. These may be terminated employees whose cards are still in the system. At a minimum, all such employee cards should automatically be suspended until the employees return. However, a good report is one that will list all active cardholders who did not use their cards. This can be done with an exclusion report comparing active cardholders against card usage.

Nesting Reports

In a parking structure that had little room for both visitors and employees, the first two floors were set aside for visitors, and the upper floors were segregated for employees by reading a toll tag-type card on the employees' windshields from an overhead reader, coupled with a vehicle gate. The old employee toll tag readers and gates at the ground-level entrances were set to "open" so that visitors could freely enter the parking structure and access the first two floors. The problem was that employees felt free to park in visitor spaces, leaving no spaces for visitors. The solution was to reengage the toll tag readers on the ground floor and have visitors check in via intercoms at the ground floor. The console officer would open the gate for each visitor and the gate would open automatically for employees, having read their employee toll tag cards on their windshields. A custom report was prepared that compared employee usage at the ground floor with the reader that granted upper floor access. If an employee parked in the first two levels instead of on the upper employee levels (if an employee did not clear past the upper tag reader within 5 minutes), the custom report identified the employee as a visitor area parking offender and the employee was counseled by his or her supervisor with a warning. If the employee reoffended, parking privileges to the structure were suspended for 30 days, requiring the employee to find parking in the surrounding neighborhood and walk to the building. For those few employees who tried to "fool" the system by stating that they were visitors, the toll tag "gave them away" as employees and they were turned away. The system proved to be very effective at making spaces available for visitors in an area with very few outside parking spaces.

SECURING THE SECURITY SYSTEM

Many TCP/IP-based security systems are installed without encryption or any other type of network security. I am fascinated by a security industry that does not secure its own systems. This could be the height of technical incompetence and moral (and possibly legal) irresponsibility.

Device and Transmission Security
Architectural Security

The OSI reference model (OSI seven-layer network model) has many opportunities to both secure and exploit weaknesses in data communications. The OSI levels have been discussed previously; here, I discuss how those layers affect the security of the system and the organization.

OSI layer 1 is the physical layer. It is imperative to prevent physical access to network switches, routers, firewalls, and servers if the security system is to be secure. All these devices should be behind locked doors and in alarmed rooms.

OSI layer 2 is defined as the data link layer. This is the layer on which switches operate. Each TCP/IP device has a physical address called a media access control (MAC) address. This address is unique for every device that is hard coded into the network interface card of every TCP/IP device. The MAC addresses of the devices within the system should be stored in a table, and those addresses should be reserved such that they are the only authorized devices on the network, allowing no other devices on the network.

OSI layer 3 is the network layer. This is the layer on which routers operate. This is often called the protocol layer. Layer 3 manages the IP protocol. Subnets, supernets, VLANs, and VPNs are all managed using OSI layer 3.

OSI layer 4 is the transport layer. Layer 4 manages TCP, UDP, RTP, and other protocols. Better network switches provide for prioritizing of certain packet types (e.g., intercom traffic over video traffic). Layer 4 devices include firewalls and layer 4 session switches.

OSI layer 5 is the session layer. Layer 5 opens and closes network sessions, controls the establishment and termination of links between network devices and users, and reports any upper layer errors. Secure Socket Layer security operates on layers 5–7. Layer 5 data management can also optimize network data traffic by establishing a TCP proxy that reduces the amount of outside network traffic allowed to see the host.

OSI layer 6 is the presentation layer. Layer 6 performs network encryption and compresses and decompresses data.

OSI layer 7 is the application layer. Layer 7 manages application usernames and passwords.

A good network designer secures his or her system at all seven layers of the OSI network model. Any layer that is not secured is vulnerable to an internal or external system hacker.

Data Encryption

Encryption is essential for any wireless network traffic and is a good idea for all data on a security system, especially alarm/access control data, which if hacked could unlock doors, open gates, and bypass alarms.

Encryption Basics[5]

Encryption is the process of converting a readable message into something that is unreadable by anyone who is not in possession of the appropriate encryption key (Fig. 18-1).

There are two common techniques of encryption: secret key and public key cryptography. These are also known as symmetric key and asymmetric key cryptography, respectively. Secret key cryptography involves using the same key for both encryption and decryption. Public key cryptography uses only one key (a public key) for encryption and its mate (a secret one) for decryption.

Public key encryption permits one to publish the public key, allowing many people to know and use the key to create messages that can only be decrypted by someone with the secret key. Once encrypted, the public key will not open the message, making it secure from everyone with the public key. Public key encryption is best used with devices such as a smart card that holds the private key. One of the best public key systems uses a smart card that continuously displays a rotating number

Figure 18-1 Encryption.

that must be input and matched to the private key. After a few seconds, the number changes, making the last number useless to anyone who has captured it on a sniffer.

Secret key encryption is best used as a single-use encryption method.

Encryption keys can be any length, from a few characters to many. Most commercial and governmental keys are from 40 to 256 bits. The longer the key, the longer it takes a hacker to conduct a "brute force attack" in which the attacker tries all possible combinations until he or she finds one that works. Encryption specialist Kevin Henson has developed a 40-kilobit encryption key that can encrypt or decrypt a megabyte of data in less than one-quarter of a second.

Internet Protocol Security

Internet Protocol Security (IPSec) is a set of protocols defined by the Internet Engineering Task Force to provide IP security at the network layer (OSI layer 3). IPSec is highly recommended if the security system is to be run on the organization's WAN, even if it is on its own VLAN.

Radio Frequency Security

When a designer specifies a radio frequency (RF) infrastructure, there are two major security concerns. I call them the CNN factor and the Chevy Vega factor. No client wants video from their cameras showing up on CNN, and no client wants an 18-year-old sitting in an old Chevy Vega with a laptop computer attaching to the wireless network security system. Other concerns include the following:[6]

- Probing/network discovery
- Denial of service (DoS) attacks
- Surveillance
- Impersonation
- Client-to-client intrusion
- Client-to-network intrusion
- Rogue APs and ad hoc networks

Countermeasures

The following measures help secure RF infrastructures:

- Probing/network discovery: Encrypt the SSID connection. There is little that a network designer can do to prevent probing and network discovery other than to turn off the SSID message. However, that does not prevent a determined hacker. I suggest using 802.11a or another less used frequency for backhaul traffic. The network cannot be probed if the hacker does not possess equipment that can see the network. Encrypting the SSID helps to prevent entry.
- DoS attacks: DoS attacks can take several forms, but all of them are carried out with the intent to deny access to the appropriate user. A common DoS method is RF jamming.
- RF jamming: RF jamming involves flooding the airwaves with 802.11 frequency energy. There is little that can be done about this. I recommend using either 802.11a or another less used frequency for backhaul (there is less equipment in use and, therefore, less chance of jamming).
- Deauthentication attacks: In a deauthentication attack, the attacker floods the airwaves with spoofed MAC address. Eventually, the system loses track of what devices it is connected to and will try to search for another AP. There are several effective means to prevent this type of attack, including detection of MAC address spoofing. Other counter-measures can log the attempts and approximate the physical location of the attacker based on signal strength in proximity to his or her nearest wireless node.
- Surveillance: Encrypt all data on the RF system using a strong encryption algorithm. This helps prevent your video from being illegally exported to other systems. I recommend the use of IPSEC for this purpose.
- Impersonation: Often, solving the surveillance problem also solves the impersonation problem. Another type of imper-sonation attack is the man-in-the-middle attack. This type of attack allows the hacker to add, delete, and modify data. An intrusion detection system can be effective in preventing man-in-the-middle attacks.

- Client-to-client intrusion: Many designers make their servers nearly impervious to outside attacks but fail to protect client devices. Diligent maintenance of network authorizations can prevent this type of attack. I strongly recommend against allowing business user clients onto the security system wireless backbone, even if a VLAN is used.
- Client-to-network intrusion: Multilayer security as described previously is effective in preventing this type of attack.
- Rogue APs and ad hoc networks: Diligent network management can prevent a client from setting up a rogue access point.

ARCHIVED DATA SECURITY
Archiving Principles

Data archiving is the process of storing the record of events within the system for future retrieval and analysis. As data flows into the server for the system to process, an archive file captures a copy of the data and stores it in a fashion that is indexed for retrieval. Data are typically stored for alarm/access control, system status change events, video streams, and audio streams. These will likely be stored on separate disk volumes or libraries.

Backups and Recoveries

Data can be stored either in its native form or as a backup for a recovery. Typically, both may be used, with native data stored for recent history on disk within the primary server and backup files being used to store older data on disk or tape on extended storage.

For extended storage beyond the capacity of the disks within the server, an extension box is created that includes a backup server and disk and/or tape storage. For large storage requirements, a tape carousel is appropriate. These should be attached to the server with a separate NIC in the server and connected directly to the backup server or, if several servers are involved, through a backup switch, separate from the primary backhaul network. This is to minimize the effect of archiving data traffic on the primary backhaul network. This architecture is called a storage area network. It is the best choice for large video archives. If the archive server is connected onto the backhaul network (network attached storage), the additional traffic caused by the archive data may cause the backhaul network to begin losing video packets, which has a negative effect on the quality of both live and archived video images.

Business Continuity Management Servers

Large enterprises value archives and often place their archive servers in a separate physical location. Such servers are called business continuity management (BCM) servers. It is common in large enterprises to have both live and archive servers locally, or in a primary data center, and BCM servers in a separate data center. In such cases, these will be an entire duplicate set of servers, usually configured as fail-over servers, ready to take over on a moment's notice. This requires a high-speed connection capable of supporting all the data.

User Classes and Authorities

Users are not all alike in terms of their access privileges. They are categorized into several major classes:

- Administrators: Administrators have all rights on the system, including the right to add, modify, and delete data and programs.
- Managers: Managers have all rights on the system except to add or delete programs or to delete data. However, a manager is permitted to issue authorizations to lower level users and to manage how they can use the system. Typically, some system reports are also reserved for managers.
- Supervisors: Supervisors can manage all live activities in the system, including screen configurations and access to high-security areas.
- Guards: Guards may be permitted access to view certain classes of cameras and not others, and they may be permitted

to lock and unlock or open certain gates. Typically, guards can see and respond to all alarms.

- Roving guards: Roving guards may be issued wireless tablets or PDAs that may grant access only to the region of their patrol.

Login/Logout Security (Card Controls Operating System)

One of the most important and most often overlooked elements of security system data integrity is solid proof of who was logged onto a guard workstation when an event took place. It is stunningly common to discover that the person who the system records as having been logged in was in fact not even at work at the time of a security event. In the hands of a skilled defense attorney, this can be argued to void the validity of the rest of the data in the system.

The most effective way to verify that the logged operator is in fact the operator on the console is to use a presence reading card reader tied to the workstation login. Using this method, login to the guard workstation is automatic when the guard places his proximity access card in a reader slot. With his keys on the same ring as his access card, logout is ensured whenever he leaves his console for a restroom break or at the end of a shift.

Cutting-Edge System Security

For extremely high-security systems, special additional security measures can be taken that can effectively make the security system invisible on the network. In the simplest method, the security system is programmed onto its own VLAN on the organization's WAN. More sophisticated methods also exist that are suspected of being used by intelligence agencies of certain governments. These are accomplished with the use of nonstandard protocol data encapsulation. One reported method even includes a "protocol diode" that could theoretically be configured to allow a "one-way mirror," allowing the system to look into the common data architecture without being seen by that WAN.

System Cutover Day

On the day on which the new security system is to be cut over to replace an older one, nerves can be frazzled. The setting up of a temporary data infrastructure to run the system can help ensure that all elements of the new system are in good working order and communicating properly prior to actual placement of the system on the primary data network. Bench testing is also a recommended option.

SUMMARY

System finalization includes commissioning, training, and acceptance. Steps include device IP addressing and startup, device communications and programming, and securing the security system.

It is the responsibility of the designer to ensure that the security system design includes securing the security system. Security measures should be taken at all seven layers of the OSI networking model, where possible.

RF systems in particular should be secured because their infrastructure has no physical security. Common RF attacks include

- Probing/network discovery
- Denial of service attacks
- Surveillance
- Impersonation
- Client-to-client intrusion
- Client-to-network intrusion
- Rogue APs and ad hoc networks

Archived data must also be secured, and a business continuity program should be developed for the security system.

User classes and authorities should be set up, and logon/ logoff security should be considered. System cutover should be well planned so as to occur smoothly.

CHAPTER NOTES

1. Department of Homeland Security, www.dhs.gov.
2. A T-1 connection is 1.5 Mbps both up and down.
3. A stateful firewall is a firewall that keeps track of the state of network connections that are moving through it. The firewall is programmed to examine each packet, searching for those that meet a predetermined state that is allowed by the firewall. All other packets will be rejected. Stateful firewalls are OSI level 3 devices.
4. A managed firewall is a network appliance that examines all of the data flowing through it and compares the data to a set of rules searching for intrusions, malformed packets, malicious packets (viruses, etc.), and the like. The system can be programmed to constantly learn what its programmer considers malicious behavior as it passes each questionable transaction up to the operator for human evaluation. Those packets that look substantially like those that have been rejected by human intervention become automated in their rejection over time.
5. Kevin Henson, Chief Cryptology Scientist, Asier (www. asiertech.com).
6. Green, J. (2004, May). *Security Considerations and Vendor Solutions*. SANS Institute, Bethesda, MD.

19

System Implementation

SYSTEM MAINTENANCE AND MANAGEMENT

Maintenance

Each integrated security system requires constant maintenance. This comes as a surprise to many owners who would never think about running their cars for 2 years without oil changes and fluid and tire pressure checks. Many system owners wait until something breaks in the system before they call a maintenance technician. These are the same owners who have a scheduled maintenance program for the elevator, building automation system, roof, windows, etc.

Integrated security systems should be maintained on a standard schedule. Depending on the size and scope of the system, the maintenance could be bimonthly, monthly, weekly, or even daily. Each component should be checked for its normal working order on at least a weekly basis. However, this does not have to be performed by a contract maintenance technician but, rather, can and should be performed by the security console officer staff.

Weekly system testing requires a console officer and a roving guard or maintenance technician. One walks and tests, and the other confirms the test results. Each access-controlled door, alarm, and output control point should be tested weekly. Access-controlled doors should be tested for operation—not just for the electronics but also for the operation of the door. This can be done easily on a guard tour. The roving tester should carry a clipboard and follow a standard checklist. Any discrepancies in operation should be noted on the clipboard. Alarms, output control points, cameras, and intercoms can all be tested while on the guard tour walk.

Any items that are found to be out of specification can be adjusted or repaired on the next scheduled maintenance visit (usually bimonthly) if it is a noncritical element or sooner if it is a system element. System maintenance must be conducted routinely on both the security system hardware and the information technology (IT) infrastructure, servers, workstations, operating systems, and software. This must be under the authority of a knowledgeable individual who:

- Understands the security program and its goals, methods, and tactics
- Understands the security equipment and its normal operating conditions
- Can determine if a problem is operational, electronic, or IT related
- Has good oversight and management skills
- Has been given responsibility, authority, and budget for maintenance

Many organizations believe that the security contractors often are not well suited to maintain the entire system since many contractors do not employ adequate IT trained service technicians. That will change. At the same time, many IT service organizations are discovering that they can install and service IT-based security systems. Some of these organizations are rushing in to fill the void.

IT-based integrated security systems must be maintained by a group that is competent in the maintenance of IT systems. That is often not the installing security contractor, whose competence is limited to the edge devices and software. I often recommend that maintenance of the IT infrastructure, operating systems, and software be placed under the authority of the organization's IT department.

The decision as to who should be in charge of maintenance is important and must be made on the basis of technical competence and political sensitivity. In the end, it is essential for the organization to understand that the security system helps to provide physical security for the entire organization. To the extent that it is well maintained, it can do that job. To the extent that it is not well maintained, it cannot, and that creates exploitable vulnerabilities in the organization's security.

Management

Electronics is a tool of the security management program, of cohesive security management, not a segregated program unto itself. The integrated electronics security system is there to assist the security operations force, not to replace it. The data that the system gathers must be acted on by patrol officers, so the two functions should both be managed by the corporate security manager or director, who makes and implements corporate security policies and procedures.

It is not uncommon in the third world to segregate the management of the guard and electronics monitoring functions to two different managers, who are culturally not inclined to work together. The reason stated for this segregation is so that neither would have total control of the security program and that there would be "checks and balances" on the overall program. This approach is doomed to fail in a security program. The result is always that there was essentially no communications between the two segregated and essential security programs. In one such case, the guard force was not receiving information from the console operators to direct it to respond to alarms; the operators were simply recording alarms and observing the independent, uncoordinated activities of the guards who were "in the dark" about events that the security console operators knew about. The guards, of course, also did not know that the console officers had a habit of "taking naps" on the night shift, turning off alarms in order to sleep. Was this critical government facility on which the entire government depended protected by its security force and electronics program? Not at all. This installation, in which the electronics security manager mostly used the available equipment to "tell on" any breaches of protocol by the guard force, served no useful security purpose. It had instead created a hopelessly uninformed guard force with a million-dollar investment in electronics that was of little value. It is important to integrate the guard and electronics programs to the advantage of the guard force.

MANAGEMENT APPROACHES: TYPES OF SYSTEM IMPLEMENTATIONS

Monitored Systems

Full-Time System Monitoring

Often, larger systems such as might be at a corporate headquarters or campus facility are monitored on a full-time basis with a console that is constantly monitored by one or more operators. In enterprise-class systems, there may be multiple console stations, each with its own operator monitoring dozens to hundreds of remote sites. Any facility that has full-time monitoring should be equipped with a complete security command center—that is, a dedicated room with appropriate lighting, ergonomic chairs, and a redundant monitoring console to ensure business continuity in the event the primary console fails. Each console should have multiple screens,[1] a microphone, speakers, a radio, a telephone and a nearby printer, a refrigerator, a snack area and a nearby restroom. A minimum of 400 square feet is recommended for a security command center. The room should be equipped with a man-trap to prevent "tailgating."

Part-Time System Monitoring

Some facilities may be monitored onsite only during certain hours (often when the building is occupied by employees).

When the building is unoccupied, it may be monitored only by a central station-type alarm system, or perhaps it may be monitored by an enterprise-class security command center at a remote location.

Unmonitored Systems

Unmonitored systems simply provide access control and video recording for use for audits if a suspicious event should occur. This is a very useful application for smaller sites where it does not make economic sense to invest in the high operating cost of full- or part-time system monitoring by a dedicated security guard.

Hybrid Systems

Systems that have a monitoring console at a reception guard post are a hybrid between monitored and unmonitored systems. They are not truly monitored since the guard has other more primary duties and may look at video screens only when time (and boredom) permits. In all types of systems, it is clear that the recording of alarm, access control, and video scenes is an important element of their successful implementation to ensure that evidence of suspicious activity is gathered that can be used to identify offenders and prevent or deter future similar events.

SECURITY COMMAND CENTER OPERATIONAL IMPLEMENTATIONS AND ISSUES

Staffing Requirements

Skills

Video command center staffers need certain skills, and there are also other skills that are helpful:

* Essential attributes

  Dependability
  Honesty
  Good computer skills

Good communications skills
Good organizational skills
An understanding of chain of command

- Helpful skills

    Police patrol experience: Many people with foot patrol experience have the ability to spot suspicious activities that others would miss.
    Telephone call center experience: Previous call center or technical support center experience is good preparation for working under stress in a calm fashion.
    Police dispatch experience: Police dispatch experience is a good background for console operators who must dispatch patrol officers.

Hours

Console hours can vary from organization to organization. Organizations should consider that it is difficult for a console officer to focus for long periods on any video. Console officers should be rotated no less than every 2 hours from console duty to patrol or guard desk duty in order to keep the officers fresh and for cross-training purposes.

Supervision

It is easy to forget the purpose of something when it becomes routine. I heard about a console guard who was assigned a "most urgent task" for a refinery graveyard shift. Focusing on the task, she was consistently distracted by "false alarms" in the perimeter detection system. After resetting the false alarms no less than five times without sending a patrol to check them out, she was amazed when a routine patrol stumbled onto a group of student activists with throw-away cameras who had climbed the fence and gotten into the refinery, claiming to be on a photography class project. Right! A photography class with throw-away cameras at night, in a refinery. What a surprise that several of the "students" were not attending any classes and were members of an environmental protest organization.

Good console operation begins with good management. Supervisors should have console officers focus on the task of console management, not other tasks, no matter how urgent the other tasks may seem. The job is to use the security system to detect, assess, and respond.

Security/Safety Policy Compliance

Interfacing the Technology to the Overall Security Program

System planning should also be in the hands of high-level corporate security managers and directors, not the security supervisors, facility managers, contractors, or the maintenance team. System planning must be done by qualified personnel who understand the organization's assets, threats, vulnerabilities, risks, and a wide range of available countermeasures. To the extent that the system is planned by a person who knows only one of these things, the planning will necessarily be incomplete and ineffective.

Skills of the Security Management Team

The organization's security team should begin at the top and end at the bottom.

C-Level Executive

A C-level executive (chief level officer of the company) should have responsibility for overall loss prevention and control. Security should be placed under this person.

Security Command Center Manager

Day-to-day corporate security management should fall to an experienced security manager. A police, FBI, CIA, or special forces background is not generally suitable because these focus more on response than on prevention or are too narrowly focused away from the kinds of activities for which the officer will have responsibilities. Do not get me wrong, one of the finest corporate security managers I know came from the police force, but that is a rarity, and he was a total maverick inside the police force as well. Some of the finest managers I have seen come from the U.S. State Department Diplomatic Security Service. These folks have worked throughout the world under hardship and understand both diplomacy and politics, as well as how to get the job done under hardship conditions. Most of them also have a wide variety of skills, including the following:

- Results-oriented management
- Surveillance and countersurveillance
- Executive protection
- Perimeter protection
- Detection and Investigations
- Assessment
- Response
- Configuring facility security to disrupt the attacker's plans
- Managing subordinates

Shift Supervisors

Shift supervisors should have good communications and organizational skills and be able to set a good example by natural leadership.

CLOSING OUT THE PROJECT

Measuring Success

- A successful enterprise-class integrated security system design is one that is used and which grows in its coverage of remote sites.
- Successful systems pay for themselves in loss prevention. For example, when a system can provide evidence identifying the perpetrators of damage to the facility or theft of goods or information or provide evidence of who perpetrated an illegal act, that system has shown value.
- Successful systems facilitate a more gracious conduct of business.

- Successful systems facilitate a uniform application of corporate security policy.
- Successful systems catch offenders.

Lessons Learned

At the conclusion of any major design, it is advisable to have an internal lessons learned session. The session should recap challenges and solutions, mistakes and corrections, and shortcomings in the design or implementation that one would like to change in the future. A series of recommendations should be put forward to limit or prevent such problems for future projects. Generally, it is advisable to consider putting those recommendations into policy or into the specifications, if they were installation related.

DEALING WITH OFFENDERS WHO TRY TO CIRCUMVENT THE SYSTEM

Where video is used in public spaces, it is not uncommon for offenders to try to circumvent the security system by wearing hats, beards, etc. or looking for areas to offend that are not well covered by cameras. Occasionally, offenders will position themselves below a camera and then spray paint the lens area to obscure their activity. Such behavior should be a sign to security management that a problem area has been detected that needs additional security effort. A log should be made of offenses vis-a-vis system effectiveness to help determine the need for additional patrol, cameras, or emergency phones or to use the system to surveil instead of simply to patrol. Remember that electronic systems do not create security; they are only one of several tools used to improve security.

Using the System for Surveillance

When surveillance is indicated, a console and operator should be dedicated for that purpose. It is unwise to mix surveillance with other duties since the event one is looking for will most likely occur while other duties are being conducted. Video can be used to look for suspicious behavior, especially where crimes have occurred previously.

For example, in a public transit environment, success can be achieved using the video system to surveil subway platforms for suspicious behavior. Since most offenders assume that even though cameras exist, they are not being actively watched, they may feel free to surround a passenger and hassle him or her. By using intercoms to intervene when they move in for the assault or robbery, positioning officers nearby to respond quickly to apprehend, and coordinating with operations to ensure that no trains stop while the officer takedown is occurring, successful apprehensions can take place. Properly advertised in the press, these methods can have good results in reducing crimes in subway environments because they put criminals on notice that they will be detected and apprehended while committing crimes on the metro's property.

Using the Archive Video System to Detect Improper Behavior

Video systems can also be used to identify offenders in other environments. Whereas the offender may try to obscure his or her identity while committing a crime in view of a camera (e.g., by wearing a hat or hood while entering and leaving an office area to steal personal effects and laptops), such behavior looks very suspicious while entering or leaving a more public access way to that area, such as clearing past the receptionist or while tailgating through an employee entry with a group of employees. By observing time–date stamps on the video of the subject entering and leaving the area where the crime took place and looking for a suspect who enters with nothing and leaves with a laptop, the security manager can observe clothes, identifying features, etc., and then look for that person on other cameras until a good full-face video of that person is found. It is often found to be an employee or a person who is escorted into the area by a receptionist, from whom a positive identification of the offender can be made.

SUMMARY

Security systems must be maintained and managed effectively. The functions of all devices should be checked weekly; and any defective devices should be scheduled for maintenance.

Cohesive system management is essential if the system is to operate to the advantage of the security program.

System implementation issues include staffing requirements and security/safety policy development and compliance programs. Each level of security management should be properly qualified.

Closing out the project should include success-measuring metrics and a lessons learned session.

CHAPTER NOTE

1. Microsoft Windows® facilitates the operation of multiple screens on the same workstation (my designs typically run four to six). Workstations that run multiple screens should be equipped with lots of fans, lots of memory, redundant power supplies, and lots of processing power.

Index